LIVING IN SCOTLAND

LIVING IN SCOTLAND

SOCIAL AND ECONOMIC CHANGE SINCE 1980

LINDSAY PATERSON, FRANK BECHHOFER AND DAVID McCRONE

EDINBURGH UNIVERSITY PRESS

Edinburgh University Press Ltd
22 George Square, Edinburgh

Typeset in Goudy Old Style
by Hewer Text Ltd, Edinburgh, and
printed and bound in Great Britain by
The Cromwell Press, Trowbridge, Wilts

A CIP record for this book is
available from the British Library

ISBN 0 7486 1785 X (paperback)

Contents

Tables in Main Text

Supplementary Tables in Appendix 1

8. Consumption, Lifestyle and Culture

Figures in Main Text

Preface

AUTHORSHIP

Dr Cristina Iannelli is full joint author of Chapter 6. All chapters were subject to extensive comment, debate and re-drafting among three (or, in the case of Chapter 6, four) authors, and so authorship is shared. Bechhofer was responsible for the first draft of Chapters 5 and 8. McCrone was responsible for the first draft of Chapters 2, 3 and 4. Paterson was responsible for the first drafts of Chapters 1, 6, 7 and 9 and of the Appendixes. Paterson was responsible for finding and compiling most of the published data (the main exceptions being the demographic data from Anderson in Chapter 2 and the Inland Revenue wealth data in Chapter 5), and for all the new analysis of surveys, and any errors in the compilation of data remain his responsibility.

REFERENCE CONVENTIONS

Where data have been obtained from a published source, that is cited in the usual way in the 'author date' format. Where no published source is cited, the data have come directly from analysis of surveys, as explained in Appendix 2. The only exception to this rule are data from the full report of the population census of Scotland of the year 2001, which is always cited as 'Census 2001' followed by the table number in the census reports. A census table number without any alphabetic prefix comes from Registrar General for Scotland (2003a), and one with such a prefix comes from Registrar General for Scotland (2003b). The preliminary population report of this census is cited as Registrar General for Scotland (2002c). Likewise, the 2001 census of England and Wales is referred to as England and Wales Census 2001. Our tables appear in two places: in the text, one series is numbered decimally within chapter (for example, Table 2.1); supplementary tables for each chapter are grouped in Appendix 1, where they are numbered decimally with the prefix A (for example, Table A2.1). Except where explicitly stated otherwise, tables and figures describe Scotland. The tables are also recorded on the CD which accompanies the book, in a format that may be read by Microsoft Word. All figures appear in the main text, and are numbered decimally within chapter.

ACKNOWLEDGEMENTS

We are particularly grateful to Michael Anderson of Edinburgh University for very generously letting us use his data on population and demography in the Figures in Chapter 2 and in Table 2.1. Further helpful advice was obtained from Robert Wright and Lynn Jamieson. Robin Rice and Stuart Macdonald of the Data Library at Edinburgh University helped us to gain access to data from social surveys. Cristina Iannelli's work for Chapter 6 was supported by the UK Economic and Social Research Council (grant number R000239915).

Notes on the Authors

Lindsay Paterson is Professor of Educational Policy at the University of Edinburgh and has academic interests in education, politics and culture. His books include *A Diverse Assembly* (1998) and *Scottish Education in the Twentieth Century* (2003). He is editor of the quarterly journal *Scottish Affairs*.

Frank Bechhofer is University Fellow and Emeritus Professor of Social Research, University of Edinburgh. In 1986 he founded the Research Centre for Social Sciences and was its Director until 1997. He has published widely in the areas of social stratification, the social structure of Scotland, individual and household strategies, national identity and research methodology. He coordinated the Edinburgh team in the Social Change and Economic Life Initiative funded by ESRC. A former chairperson of the British Sociological Association, he co-authored *Principles of Research Design in the Social Sciences* (2000) with Lindsay Paterson.

David McCrone is Professor of Sociology, and director of the University of Edinburgh's Institute of Governance. His recent books include *Understanding Scotland* (2nd edn, 2001) and *The Sociology of Nationalism* (1998). He is coordinator of the research programme funded by the Leverhulme Trust on Constitutional Change and National Identity (1999–2004) and a Fellow of the Royal Society of Edinburgh.

CHAPTER I

Introduction

This book outlines the main changes in the structure of Scottish society that have taken place in the last two or three decades. It does that in a quantitative way, because during that period Scotland has acquired a wealth of reliable, good-quality statistical information to a hitherto unprecedented degree. This is not to imply that this is the only means of assessing social change, but such data do provide a reliable basis for making judgements about its extent and its implications. The process of deriving and constructing statistics is, of course, a deeply social one, surrounded by inevitable controversy, but the relative precision of statistical measures allows for a well-informed and reasonably dispassionate debate. We hope that this book may stimulate that kind of methodological debate as well as discussion about the changes it charts. We must stress at the outset that the book is not about the data for their own sake, but about the issues which they illuminate, issues which affect everyone who lives in Scotland. We believe that there is a solid base of evidence for what we say. We hope readers will use the statistical material to come to their own conclusions, whether or not they match ours.

Our seven substantive chapters are primarily about large-scale changes that have been profoundly altering Scottish society. Chapter 2 deals with basic demographic features: the size and shape of the population, its age structure and gender composition, the patterns of migration – including regional migration within Scotland – and of de-urbanisation, suburbanisation, and rural repopulation. Chapter 3 is about changes of which, to some extent and in a personal way, we are all aware. It discusses the restructuring of families and the formation of new household structures, the decline in family size, the changes in patterns of marriage and divorce, and the increase in cohabitation. Chapter 4 deals with the ways in which we earn our living, perhaps no longer our central life interest but fundamental to the kind of lives we are able to live. It looks at the changing nature of work, the decline of male manual work and the rise of new forms of employment often dominated by women. We examine the context in which this has occurred: that is, industrial change and occupational change, de-industrialisation, and the impact of globalisation and the new international division of labour in its effects on such matters as inward investment in Scotland. Chapter 5 is about money and resources. It assesses how Scotland's resources are shared, looking at the distribution of income and wealth and at the opportunities which these confer or which their absence withholds. Chapter 6 explores the changing nature of social class: has Scotland become a 'middle class' society? Is social mobility easier or more difficult than hitherto? How important is social class compared to other matters – gender, age, ethnicity, for example? Chapter 7 examines the role of education in determining people's life chances, tracking the enormous expansion of formal education that has taken place in recent decades. Does education drive social opportunity? What is the role of education in generating social advantage? Is education a cause or an effect of social position and of social change? What are the relevance to educational opportunity of class, gender, religion and ethnicity? Chapter 8 is about the way we use the resources we have, be they financial, educational or cultural, and about some of the implications of general standards of living which were unthought of thirty years ago. It asks how the patterns of social and cultural consumption have changed. How do people choose to spend their money, and how, for example, have their leisure patterns altered? Are the less affluent, and especially the younger groups, doubly disadvantaged by an inability to enjoy, and especially to share socially, the lifestyles, access to knowledge and communication of their peers? Chapter 9 then draws the themes together in conclusion. The Appendixes provide supplementary tables, an outline of the sources of data on which we have drawn, a discussion of various ways of measuring social class, and an explanation of the concealed complexities that are involved in comparing percentages (including the rather technical matter of 'odds ratios'), something which we have to do frequently throughout the book.

This introductory chapter sets the scene for the empirical analysis by summarising key processes of social change that have been raised in discussions of many developed societies. The point here is not to claim that these processes in the abstract may be applied unproblematically to understanding the Scottish experience. One of the main points that we will return to in the final chapter is that, like the reaction in any country, the reaction of Scotland to what are common social changes is also unique, being shaped by its own history and culture. Nevertheless, the themes provide a succinct framework through which to interpret Scottish experience. Further discussion of the

themes outlined here may be found in many recent boo.
change. The book that comes closest in purpose to the presei.
written at a more specialised level, and for Britain as a whole
differentiated attention to Scotland, is the edited collection by Hals
Webb (2000); especially relevant are the chapters by Halsey (2000), G.
(2000), Heath and Payne (2000), Dilnot and Emmerson (2000), Atkinso.
(2000), and Gershuny and Fisher (2000). Other notable books on these
introductory themes are by Hobsbawm (1994), Giddens (1984, 1998), Beck
(1992), Hirst and Thompson (1999), Turner (2001), Savage (2000), Bell (1976)
and McCrone (2001).

ECONOMY AND EMPLOYMENT

Four broad economic trends have been evident in most developed societies
since the 1970s. The first is a wholesale shift in the basis of production. At
the end of the 1970s, most developed economies still had a significant
manufacturing sector, still had quite important sectors of primary production – such as coal mining – and still therefore had the structures of
employment around these that had been first established before the First
World War. That world has largely now gone, although it disappeared at
varying rates in different countries, and in the UK was helped on its way by
political decisions made by governments during the 1970s and 1980s. Even
within manufacturing, the products have changed, for example from heavy
to light engineering and computers. It is no longer the case that the
developed economies depend on making the kinds of things which were
the staple until the middle of the twentieth century, and which, in Scotland, underpinned culture, politics, and even the identity of particular
locales and the nation as a whole.

The second trend relates to the emergence of an economy offering
services of two types. One set require high-level skills, depend on rapidly
changing technology, and are – in principle – readily exportable across
borders. The prime example is financial services, the deregulation of which
in the 1980s and 1990s has helped to drive many other aspects of social and
political change. The world financial markets are now largely a law unto
themselves, generating their own growth by their own activities, and able to
challenge even the most powerful governments for sovereignty. Their
personnel are highly skilled, and indeed the most skilled are among the
best graduates in mathematical and economic disciplines. Scotland is a
small player in all this, but at least it is a player, with its legacy of financial
institutions from an era in which their main function was providing
financial capital for manufacturing, going right back to the advent of

pitalism itself. But finance is not the only example of the highly skilled, high-status service economy. Formal education is another, vastly expanded in all countries over the past century, not only the developed ones: education engenders its own demand, because well-educated people, and their children, are far more likely to want more education than people who have had a rather abbreviated initial experience of it. Health-care is another example. The creation of the National Health Service and the benefits it brought depended on what now seems very basic medicine; even the much more developed systems of the middle of the twentieth century seem rudimentary today and have been superseded by more and more subtle and expensive types of treatment, as approaches to health generally have become more sophisticated and greater longevity has increased the incidence of diseases that used to be quite rare. Scotland has shared very readily in the growth of education and health-care, partly because it already had relatively well-developed educational and health systems by the middle of the century. Employment in health and education thus forms an important part of the new middle class.

The service sector is not all so liberating, however. There are also the precarious and poorly paid jobs that surround the relative affluence of the high-status ones – working in fast-food, cleaning, personal services of various other sorts, and also, slightly less riskily, in call centres and other kinds of service employment fuelled by the new technology. The key feature of all of these jobs is that they may disappear overnight, either because of automation, or because – in the case of call centres, for example – further technological developments allow them to follow the manufacturing jobs to regions of the world where labour is cheaper. Some of the residual manufacturing jobs have been of a similar sort – assembling computers rather than developing them – and hence are equally likely to disappear elsewhere. The 'service economy' is just as much about these shadowy jobs as about the glitter of the stock market or the pioneering excitement of the laboratory.

One consequence of the sectoral changes has been a growth of different patterns of working, the third economic trend. Sometimes, especially in the high-status sectors, workers are able to exercise choice, with some, especially women, choosing part-time work (although they are often constrained to do so by caring responsibilities) or interrupted careers, or so-called portfolio careers in which income is derived from a variety of sources. The most flexible versions of this are quite rare, but the idea of having to change occupation or working patterns several times during a lifetime is common. But for people in the most risky parts of the economy, working part-time or in temporary jobs is not a choice, but, rather, something that cannot be avoided.

The fourth and final economic trend is the withdrawal of the state from providing jobs directly. In many European countries, large segments of the manufacturing and primary-production economy were nationalised, for example coal mining and steel making in the UK. In contrast, very little of the new financial sector is publicly owned, and in the low-status parts of the service sector most of the worst-paid and most insecure jobs depend on the least socially responsible employers. Nevertheless, the extent of the decline in public-sector employment should not be exaggerated (as it often is). With the exception of the financial sector, the expansion of better-paid and more secure service-sector employment has been largely in the public sector, education and health-care being prime examples.

SOCIAL RELATIONS OF PRODUCTION

Along with these changes have come equally significant changes in the social relations that accompany employment. The one that most immediately arises out of the employment trends noted above concerns gender. With notable caveats (such as those concerning the finance sector), it may be said that the old economy was dominated by male jobs and the new one by female ones, whether high-status or not. Women make up the majority of employees in health, education, and other segments of the public-sector service economy such as social work. They have begun to enter some of the highest-status professions – such as the law and medicine – in proportions that would have been unthinkable a generation ago. They also dominate the most precarious and low-status service jobs, such as cleaning. Men used to dominate manufacturing employment, but even the new types of manufacturing (such as of computers) tend to employ many more women than men.

Underlying this radically different economic role for women have been changes to the family – smaller family sizes, later age at marriage, later and safer child-bearing, and to some extent more sharing of domestic work by men and women. As important as these, however, has been the automation of much domestic drudgery, and the reduction in the need for full-time home workers resulting from a generally cleaner environment. If reliable means of contraception have been a crucial factor in the economic liberation of women, so also have been the washing machine and the end of coal as the main source of industrial and domestic energy.

There are other important changes in the social relations of production, though, with some cutting across this one. On the whole, workplaces are much smaller than in the days when the socialist MP James Maxton could address almost the entire male electorate of his constituency coming through the gates of the Parkhead Forge in the Bridgeton area of Glasgow. Along with the growth of the insecure service sector, this greater isolation of employment has been a significant factor in the decline of trade unions. Unions have now become much more the professional associations of the secure worker in the public-service sector – teachers and health care workers, for example – rather than simply the communal representatives of manufacturing labour. The people who now most need the protection which union representation can provide – the low-paid, insecure workers in the low-status service sector – are those who are least likely to have it, through choice, through the absence of a trade union culture or through pressure from anti-union employers. In practice, this means that large numbers of female workers are not represented by a trade union.

The power of women in the workplace is disproportionately low for the further reasons that managerial positions tend still to be in the hands of men, and that, even within secure sectors where women dominate numerically, the highest-status roles tend still to be filled by men. Women are still strikingly under-represented among senior private-sector managers, hospital consultants, partners in law firms, school headteachers, or university professors.

So the regulatory role of the state matters much more than ever before for ensuring that working conditions are decent and fair. Laws against invidious discrimination may not have ended it, but they have mitigated its worst effects, and have probably enabled a gradual increase in the relative salaries of female workers, although more so in the secure sectors than elsewhere. Legal challenges are slowly improving women's chances of promotion to the most senior jobs. If trade unions are weaker than they have been for a century, the role of employment law and of laws governing health and safety is all the greater. If communal support for matters such as child-rearing is in decline, because of the dwindling of extended, local families, then state-provided child-care becomes very important in allowing women to enter the paid labour force. This is not to say that the state actually is doing all these things, but rather to say that the political decisions on these matters now are even more important than they have ever been.

SOCIAL SELECTION

The changes have not all been to do with work, although the economy underpins everything else. There have also been profound changes in the manner in which individuals are selected into social roles, including but not confined to work roles. The first point here, world-wide again, is the growing importance of educational credentials. As apprenticeships declined, both for manual jobs and for entry to certain professions such as accountancy, it became increasingly important to hold worthwhile certificates as evidence of competence and potential. One (but only one) of the explanations of educational expansion is this: schools and universities, by providing educational credentials have, to some extent, taken over the role of selecting people for particular jobs.

The point here is not that developed societies are necessarily more meritocratic than before, although they may be. It is that the means by which people are allocated to particular roles in life have come to depend increasingly on education. That might not be more meritocratic if educational success depends more on family social circumstances than on actual merit and effort, and there is certainly abundant evidence that the expanded post-16 and then post-school education systems have been used most enthusiastically and most efficiently by the middle class. Doing so seems a legitimate way of conferring advantage where direct buying of influence, or actual nepotism, would not. Teachers in public-sector schools have struggled against this at least since the middle of the twentieth century, with some, although only limited, success in most countries.

The ability to exploit effectively the new types of selection does not just replicate old patterns of class domination. There are more positive consequences. An economy where credentials matter a great deal may be one where women do best, because girls and women, on average, have higher levels of educational attainment than males. Likewise, the sons and daughters of the most recent immigrants to developed countries may be expected to do well too, in due course. Just as with previous waves of immigration, relatively powerless incomers seem to be using formal equality within a meritocratic education system to demonstrate their economic potential, despite dominant social attitudes to their skin colour or religion.

Education may also lubricate the fluidity of the new labour markets – the necessity to change jobs relatively often, to retrain during periods of unemployment, or (especially for women) to return to the labour market after having children.

But if education achieves all these things, it also condemns to even more inescapable subjugation the minority of people who have not gained its benefits. Whether or not we use the term 'underclass' to label those who seem to be almost permanently excluded from the labour market and from other kinds of social participation, the point that is most important about them is that they have dropped out of school early, have taken no part in any kind of lifelong learning, and have no access to most of the new media of communication. That is why some writers have referred to the importance of considering the implications of a 'knowledge society'. It is a slogan, but it also sums up the problems faced by people who do not have knowledge.

FORMS OF LIVING

These changes are also about cultural selection, not just economic selection. Education confers a predisposition to a certain kind of lifestyle (including, as we have noted, to wanting more education), something which has frequently but inaccurately been called 'middle class culture'. The case of Scotland, as we will see in Chapter 6 especially, should warn us against that rather rhetorical label, insofar as a large majority of people refuse that class identity, but so also should the history of attitudes to education, in Scotland and elsewhere. Throughout the twentieth century, the labour movement and other educational reformers campaigned for expanded education, not only to open up economic opportunities, but also to democratise access to human culture, to what the nineteenth-century English liberal Matthew Arnold called 'the best which has been thought and said in the world'. The most optimistic reading of the changes of the past three decades or so is that, in developed countries like Scotland, a far larger proportion of people now than ever previously do have access to the fruits of human culture.

The long-term implications of this cultural revolution will take many further decades to work through. There is the potentially greater human understanding that comes from a more educated sensibility, another goal which reforming educators have set themselves for a century. There is the greater individualism of personal style, enabled but not caused by the rise in disposable income and drastic reduction in the cost of all kinds of personal possessions compared to the middle of the twentieth century. People in the developed countries may now own such wardrobes and libraries, may eat such food from all over the world, may have access to such music, film and other sources of entertainment that only the very richest could have enjoyed in the austere aftermath of the Second World War or earlier. That they choose to exercise these choices is not down to the cost alone, however: the economic system that provides the goods is the occasion, not the reason, why people want these things. As Eric Hobsbawm has noted (Hobsbawm 2002: 275, 414), one of the ironies for old communists is that, in the affluent parts of the world, capitalism has delivered the material abundance that socialists used to claim it could never do. But a proper historical perspective would also conclude that it is not capitalism on its own that has caused the cultural revolution by which people's tastes have broadened, but rather the processes of democratisation which were forced upon capitalism by the political campaigning of radical reformers, including communists themselves: in Hobsbawm's words, 'the world will not get better on its own' (ibid.: 418).

The cultural revolution also has implications for how people imagine society, no longer perhaps as a collectivity, but now rather as a web of individual opportunity and choice. Beyond that, there is potentially an implication for their role as citizens. The majority is potentially more assertive, and more capable of being effective, on account of its much improved levels of education and much more discerning levels of culture. But, for the very reasons of its apparently secure opportunity and affluence, it may no longer see much relevance in the intrinsically collective world of politics at all. Only the minority who see that a great deal of the affluence (though not the education) actually depends on a rather ruinous exploitation of the earth's natural resources might then find a new set of collective concerns to replace the distributive goals of the reforming politics of the past.

CONCLUSION

The paradox for Scotland is that the country has embarked on a new constitutional and political trajectory that seems to contradict some of these conclusions. The movement for self-government has asserted the value of community, the efficacy of active citizenship, the dignity of the nation's ancient collective principles. Community has often manifested itself as class, and class identity and class politics remain potent forces, even when – perhaps especially when – they are now more a matter of choice than fate. The new parliament has been taken to task, not for its inadequate attention to individualistic consumerism, say, but for its alleged failure to engage with communities. By that is meant people beyond the circles of news media, civic institutions and academic analysts who surround the politicians and perhaps hem them in. The communities of Scotland are believed to be the repositories of sovereignty. They may have changed profoundly but they are still, in people's minds, collectivities.

This book is not itself an examination of matters of identity, and it only touches on questions of politics: these topics have been covered extensively elsewhere. Our main purpose here is to look at deeper matters, at the changing social structure which the new Scottish polity has to work with. But we return to this apparent paradox in the final chapter – to the seeming contradiction between the collective allegiance that has now transformed Scotland's governing system and the erosion of the old social basis of collective identity that the book traces.

CHAPTER 2

Population and Demography

Scotland has a population of about five million people, and has had for much of the last hundred years. That may seem a fairly uncontroversial and somewhat boring fact, but behind it lies a much more interesting set of processes. In much of this book we will be focusing on processes which Scotland shares with other western societies, but, as regards its demography, it is something of an outlier. The population of any country is the outcome of the complex balance of birth rates, death rates and migration patterns. Like other industrialised countries, Scotland entered the twentieth century with a high but falling birth rate and a lower but falling death rate, so that it more or less corresponded to the central phase of what demographers used to call the 'demographic transition': from high fertility and high mortality, to low fertility and low mortality. Why, then, should it be interesting that Scotland's population, the outcome of these balances between births, deaths and migration, has not been growing for much of the last century?

The fact is that Scotland has been losing population in relative and in absolute terms. Compared with England, Scotland's population growth has been slower in every decade for almost 200 years. Since 1931 it has been slower than Northern Ireland, and since the 1960s it has also been slower than Wales (see Table 2.1). In the course of the twentieth century, the population of the UK increased by about 22 million, but, whereas the population of England grew by 64 per cent, Scotland experienced growth of only 14 per cent, lower than Wales and Northern Ireland too (Office of National Statistics 2002a: Table 1.1). Its population is now roughly equal to what it was in 1951, and 3 per cent lower than 1971, at a time when England's is almost 20 per cent above that of 1951, and 7 per cent above 1971. Indeed, there is no other European country with lower levels of population growth (see Figure 2.1). Scotland's population is the only one to fall since 1918, and its static and falling population compared with 1951 and 1971 respectively compares with growth rates of between 20 per cent and 60 per cent elsewhere (since the 1950s), and 6 per cent and

20 per cent or more since the 1970s. Even its near neighbour across the North Sea – Norway – which also has a strong tradition of emigration has had much more buoyant population growth (16 per cent since 1971).

Table 2.1 Population (thousands) and percentage rates of change per decade in population, Scotland, England and Wales, 1851–2001

Year	Population (thousands)			Percent change per decade		
	Scotland	England	Wales	Scotland	England	Wales
1851	2889	16763	1163			
1861	3062	18770	1296	6.0	12.0	11.4
1871	3360	21295	1417	9.7	13.5	9.3
1881	3736	24402	1572	11.2	14.6	10.9
1891	4026	27231	1771	7.8	11.6	12.7
1901	4472	30516	2012	11.1	12.1	13.6
1911	4761	33651	2421	6.5	10.3	20.3
1921	4882	35229	2658	2.5	4.7	9.8
1931	4843	37359	2593	–0.8	6.0	–2.4
1951	5096	41159	2599	2.6	5.0	0.1
1961	5184	43461	2635	1.7	5.6	1.4
1971	5236	46018	2740	1.0	5.9	4.0
1981	5180	46821	2813	–1.1	1.7	2.7
1991	5107	47875	2891	–1.4	2.3	2.8
2001	5064	49181	2903	–0.8	2.7	0.4

Source: Michael Anderson (see Appendix 2).

Figure 2.1 Population of selected European countries, c. 1870–c. 2001

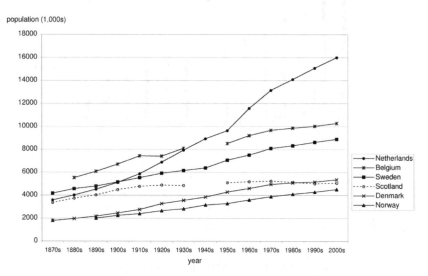

Source: Michael Anderson (see note in Appendix 2). The dates within decades of countries' censuses vary, and so the census closest to the decade noted is used; there was no census in Scotland or Belgium in the 1940s.

In this chapter, we will explore this puzzle, while sketching out the patterns of similarity which Scotland shares with other western European countries in terms of its demographic patterns and processes. The trends can be seen in Figure 2.2. Death rates in Scotland fell decade on decade until the 1920s, before levelling out at their lowest level in its history. Birth rates fell fast until the 1930s, rose slightly in the post-war period, and collapsed from the 1970s. Net migration has slowed in recent decades in comparison with the pervasive trends of much of the previous century, but this does not make up for the declining rate of natural increase. In short, modern Scotland is not able to reproduce itself, and will decreasingly be able to do so on present trends.[1] This, together with an ageing population, has led many to be concerned about the future, particularly in terms of how Scotland's labour force is to reproduce itself in the next few decades. The relationship between economic growth and population growth is an emerging issue in Scottish politics, especially as immigration is a reserved rather than a devolved power.

Let us disentangle the various strands which go to make up Scotland's population.

Figure 2.2 Components of population change, 1861–2001

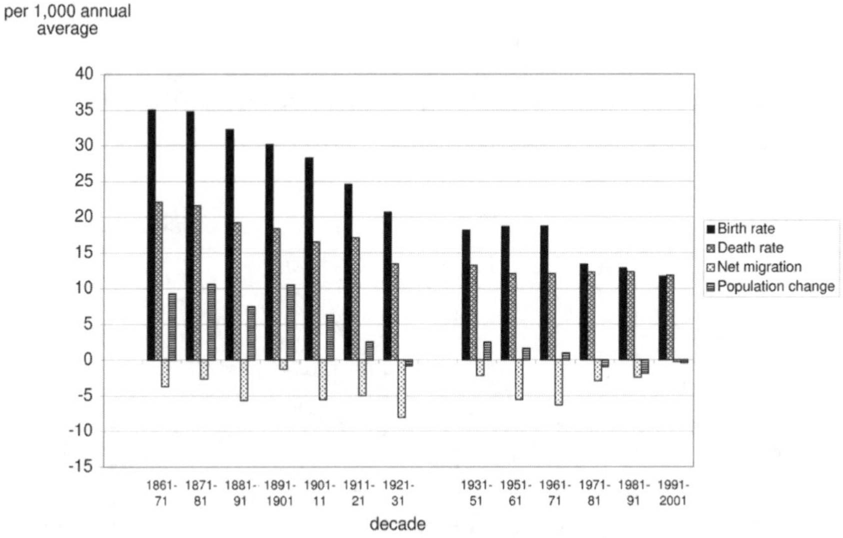

Source: Michael Anderson (see note in Appendix 2).

FERTILITY AND NUPTIALITY

In 2001, just over 52,000 babies were born in Scotland, compared with over 66,000 ten years earlier. Put in context, this is around 40 per cent of what it was at the beginning of the twentieth century, and around half of the 1961 figure (see Figure 2.3). There was some stabilising in the 1980s as the age cohort born in the 1960s grew to motherhood, and then a steady decline during the 1990s. This absolute decline is shared with other comparable countries, but what makes Scotland unusual is the relative rate of decline. The Total Fertility Rate (TFR) is the average number of children which would be born to a woman if the current pattern of fertility persisted throughout her child-bearing years. Rates for live births per 1,000 women are significantly lower in Scotland than in other parts of the UK. For example, the TFR for Scotland in 2000 was 1.47, compared with 1.64 for the UK as a whole, England's 1.65, Wales's 1.70, and Northern Ireland's 1.74. Scotland's rate is also lower than any of the nine standard English regions (Office of National Statistics 2001: Table 3.13). Given that a fertility rate of just over two children among live births is required for a population to reproduce itself without substantial inward migration, then Scotland has a particular problem, leading to claims that it is threatened by a 'demographic time-bomb'. Fertility rates have fallen year on year since the 1960s, stabilising in the 1980s before falling again, and there would need to be a substantial increase in the birth rate – possibly by as much as 40 per cent – to hold the population steady in the longer term.

Figure 2.3 Births to married and non-married parents, 1900–2001

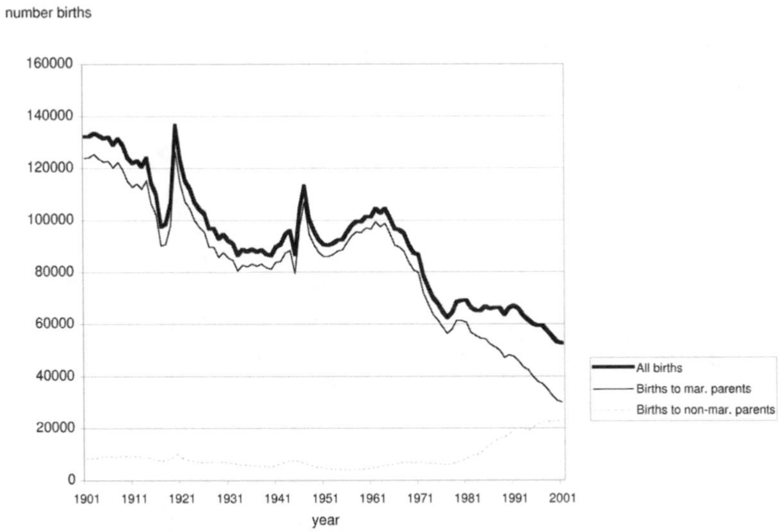

number births

Source: Michael Anderson (see note in Appendix 2).

What makes this process of birth rate decline especially intriguing is that it combines with shifts in the ages at which people marry and have children (Figure 2.4). The past 30 years have seen a dramatic rise in the age at which people get married for the first time, and this has a concomitant effect on opportunities for child-bearing. There has, of course, been a steep rise in cohabitation, and most of the recent rise in non-marital fertility is to couples who are cohabiting (see Chapter 3). Nevertheless, marital and non-marital fertility is still well below the boom years of the 1950s to 1980s. For example, 60 per cent of all live births in the late 1940s – commonly referred to as the period of the baby boom – were to mothers aged under 30 (see Table 2.2). By the early 1970s, this had risen to 79 per cent, but by 2001 had fallen right back to 52 per cent. Concomitantly, live births to mothers in their 40s were at their lowest in the 1970s and 1980s, and had begun to rise by the end of the century. Put another way (Table 2.3), we can see the fairly dramatic drop in cumulative fertility by comparing the female birth cohort for 1940, which attained on average just under 2.5 children by the age of 45, with that for 1955, where the average was less than 2. For each age, on the other hand, there has been a substantial reduction over time, and for those aged 25 and 30 there has been a halving of cumulative fertility. What seems to be happening is not simply fewer women having children, but a delay in them so doing (Figure 2.5). The most dramatic falls have occurred among women in their 20s, such that the norm is for many women to wait until their 30s, by which time their fecundity is reduced.

Figure 2.4 Mean age at first marriage, 1860–2001

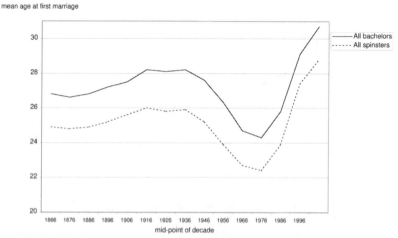

Source: Michael Anderson (see note in Appendix 2).

Table 2.2 Live births, by age of mother, 1946–2001

| % in rows | | | | Age | | | |
Year	<20	20–24	25–29	30–34	35–39	40–44	45+
1946–50	3.9	25.3	31.1	21.7	13.6	3.9	0.3
1951–55	4.3	28.2	31.2	21.6	11.2	3.4	0.2
1956–60	5.5	30.3	31.4	19.7	10.4	2.6	0.2
1961–65	7.3	31.1	30.9	18.6	9.3	2.6	0.2
1966–70	9.9	34.1	29.7	16.2	7.8	2.1	0.1
1971–75	11.8	34.5	32.5	14.1	5.6	1.4	0.1
1976–80	10.9	32.7	34.6	16.2	4.4	0.9	0.0
1981–85	9.9	32.4	34.2	17.3	5.2	0.8	0.0
1986–90	9.2	28.2	36.0	19.8	5.8	0.9	0.0
1991–95	7.6	22.2	35.5	25.4	8.1	1.1	0.0
1996–2000	8.3	17.5	30.4	29.8	12.0	1.8	0.1
2001	8.5	17.4	26.2	30.9	14.7	2.3	0.1

Source: Registrar General for Scotland (2002a: Table 3.1).

Table 2.3 Cumulative fertility,[1] by selected female birth cohort (1940–80) and selected age

| | Cumulative fertility at exact age | | | | | |
Female birth cohort[2]	20	25	30	35	40	45
1940	0.15	1.09	1.99	2.37	2.47	2.48
1945	0.20	1.10	1.85	2.14	2.24	2.26
1950	0.23	0.97	1.62	1.95	2.06	2.08
1955	0.23	0.80	1.43	1.79	1.92	1.95
1960	0.17	0.69	1.29	1.68	1.84	
1965	0.14	0.57	1.15	1.56		
1970	0.15	0.52	0.99			
1975	0.15	0.46				
1980	0.15					

Source: Registrar General for Scotland (2002a: Table 3.7).
1. Cumulative fertility is the average number of children per woman born in the year specified.
2. Exact birth ages (i.e. selected from full set).

Figure 2.5 Births per 1,000 women, by age group, 1938–2001

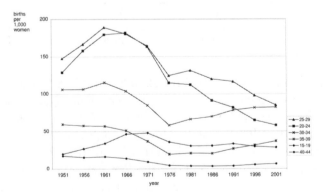

Source: Michael Anderson (see note in Appendix 2).

The fall in the number of live births does not seem to be the result of increasing rates of abortion, although there has been an increase in the rate from 8.9 per 1,000 in 1985, to 11.5 by 1999 (Table 2.4). Most of this increase results from greater use of abortion by younger women, especially those under 25, who have in any case always had higher rates than older women. The greater use of contraception by women in Scotland has also seen a shift away from oral contraceptive methods in favour of use of the sheath, although the former remains by far the most popular method of contraception (Table 2.5).

Table 2.4 Abortion rates, 1985–99

	Rate per 1,000 women aged 15–44			Rate per 1,000 women in age group					
Year	Total	Performed in Scotland	Performed in England or Wales	16–19	20–24	25–29	30–34	35–39	40–44
1985	8.9	8.2	0.6	15.7	14.2	9.2	6.2	4.1	1.7
1990	9.8	9.1	0.7	18.7	16.9	11.0	6.8	4.4	1.5
1995	10.4	10.1	0.3	18.4	19.5	12.4	8.0	4.8	1.8
1999	11.5	11.2	0.3	20.6	21.6	14.4	8.8	5.7	2.0

Source: Common Services Agency (2000: Table A2.2).

Table 2.5 Contraceptive method,[1] 1980–99

	Year				
Contraceptive method chosen	1980	1985	1990	1995	1999
Oral contraceptive	55	58	54	49	43
Intra-uterine device	17	16	11	5	6
Cap/diaphragm	6	7	6	3	1
Sheath	10	10	13	21	24
Other	5	4	9	14	14
None	8	5	7	8	13

Source: Common Services Agency (2000: Table A3.2).
1. As practised by people attending Family Planning Clinics. From 1989 includes figures for Lothian Brook Advisory Centre, and from 1997 includes figures for Highland Brook Advisory Centre.

The reduction in family size and child-bearing is a function of many things: increased labour-market participation by women (see Chapter 4), as well as shifts in personal and family lifestyles in the later decades of the twentieth century: 'Both the employment aspirations and the leisure interests of many women in the later 1970s and the 1980s were inimical to a child-centred existence, and, for the first time, they had available to them the means almost to guarantee that they could avoid pregnancy if they wished' (Anderson 1992: 37).

AGE STRUCTURE

The overall effect of limits to child-bearing has been to age the population significantly, compounded by greater longevity. Whereas in 1981 for every person over 60 there were 1.6 under 20, a mere twenty years later there was approaching parity (Table 2.6). Similarly, the proportion over 70 years of age rose from 9.4 per cent in 1981 to 11.2 per cent in 2001, whereas those under 10 years of age fell from 13 per cent to 11.5 per cent; so there are virtually as many over 70 as under 10. As in other advanced industrial countries, women outnumber men (by 52 per cent to 48 per cent), especially in the older age groups, where fully seven out of ten people over 80 years of age are female (Table 2.7). There has been a modest reduction in this female preponderance in older age groups – in 1981, 73 per cent of the over 80s were women – but this reflects increasing longevity of the population as a whole. The overall effect is to produce a bell-shaped curve with more people in their 30s than in younger age groups, and many more surviving into old age (Figure 2.6).

Table 2.6 Population distribution by age, 1981–2001

Age:	1981	1991	2001
0–9	13.0	12.7	11.5
10–19	17.3	12.9	12.6
20–29	14.6	15.3	12.5
30–39	13.1	14.3	15.5
40–49	11.4	13.1	14.1
50–59	11.5	11.1	12.6
60–69	9.8	10.2	9.9
70–79	6.9	7.0	7.4
80 and over	2.5	3.4	3.8
Total (=100%)	5,035,315	4,998,567	5,062,011

Sources: Registrar General for Scotland (1983a: Table 6); Registrar General for Scotland (1994a: Table 2); Registrar General for Scotland (2002c: Table 1).

MORTALITY AND MORBIDITY

Just as the Scottish birth rate has fallen, so has the death rate since the mid-twentieth century, in a dramatic fashion for both sexes, although these rates have stabilised in recent years (Table A2.1). The death rate of males aged 45–54 is now only 5.3 per 1,000, compared with twice that proportion in the post-war period. The decline in female deaths in this age group is equally dramatic, from 6.6 per 1,000 to 3.2 by 2001. Nevertheless, at most ages for both males and females, death rates in 2000 were higher in Scotland than in any other constituent country of the United Kingdom, a trend especially noticeable for people over 55.[2] There is a differential improvement in life expectancy for all age groups, although, as one might expect, it is greater for the mid-life groups where the death rate halves over 50 years, than for older age groups where it reduces by about one-third. Death rates among men are higher than for women in all age groups.

Table 2.7 Proportion female, by age, 1981–2001

Age:	1981	1991	2001
0–9	48.7	48.8	48.7
10–19	48.8	49.0	49.0
20–29	49.5	51.1	50.7
30–39	49.9	50.9	51.7
40–49	51.1	50.4	50.9
50–59	52.0	51.7	50.7
60–69	55.3	54.1	53.1
70–79	61.2	60.4	58.1
80 and over	73.4	71.8	69.4
All	51.8	52.1	51.9

Sources: Registrar General for Scotland (1983a: Table 6); Registrar General for Scotland (1994a: Table 2); Registrar General for Scotland (2002c: Table 1).

Figure 2.6 Age structure of population, by gender, 2001

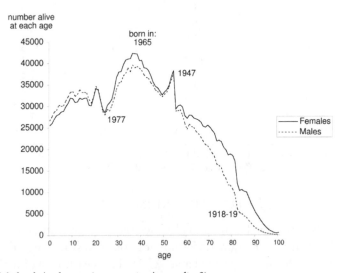

Source: Michael Anderson (see note in Appendix 2).

Improvements in longevity are equally dramatic (Table 2.8). Whereas among those born in 1950 men might have expected to live to be 64, and women to 69, if no further changes in mortality rates had occurred, by the turn of the century men had improved their life expectancy by almost nine years (to 73) and women by even more (almost ten years) to 79. The benefits of being female when it comes to living longer are consistently held for all age groups, from birth to 65, and have, if anything, grown over the 50-year period.

Table 2.8 Expectation of life by sex and selected ages, 1950–2001

Age	Birth		1		15		45		65	
Year	male	female	male	female	male	female	male	female	male	female
1950–52	64.4	68.7	66.2	69.9	53.1	56.7	25.5	29.1	11.4	13.2
1960–62	66.2	72.0	67.3	72.7	53.9	59.1	25.8	30.5	11.5	14.2
1970–72	67.3	73.7	67.8	73.9	54.3	60.3	26.2	31.5	11.6	15.4
1980–82	69.1	75.3	69.0	75.1	55.4	61.3	27.2	32.4	12.3	16.0
1990–92	71.4	77.1	71.0	76.5	57.3	62.7	29.0	33.7	13.2	16.8
1991–93	71.5	77.1	71.1	76.5	57.3	62.7	29.0	33.7	13.2	16.8
1992–94	71.7	77.3	71.2	76.7	57.5	62.9	29.2	33.9	13.4	16.9
1993–95	71.9	77.4	71.4	76.8	57.6	63.0	29.3	34.0	13.5	16.9
1994–96	72.1	77.6	71.6	77.1	57.8	63.2	29.6	34.2	13.7	17.2
1995–97	72.2	77.8	71.7	77.2	57.9	63.3	29.7	34.3	13.8	17.2
1996–98	72.4	77.9	71.9	77.3	58.1	63.5	29.9	34.4	14.0	17.3
1997–99	72.6	78.1	72.1	77.4	58.3	63.6	30.1	34.5	14.2	17.4
1999–2001	73.1	78.5	72.5	77.9	58.7	64.0	30.7	35.0	14.7	17.8

Source: Registrar General for Scotland (2002a: Table 5.4).

The most stark decline in mortality relates to perinatal and infant mortality, as infectious diseases are controlled by antibiotics and improved treatments (Table A2.2). Perinatal death (stillbirths, and deaths during the first week of life) fell, for males, from 51.5 per 1,000 live births in 1946–50, to 8.0 in 2001, a factor of more than six. A similar decline occurred among females, from 44.9 to 6.7 in the same period. Infant deaths (those occurring in the first year of life) had an even more dramatic fall, a factor of nine for males (53.2 to 5.8), and of eight for females (41.1 to 5.2). In broad terms, in the post-war period, it took 25 years to halve the rate, then a decade to halve it again, but two decades to halve it once more. Thus, at a time when the birth rate was already falling, those (fewer) babies who were being born had a much better chance than ever before of surviving into childhood.

Men and women in Scotland not only have different life trajectories, but they have different patterns of mortality (Table A2.3). There has been a similar rate of increase since 1950 for both sexes as regards dying of cancer, although the types of cancer are different. Both genders increasingly converge as regards lung and related cancers, and while the rate for men has doubled (from 48 to 94 per 100,000), that for women has gone up sixfold (from 10 to 62 per 100,000). Ischaemic heart disease is a major killer for men and for women, although there are signs that its peak rate was reached in the 1970s and 1980s.

In a population notorious for ill health by international standards, patterns of morbidity (disease) reflect social change (Table A2.4). Thus, Scots today are most likely to consult their GPs about mental problems, hypertension, upper respiratory tract infections, and back problems. No directly comparable data are available for earlier periods, though a 1939 report for the Department of Health of the Scottish Office (Brotherston 1987: 74) found that the common causes of sickness were respiratory diseases, diseases of the digestive system, accidents, rheumatism, and skin diseases. The general improvement in levels of diet and cleanliness, the increase in safety, and the rise of stress-related disorders are all evident in the contrast.

The old killer diseases and epidemics which had been so familiar – the communicable infectious diseases caused by viruses and bacteria – have all but been eradicated. By the 1990s, people were dying mainly of cancers and ischaemic heart disease, and these alone were each responsible for around a quarter of all adult deaths in Scotland (Anderson 1996: 375). Considerable class differentials remained, so that the death rate in eastern Glasgow in 1991, even allowing for age and sex differences, was 77 per cent above middle class Bearsden and Milngavie, and even considerably higher than in the Western Isles.

What seems to have brought about this dramatic improvement in health was less the discovery of new medical techniques and treatments, and more the impact of rising living standards during much of the second half of the twentieth century. Only after 1945 did families expect all their children to survive into adulthood, and the death of a child became even more of a tragedy because it was so uncommon.

Social deprivation remains a stubborn determinant of health inequalities. The ill-health of Scotland's population is an issue to which we will return in later chapters, but it is worth developing at some length at this point in the book. The authors of the report *Health in Scotland 2002* comment: 'Poverty and social exclusion go hand in hand with a propensity to suffer more ill-health and to die younger than more affluent citizens. While such differences are a common feature of health experience across the UK and the EU, they are generally greater in Scotland than elsewhere' (Scottish Executive 2003a: 3; see also Hanlon et al. 2001: 17). Children of families in the Registrar General social class V are approximately three times more likely to have a mental health problem than those in social class I (Scottish Executive 2003a: 14). Similarly, young people living in the most deprived areas are almost four times more likely than those living in the least deprived areas to commit suicide; women in the most deprived areas are 3.5 times more likely to suffer from acute myocardial infarction, and 3.1 times more likely to have lung and related cancers (Table 2.9).

Inequalities among men are less stark, with ratios of 1.9 for acute myocardial infarction, and 2.9 for lung and related cancers. The Social Disadvantage Research Centre, in the Department of Social Policy and Social Work at the University of Oxford, carried out and published in 2003 a very careful and complex statistical exercise on behalf of the Scottish Executive to examine various kinds of social deprivation, and construct indices at a small area level (Social Disadvantage Research Centre 2003). Deprivation is examined within five domains: Income Deprivation; Employment Deprivation; Health Deprivation and Disability; Education, Skills and Training Deprivation; and Geographical Access to Services. In each domain an index is constructed from various indicators. Health deprivation is much more a feature of urban Scotland, with local authority divisions in the Highlands and Western Isles not figuring among the most deprived as regards health. Forty three per cent of the tenth of divisions that have the greatest health deprivation in Scotland are located in Glasgow (Social Disadvantage Research Centre 2003: 41).

Table 2.9 Health and social deprivation

| | Suicide[2] | | Depression[3] | | Acute myocardial infarction[4] | | Cancer[5] | | |
| | | | | | | | | Illness/condition | |
Deprivation category[1]	age 15–29	age 30+	male	female	male	female	breast[6]	trachea, bronchus and lung male	female
1 (least deprived)	62.3	60.3	66.1	70.2	103.4	25.6	105.5	70.9	31.7
2	74.2	73.3	84.4	90.9	118.4	36.2	104.1	82.8	34.2
3	78.8	90.4	90.6	86.4	135.8	43.6	102.1	94.0	38.3
4	79.7	97.3	94.9	101.1	149.3	55.3	97.9	118.5	46.5
5	111.9	104.0	122.2	113.8	169.3	64.4	93.4	136.8	53.3
6	126.8	106.9	128.5	119.2	184.5	71.7	91.3	159.0	61.1
7 (most deprived)	236.9	170.8	121.6	124.2	192.0	90.4	92.7	208.1	97.0

Source: McLaren and Bain (1998: Appendix).
1. The deprivation categories are explained in the source, and are based on the work of Carstairs and Morris which is discussed in the text.
2. 1991–95, crude mortality rates per 100,000 population.
3. 1991–95, age-standardised first admissions ratios.
4. 1991–93, ages 0–64, age-standardised rate per 100,000 population.
5. 1986–95, age-standardised registration rates.
6. Female only.

For men, Scotland has the highest mortality rate in industrialised countries from coronary heart diseases; for women it has the second highest rate (Falaschetti et al. 2000: 12). The Scottish Health Survey has also found a clear social class gradient in this respect, most notably among women: see Table A8.10 in Chapter 8. The age-standardised incidence runs from 18.2 per cent for men in Registrar General's social class I to 30.4 per cent in social class V; for women, it runs from 14.0 per cent to 28.8 per cent. Similarly, the age-standardised incidence of ischaemic heart disease and strokes is lower among men in social classes I and II (4.1 per cent and 5.9 per cent respectively) than in social classes IV and V (7.9 per cent and 9.2 per cent) (Falaschetti et al. 2000: Table 2.11).

While there is no clear relationship between social class and the non-work accident rate, the rate as regards work-based accidents is, for men, some four times higher for social classes III (manual), IV and V than for social classes I, II and III (non-manual) (Laiho and Purdon 2000: Table 5.20). There is not such a clear relationship between class and the work-based accident rate for women. On the other hand, men in manual work are, in the course of their work, much more likely than non-manual men to meet overall guidelines for physical activity, as we discuss in Chapter 8.

There is a strong and continuing social class gradient in the prevalence of smoking among both men and women, again as discussed more fully in Chapter 8: see Table A8.5 and also Boreham (2000). Similarly, on a 22–item table of adults' diets, the consumption of healthy foods is much more prevalent among classes I and II than among IV and V (Deepchand et al. 2000). For example:

> one half of men and women in Classes I and II ate green vegetables five or more times a week compared with around one-third of those in Classes IV and V. Similar differences were apparent for using semi-skimmed or skimmed milk and eating oily fish, wholemeal bread, fruit and raw vegetables. (Deepchand et al. 2000: 331)

We discuss some further examples in Chapter 8 (Table 8.2). Deepchand et al. (2000: 333) also found that Scotland and England are broadly similar in terms of eating habits, although in Scotland there is marginally less eating of wholemeal bread, high-fibre cereal and non-fat milk, and a greater propensity to consume fried food, chocolate, crisps and biscuits.

A SCOTTISH EFFECT?

The debates about Scotland's health record have been enlivened since the late 1980s by the discovery of a so-called 'Scottish effect'. In 1989, Carstairs and Morris used 1981 census data to establish that the vast majority of excess mortality in Scotland, compared with England and Wales, could be explained by higher levels of deprivation as measured by a composite of social class, unemployment, non-car-ownership, and overcrowding (Carstairs and Morris 1989). Using 1991 census data, however, later researchers concluded that 'deprivation' accounted for around 40 per cent of excess deaths in Scotland at all ages, and 60 per cent of those younger than 65 (Hanlon et al. 2001: 19). Take mortality ratios standardised for age, sex and deprivation, for example. The normal standardised mortality ratio is the ratio between the number of observed deaths in Scotland and the number of deaths that would have been expected if the age and sex structure of Scotland had been the same as in the rest of the UK. When this ratio is further adjusted to estimate what Scottish mortality would be if its deprivation pattern had also been the same as in the rest of the UK, Scotland scored 107.4. That means that, adjusting for age, sex and deprivation, Scotland was 7–plus percentage points above what one would expect. In other words, there seemed to be a 'Scottish effect'.

One key difficulty with such indicators of deprivation as devised originally by Carstairs and Morris is that they are based on aggregate rather than individual level data, and there is a possibility that they are an artefact of using certain aggregated census data. It has been calculated, for example, that up to half of the most deprived *individuals* in Scotland live outwith the most deprived *areas* (Bain 2002: 25).

Later work on international comparisons taking Scotland as a unit seems both to confirm the poor state of the nation's health and also to point to interesting counter-intuitive findings (Leon et al. 2003: 5–6, 8). This research reaches the following conclusions:

- Life expectancy for Scottish women is the lowest in the EU; for men, it is the second lowest. This puts Scotland on an international par with Costa Rica, Cuba, and the Czech Republic, and below other parts of the UK.
- It was only from the mid-twentieth century that Scotland declined relative to others, suggesting that, while other countries improved, Scotland slid down the league table of life expectancy.
- Scotland's poor overall position seems to be driven by very high mortality among adults of working age, rather than among young and old people.
- Not all causes of death show the worst rates in Europe. For example, while male deaths from cardiovascular disease and lung cancer are the highest in Europe (and for women, the highest in the world), Scotland performs relatively well in terms of deaths from injury and violence. Until recently, and contrary to expectations, this was also true for cirrhosis of the liver, rates for which are rapidly deteriorating. What such data

suggest is that Scotland's comparatively poor position as regards health is not simply the result of longstanding factors, but of relative changes in recent history.

• Patterns of premature mortality may be related to complex interactions between, for example, smoking and diet, notably with regard to lung cancer and cardiovascular disease.

In sum, the notion of a 'Scottish effect' might be treated with some caution, designed as it was initially to identify differences in mortality between constituent countries and regions of the UK, and based on aggregate rather than individual-level data. What we can say is that life expectancies have improved across the whole of the twentieth century, but that rates of improvement in the past 50 years have been slower in Scotland than in most western European countries.

DOES RELIGION MATTER?

The Scottish Household Survey of 2001 (Tables A2.5 and A2.6) allows us to relate people's perception of their health to their religion and their ethnicity defined as 'white' or 'non-white'. While a higher percentage of Catholics than of the population as a whole fell into the 'not good' general health category (17.4 per cent compared with 13.8 per cent), non-whites were less likely than the general population to fall into this category. One difficulty in treating religion as an explanatory variable is that it cannot be easily dissociated from other variables such as social class and ethnicity. Thus, in the Scottish context, most Catholics live in west central Scotland and are descended from people of Irish origin who entered the labour market at the lowest manual levels. Hence, the association between religion and health is not a simple one. Is, for example, this association a function of religion per se, or of people's ethnic origins, or of their social class, or possibly of all three operating interactively? Research carried out in the west of Scotland suggests that, for a series of health-related measures, 'it is those respondents with a Catholic parent or who were born Catholic who experience poorer health or physical development' (Abbotts et al. 1997: 3). That study suggests that health risks are most severe among older Catholics, and that these are mediated by social class. In general, religion and social class seem to be operating in the same direction, and interact with each other. Given that much depends on age and social class, for example, one cannot simply conclude that religion and ethnicity in and of themselves are causally related to health, although such research is indicative of such a relationship.

MIGRATION

Fertility and mortality trends in Scotland mainly followed those in the rest of Great Britain. In broad terms, where Scotland did differ was that, historically, more people had emigrated, but far fewer had in-migrated (Figure 2.7). This is the key to understanding why its population has been so static, compared with other western European countries. Scotland had long had a history of emigration which continued in the inter-war period when many Scots emigrated to Australia, New Zealand and Canada, thereby continuing patterns laid down in the previous century. For example, in the 1920s the small increase in improving birth over death rates was reversed by net emigration which totalled almost 400,000, an enormous proportion in a country of only five million people. The rates of emigration slackened in the following decade, only to increase once more during the 1950s and 1960s when Scotland had a net loss of over 0.5 million people.

Figure 2.7 Migration and population change, Scotland and England and Wales, 1901–2001

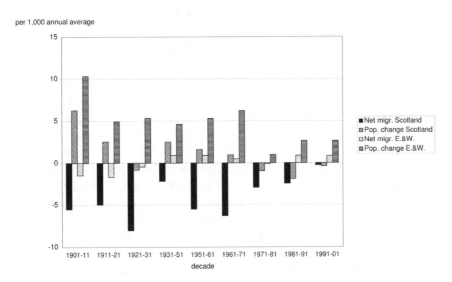

Source: Michael Anderson (see note in Appendix 2).

There was no counter in-migration to Scotland such as occurred in England from New Commonwealth countries after the Second World War, no major net incoming of population after the Irish arrived in the nineteenth century. This helped to reinforce the sense that Scotland was manifestly a society of emigrants, not immigrants. By 2001, over 800,000 people living in England and Wales had been born in Scotland (England and Wales Census 2001: Table KS05). In return, about 13 per cent of people living in Scotland were born elsewhere (Census 2001: Table CAS015), the largest group – 8 per cent – having been born in England. Until the 1980s, Scotland never had more than 10 per cent of its population born elsewhere. The 2001 figure of 13 per cent is much the same as in England (also 13 per cent) and is lower than in Wales (25 per cent). Nevertheless, whereas 9 per cent of Scotland's 2001 population were born in the rest of the UK, in England this figure was only 3 per cent, half of them born in Scotland and reflecting the integrated labour market of the UK. In Wales, 21 per cent were born in the rest of the UK, but under 1 per cent were born in Scotland; 20 per cent were born in England. Over 9 per cent of the population of England was born outwith the UK, compared with just under 4 per cent of Scotland's and about 3 per cent of that of Wales.

The areas with the highest proportions of people born outside Scotland are – with the exception of Edinburgh – not the large urban areas but the rural regions of southern Scotland and some parts of the north and the Highlands and Islands (Census 2001: Table KS05). The proportions born outside Scotland were 20 per cent or over in Argyll and Bute (22 per cent), Edinburgh (22 per cent), Moray (22 per cent), the Borders (21 per cent) and Dumfries and Galloway (20 per cent). In all 32 council areas, the largest group of people born outside Scotland were born in England: for example, 17 per cent of the total resident population in Argyll and Bute, 12 per cent in Edinburgh, 16 per cent in Moray, 17 per cent in the Borders and 16 per cent in Dumfries and Galloway. Data from the British Household Panel Survey broadly confirm this (Table A2.7), and allow us to investigate movement within and among broad regions of Scotland: in both Tayside and the north-east, two-thirds of residents were born in the same broad area, in contrast to only 46 per cent in the Highlands and Islands and 40 per cent in the south-west. Data in that same table also show that, in every broad region, most incomers were from another region of Scotland, not from outside the country.

The post-war period did see a substantial redistribution of population within Scotland from south-west and west-central areas to the east and the north-east (Registrar General for Scotland 2002b: Figure 2.5). Glasgow, whose population stood at over one million as late as 1961, tried to solve its overcrowding problems by exporting significant numbers to New Towns via its overspill policies, first in East Kilbride and then in Cumbernauld. Only later did it discover that those who went were disproportionately the younger and more skilled, and that it was retaining within the city's boundaries a disproportionately ageing and low-skilled workforce. Scotland was one of the most urbanised societies in the world by the early twentieth century: by 1911, 30 per cent of Scots lived in one of the four main cities, rising to 38 per cent by 1951. But that trend has reversed, and the proportion in these four cities was back to 27 per cent by the turn of the century (Registrar General for Scotland 1961: 8–9; City of Edinburgh Council 2003: Table 1).

CONCLUSION

What broad conclusions can we come to about Scotland's demography? The first thing to be said is that, in general terms, Scotland has followed the broad trends in western societies: from high to low birth and death rates. It is, however, different in one crucial respect. It is failing to reproduce itself in comparison with other countries of the UK, as well as in western Europe. Although its historically high levels of emigration have fallen off – if only because the traditional routes to the likes of Canada, Australia and New Zealand have been restricted – it is fairly clear that its population loss is longstanding and pervasive, reinforcing a culture of geographical mobility furth of Scotland. In broad terms, it is not the loss of its population through emigration which is the issue today, but the fact that a dramatically falling birth rate is not compensated for by sufficient inward migration. At a UK level, for example, this makes a crucial difference, given that projections suggest that net migration will account for 70 per cent of overall population change between 2001 and 2011 (Office of National Statistics 2002a: 31). In some respects, internal shifts of population compound the issue. Within Scotland, there has been a population shift from west to east: Glasgow's and Edinburgh's populations are converging, the size of Edinburgh being 78 per cent of that of Glasgow, compared with 50 per cent in the 1960s (Registrar General for Scotland 1961: 9; City of Edinburgh Council 2003: Table 1). Scotland's policy makers are having to juggle with different sets of demographic issues. Thus, rural, small-town Scotland, including much of the Highlands, shows modest natural increases with above-average fertility and low mortality, and is able to attract net in-migration (Anderson 2004). Similarly, the east coast regions around Edinburgh and Aberdeen have high levels of inward migration, often from overseas, though constrained housing markets and full employment appear to impact upon low fertility rates as many women in child-bearing ages are working outwith the home. Post-industrial Scotland, as typified by Glasgow and west central Scotland, has very low birth rates, high mortality, levels of morbidity well above the average, and continuing out-migration; these present the country's leaders with perhaps their greatest challenge.

NOTES

1. Scotland and Wales, unlike England and Northern Ireland, had an excess of deaths over births between, for example, mid-1999 and mid-2000, but in Wales, this shortfall was compensated for by net inward migration (Office of National Statistics 2001: Table 3.11).
2. The standardised mortality ratio for Scotland in 2000 was 118 compared to a UK average of 100 (Office of National Statistics 2001: Table 1.21).

CHAPTER 3

Families and Households

The twentieth century saw a dramatic fall in family size. At the beginning of the century it was not uncommon for completed families to have six or more children. Family size at this time was also class dependent, for manual labourers had almost twice the number of children of middle-class professionals. The lower the social class you belonged to, the more children you tended to have (Anderson 1996: 386). Only in the second half of the century did these social class differences come to narrow significantly. The control of family size in Scotland, as elsewhere, was the result of a complex of factors including changing social aspirations coupled with birth control technology and lengthening child dependency, especially for the middle classes. Michael Anderson observes: 'For the increasingly child-centred middle classes, the aspiration for each child to have his or her own bedroom and to own special and increasingly expensive toys was equally challenging' (Anderson 1992: 37). Not only did family size fall as the century progressed, but families were completed earlier as child-bearing was concentrated into shorter periods of time.

HOUSING AND HOUSEHOLDS

In the first part of the twentieth century, the size of families, combined with the kind of housing available at the time, led to overcrowding. In 1911, over half of all Scottish households lived in houses with two rooms or fewer, compared with only 7 per cent in England (in Scotland the term 'house' includes flats). More than one in ten Scots at this time lived in houses with only one room. This state of affairs took a considerable time to change, so that even as late as 1951 over a quarter of Scotland's urban population still lived in two-roomed accommodation. 'Overcrowding' remained a fact of everyday life in Scotland for much of the twentieth century (Rodger 1989).

Smaller family sizes, the fact that children survived infancy more successfully, and the fact that there was a lengthening period of childhood and adolescence brought about by education put greater emphasis on the family. A major programme of house-building which sought to ensure that every nuclear family had its own domestic space helped to generate home-centredness or 'privatism' which became the norm, or at least the ideal (Smout 1992: 277). By the beginning of the twenty-first century, most Scottish households enjoyed space provision which allowed for a more privatised existence, although, as we shall see in Chapter 8, this does not necessarily imply that all leisure takes place within the family house. Most households are happily provided for in terms of space and amenities. It is a measure of the housing revolution of the last few decades that as many as 93 per cent of households have central heating, and fewer than one in 2,000 households do not have sole use of a bath/shower and toilet (Census 2001: Table CAS055).

The turn-around in housing conditions is reflected in the fact that while the average size of Scottish households is now 2.3 persons, the average number of rooms they occupy is 4.7 (Census 2001: Table S51). In other words, each person has the equivalent of two rooms, although around 12 per cent of households were judged to have 'too few rooms per resident' (Census 2001: Table CAS053).[1] Such households are more likely to be found in the 'other rented sector' (housing associations and co-operatives) or in the private rented sector. In these sectors, 31 per cent and 26 per cent respectively are 'overcrowded' according to this measure.

The character of Scottish housing has also changed. By 2001, almost two-thirds (63 per cent) of Scottish households live in a house or a bungalow, and a third (33 per cent) in flats or apartments (Census 2001: Table CAS048). Tenements may dominate the centre of Scottish cities, but most Scots now live in 'houses' in the English sense of that term. There is of course considerable variation across Scotland. In Glasgow, for example, 68 per cent of households live in flats or apartments, and 30 per cent in houses (detached, semi-detached or terraced), while in Edinburgh, the figures are 55 per cent and 40 per cent respectively (City of Edinburgh Council 2003: Table 4). Only in Aberdeen is there a rough balance between flats (47 per cent) and houses (48 per cent).

There has also been a dramatic shift in terms of housing tenure (see Figure 8.2 in Chapter 8). Whereas in 1979 only 35 per cent of dwellings were owner-occupied, and 54 per cent were rented from the council, by 1999, 62 per cent were owner-occupied, and only 25 per cent were rented from the council, with a further 6 per cent rented from housing associations. Once more, there is considerable variation between Scotland's main cities.

Households in Edinburgh (69 per cent) and Aberdeen (61 per cent) are more likely to be owner-occupied, but even in Glasgow nearly a majority (49 per cent) of households are owner-occupied (City of Edinburgh Council 2003: Table 5).

CHANGING HOUSEHOLDS

Small households are now the clear norm in Scotland (Table 3.1). Those consisting of one or two people account for 63 per cent of all households, roughly split between one and two persons (in the table, the categories 'single adult', 'small adult', 'older smaller' and 'single pensioner'). The percentage of households falling into the Census definition of a 'family household' has fallen over 20 years from 34 per cent to 20 per cent. In a nice symmetry, single adult and small adult households (those with one or two adults of non-pensionable age and without children) have risen as a proportion from 21 per cent in 1981 to 35 per cent in 2001. At the same time, the proportion described as 'single parent' tripled, from 2 per cent to

Table 3.1 Household type, 1981–2001

% of households	Year		
Household type[1]	1981	1991	2001
single adult	7	13	18
small adult	14	16	17
single parent	2	5	6
small family[2]	19	15	13
large family[2]	15	9	7
large adult	14	13	11
older smaller	14	13	13
single pensioner	15	16	15

Sources: Census 2001 (Table 3); Registrar General for Scotland (1983c: Table 25).
1. Terminology is from Scottish Household Survey, for example, Scottish Executive (2002c: 206–7):
    single adult: one adult of non-pensionable age, no children;
    small adult: two adults of non-pensionable age, no children;
    single parent: one adult of any age, one or more children;
    small family: two adults of any age, one or two children;
    large family: two adults of any age, three or more children; or three or more adults of any age, one or more children;
    large adult: three or more adults of any age, no children;
    older smaller: two adults, at least one of pensionable age, no children;
    single pensioner: one adult of pensionable age, no children.
    (pensionable age means 60 for women and 65 for men).
2. In 1981, families with two unmarried adults and three or more children (less than 1.5 per cent of all households) are grouped with 'small family'; in 1991 and 2001 they are grouped with 'large family'.

6 per cent. The most significant rise occurred among single adult households (from 7 per cent in 1981 to 18 per cent in 2001), as young people in particular set up home at a much earlier age than their counterparts in southern Europe. Scotland seems to share with other northern European countries such expectations for making the life-course transitions of leaving home. Iacovou (2001) and Iacovou and Berthoud (2001) contrast the 'northern' pattern exemplified by Denmark, the Netherlands, the UK, France, Belgium and Luxembourg, with the 'southern' pattern of the more traditional, family-oriented and predominantly Catholic countries of Italy, Spain, Portugal, Ireland and Greece.

While Scotland has an ageing population, pensioner households remain at just under 30 per cent of all households. Calculated on the basis of persons rather than households, the largest proportion of individuals (36 per cent) still live in 'family' units with one or more children (42 per cent when lone-parent households are included), and the archetypal 'family' unit of two adults and one or two dependent children now accounts for just over one-fifth of all persons, but only 13 per cent of all households (Census 2001: Table 3).

Table 3.2 is based on data from the Scottish Household Survey 2001, and helps to portray how different age groups move through household types over time. Thus, 16–24 year olds are mainly to be found in large family (22 per cent) and large adult (38 per cent) households, indicating that most have not yet left their families of origin. Indeed, despite all these changes in household forms, it is still the case that a large majority of young people live with two natural parents at least until they reach school-leaving age. From the School Leavers Surveys that are referred to in the footnote of Table A3.1, we can calculate that the proportion of young people who normally lived with two natural parents when they were in fourth year at secondary school was 82 per cent among school leavers in 1980 and 74 per cent among people who were in fourth year in 1997–8. Indeed, if we add in people who lived with a parent and a step-parent, the proportions were 86 per cent and 81 per cent.

By the time people are aged 25–34, however, Table 3.2 shows they are mainly in small family units (34 per cent) or in small adult (24 per cent) households. The 35–44 age group are in small family units (38 per cent) or large family units (21 per cent), whereas the 45–59 year olds are in small adult (38 per cent) or large adult (26 per cent) households. By the time people are aged 60–74, they tend to live in older smaller households (57 per cent) or single pensioner households (25 per cent), a situation somewhat reversed for people aged 75 and over, who occupy single pensioner (54 per cent) or older smaller (42 per cent) households.

Table 3.2 Household type by age of adult population, 2001

% of individuals				Age			All
Household type[1]	16–24	25–34	35–44	45–59	60–74	75 +	
single adult	11	15	10	14	3	0	9
small adult	17	24	13	38	5	0	19
single parent	4	10	7	1	0	0	3
small family	8	34	38	7	1	0	16
large family	22	8	21	9	1	1	10
large adult	38	9	9	26	9	3	16
older smaller	0	1	1	4	57	42	17
single pensioner	0	0	0	0	25	54	10
Sample size	1,204	2,365	2,704	3,344	3,215	1,811	14,643

Source: Scottish Executive (2002c: Table 1.10), using Scottish Household Survey 2001, weighted (sample sizes unweighted).
1. For terminology, see Table 3.1.

Looking at the data on households in another way, we find that most people in single adult households (59 per cent) have never been married, that 21 per cent are divorced, and 10 per cent separated (Scottish Executive 2002c: Table 1.12). On the other hand, among people in small family, large family and small adult households, marriage is the main relationship (79 per cent, 67 per cent and 66 per cent respectively). Almost half of all lone parents (48 per cent) have never been married, while a further 22 per cent are divorced, and 23 per cent separated.

Family and household sizes are of course the outcome of complex and dynamic social processes. Almost three-quarters of households in Scotland do not have any children under 16 years of age living in them, compared with just under two-thirds two decades ago (Table 3.3). What this means is that only about one in four households in Scotland have dependent children living at home. Furthermore, large families have virtually disappeared, as a mere 4 per cent have three or more children under 16 in the household, less than two-thirds the proportion only two decades ago.

Table 3.3 Number of dependent children[1] in household, 1981–2001

% of households		Year	
Number children	1981	1991	2001
0	64.4	71.8	73.8
1	14.8	12.5	12.1
2	14.3	11.3	10.4
3+	6.5	4.4	3.9

Sources: Census 2001 (Table 4); Registrar General for Scotland (1983a: Table 36).
1. Children aged 15 or under in 1981.

In the previous chapter, we explored patterns of migration into and out of Scotland, showing, for example, that over 800,000 people living in England and Wales had been born in Scotland. While levels of emigration furth of the UK have tailed off in recent years, there is still a considerable amount of geographical mobility, differentiated by types of household (Figure 3.1). These data show the place of birth of individuals in Scotland in 1999, according to the type of household in which they lived.

Figure 3.1 Place of birth of individuals, by household type in which living, 1999

% within household type

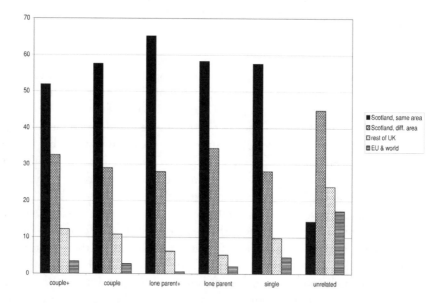

Source: Table A3.2.
Key to household type:
    couple+: couple, married or cohabiting, with dependent child(ren).
    couple: couple with no dependent child(ren).
    lone parent+: lone parent with dependent child(ren).
    lone parent: lone parent with no dependent child(ren).
    single: single person.
    unrelated: unrelated adults.

We can see that the least mobile households are those likely to be among the least affluent, notably lone parents, with or without dependent children living with them. As many as 65 per cent of lone parents with dependent children, for example, still live in the same area in which they were born, compared with 52 per cent of couples with dependent children. The most mobile, on the other hand, are unrelated adults, as many as 41 per cent of whom were born outwith Scotland, including 17 per cent outwith the UK; 55 per cent of people in this category were full-time students. The category 'single person' could have been divided into 'elderly' and 'non-elderly', but in fact the pattern for these sub-categories was very similar.

We began this chapter observing the significant class differential in family size at the beginning of the twentieth century, where manual working class families were twice the size of middle class ones. It is hard to find equivalent data 100 years on, but the Scottish School Leavers survey can be used, with caution, to support the view that class differences in family size have dwindled: see Figure 3.2. For example, the ratio as regards family size between the professional and managerial group and the unskilled manual group was 1.4 to 1 in 1981, and down to almost parity (1 to 1.1) by 1999.

Figure 3.2 Family size and socio-economic group, among school leavers, 1981–99

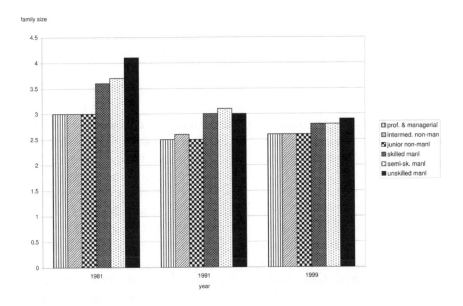

Source: Table A3.1.

FORMING AND RE-FORMING HOUSEHOLDS

What can be said about the process of household formation? First of all, fewer people are getting married, and at a later age. From the 1930s until the

1970s, the percentage of people in the relevant age groups (20–34) never marrying fell, and then climbed steadily so that more Scots today are not marrying than at any time since the 1850s (see Figure 3.3).

Figure 3.3 Never married women per 1,000 population by selected age group, 1901–2001

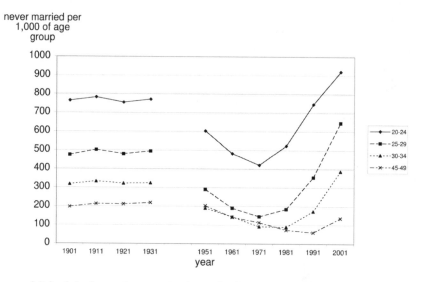

Source: Michael Anderson (see note in Appendix 2); no census in 1941.

Might this simply be a function of people forming cohabiting partnerships without actually marrying? Certainly far more people are cohabiting than before, but this does not explain the phenomenon, for the trends in both marriage and cohabitation (at least for women) both show a growing propensity to do neither. In other words, while the trend lines for non-marriage among 20–24, 25–29 and 30–34 year olds are steep, especially since the 1980s, there are comparable inclines as regards (non-)cohabitation. In other words, young people seem to be choosing to remain unattached rather than to enter into formal or informal relationships. Barlow (2002) has observed that age is an important indicator of the likelihood of cohabitation, as is religion, or, rather, the lack of it, given that the decline in adherence to religious beliefs appears to have contributed to the social acceptability of cohabitation.

There has also been a dramatically steep rise in the age of marriage since the 1970s (Figure 3.4). By 2001, the average age of marriage for men was 34.8, compared with a low of 26.5 in the 1960s, and much higher than the 1920s and 1930s when it rose to around age 28 for men (Anderson 1992: 33). The trends for women are comparable, with the average age of marriage for women standing at 32.3 in 2001, from a previous low of 24.1 in the 1960s. One might be tempted to argue that these rising averages are simply the result of the rise in divorce rates and re-marriage thereafter. Table A3.3 shows, however, that this cannot be the explanation, for the rise in the average age of marriage holds for women and men, and, crucially, for bachelors, divorcees, and even for widows/widowers. In other words, we can be fairly sure that there is a clear trend to postpone marriage regardless of sex and marital status. With respect to first marriages, some of the rise is due to cohabitation for a year or two before getting married. Hinds and Jamieson (2002: 35) cite Haskey (1999) to say that 'by the 1990s the majority of couples marrying for the first time had lived together before marriage' and Ermisch (2000) in support of the view that 'cohabitation has become part of the process of finding someone to marry'.

Figure 3.4 Mean age at marriage, by sex, 1941–2001

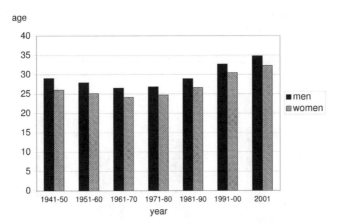

Source: Table A3.3.

We can look at the issue in a slightly different way, by focusing on the profile of all people over the legal age of marriage (Figure 3.5). By 2001, only 50 per cent of people over 16 were in marriages and not separated, compared with 63 per cent twenty years earlier. (This latter figure somewhat exaggerates the fall as it contains people who were separated, a category disaggregated in 2001.) The major increase is in single people (from 25 per cent to 31 per cent), pointing in part to the decline in the popularity of formal marriage. Cohabiting is most common among people aged 25–34, with 20 per cent living together, and then falls steadily, already down to 9 per cent for those aged 35–44 (Scottish Executive 2002c: Table 1.11). Overall, 20 per cent of small adult households are based on cohabitation.

Half of all cohabitees are to be found in small adult households but a further third (31 per cent) are in small family households with one or more children (Scottish Executive 2002c: Table 1.12). Anne Barlow (2002: 74) cites data from the Scottish Social Attitudes Survey of 2000 showing that 37 per cent of cohabitants have children from that relationship, and comments: 'This confirms that the traditional social norm of child-rearing within marriage has lost much of its force and that, for many, parenting and cohabitation now go hand in hand'. She further cites data showing 'that whilst marriage is still recognised as a valuable parenting structure, there is undoubted appreciation of the fact that it is not necessarily the best or most effective'. She goes on to show (74–5) that it is women under 25 who have shifted most markedly from a traditional view and suggests that 'they may also be the most influential in how family patterns do actually change in the coming years'. She also reports (66–7) that 31 per cent of the whole sample had experienced cohabitation, while 22 per cent of those now married had cohabited in the past. Just under half of those who had ever cohabited had subsequently married that partner.

Figure 3.5 Marital status of people aged 16 and over, 1981–2001

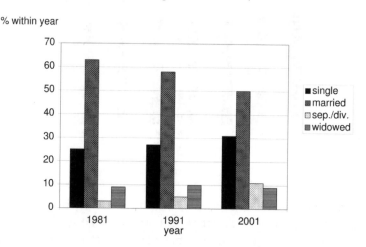

Source: Table A3.4.
Note that 'separated' was not available as a category in 1991 or 1981, and so has been combined with 'divorced' in the graph. Likewise, 're-married' is included with 'married' in the graph because it was not available as a category in 1981. The full figures are in the source table.

These figures confirm that many of cohabiting relationships are long-lived, although there is also evidence of a higher rate of breakdown of cohabiting relationships than marriage relationships (Haskey 1999). Barlow

(2002: 73–4) discusses the issue in some detail and argues that 'we are right to expect not only the incidence of cohabitation to increase as has been predicted (Shaw and Haskey 1999) but also an increase as time goes on in the average duration of such relationships'. What suggests further that these are not fleeting arrangements is the dramatic rise in live births to unmarried parents (Table A3.5). Whereas in 1981, for example, the ratio of live births to married and unmarried parents was roughly nine to one, by 2001 it was just over 1.5 to one, and, crucially, by far the largest proportion of births to unmarried parents (around 75 per cent) were to those living at the same address.

Do people marry people like themselves? In other words, how much homogamy is there? Much has been made about the significance of religious sectarianism in Scotland, and it does seem that people tend to marry those like themselves in terms of religious beliefs and practices (Table A3.6). Thus, in almost nine out of ten households in which the highest income earner is a member of the Church of Scotland, that member is married to another member of the Kirk, just as almost eight out of ten people with no religious affiliation marry those with none. Somewhat surprisingly, however, only seven in ten Catholics are married to fellow co-religionists, suggesting that there is a significant minority of Catholics in 'mixed' marriages, with Catholic/Church of Scotland partnerships being the most common at almost one in six of all marriages where there is a Catholic main-income householder. The extent of inter-marriage is even higher if the calculations are done on the basis of individuals rather than households (Bruce and Glendinning 2003: 106–7).

Scotland is a country with a relatively small number of ethnic minorities (around 2 per cent, and mainly of Pakistani, Indian or Chinese origin) but fully one-third of main-income householders from non-white backgrounds are married to or cohabiting with white partners (Table A3.7). One does not get the sense, then, of an ethnically segregated society if there are, in fact, more mixed ethnic partnerships proportionally than mixed religious ones.

While people are living longer, they are far less likely to remain with the same marriage partner. Michael Anderson observes that the rapid growth in divorce in Scotland began in the mid-1960s, well before the 1976 Divorce Act, and was spread across all durations of marriage: 'It thus probably reflected a rise in tensions within marriages as expectations of men and women about family and work life changed, together with an increasing willingness to resolve these tensions by terminating marriages that had become unsatisfactory to one or both of the partners' (Anderson 1992: 38). Barlow (2002: 65) reports Scottish Executive figures showing 1,200 divorce actions being filed in 1999, an increase of 41 per cent over the 850 in 1979. While it is true that marriages of less than ten years are more likely to fail than those lasting longer (Table A3.8), we are beginning to see a lengthening in the duration of marriages which end in divorce (a median of ten years in the 1980s, and 13 years in 2000). There has also been a significant increase in the percentage of marriages of 25 years and over which end in divorce (up from one in ten of all divorces in the early 1980s, to one in six by 2001). The changing social significance of divorce is also reflected in the legal grounds given (Table A3.9). Whereas, for example, 'behaviour' was the most common reason given in 1981 (42 per cent), by 2001 only 15 per cent of divorces took place on these grounds, with almost eight out of ten ending on grounds of non-cohabitation, mainly within two years which requires mutual consent. In other words, the accusatory 'guilty party' nature of divorce seems to have been replaced by more 'neutral' grounds of irretrievable breakdown, something the legal process both reflects and amplifies.

What can we glean from such data about how marriages and partnerships form and re-form? The most striking feature of the last few decades is that far fewer people are choosing to enter such relationships, whether marriages or cohabitations but especially the former. This, of course, tells us nothing about the short-term and more casual relationships which people have. Marriage has, probably for the first time, become something of a minority pursuit, while at the same time over a quarter of people over 16 have some experience of being married but are no longer married to their original partner, being either divorced, separated, widowed or subsequently married to someone else. People enter into marriage far later than at any time for over 150 years. Not only are people having fewer children, but more are being born to unmarried parents such that, on present trends, a majority will be so born by the end of the first decade of the new century (based on an extrapolation from Table A3.5). More marriages are ending in divorce, and not simply those entered into more recently. Further, it seems that fewer end in court action, given the rise in non-cohabitation as the main grounds for divorce. This process of partnering, break-up and re-partnering is also reflected in the diversity of household types, and the increase in single adult and small adult households.

CONCLUSION

What is striking about the past twenty years is how diverse and varied households have become. The classical 'family' of two parents and dependent children is now the exception rather than the rule, and there is a much more complex process of household formation and re-formation than ever before. People move in and out of household forms as they age and as their socio-economic circumstances change. Change in economic opportunities are reflected in household structures, most notably driven by a higher percentage of women in employment, a postponement of the age of marriage and of child-bearing, as well as greater economic independence for women and young people in particular. We develop these economic themes further in the next chapter, where we focus on changes in work and employment which remain the greatest determinant of people's life chances in modern Scotland, as in advanced industrial societies more generally.

NOTES

1. The occupancy rating used in the census assumes that every household, including one-person households, requires a minimum of two common rooms (excluding bathrooms) (Census 2001: Table CAS053, note 1).

CHAPTER 4

Work and Employment

In this chapter we will explore what Scots do for a living, and how it has changed over the last few decades. We will confine ourselves to issues of economic activity as defined by census and other official sources, without implying that non-paid work is unimportant. Indeed, sustaining the household – 'looking after the home and family' in census terminology – is an integral part of economic activity. What is interesting in this respect is that only 9 per cent of all women between the ages of 16 and 74 are so recorded, down one half in ten years, suggesting that more women are having to juggle the life/work balance (Table 4.1). We will focus too on work and employment status in the main, and would alert the reader to the fact that an analysis of social class, which relies heavily but not exclusively on occupational data, can be found in Chapter 6 which should be read in close conjunction with this one.

EMPLOYMENT STATUS

Around seven out of ten people in Scotland are defined as 'economically active', in that they are working, unemployed or a student, virtually the same as in 1991 and 1981 (Table 4.1). Within this category, however, there are interesting changes, notably the halving of persons unemployed (from 7.1 per cent to 3.8 per cent), with modest increases in part-time working and the self-employed. The most notable change, however, is with respect to gender: the proportion of men who were economically active fell over the two decades from 85 per cent to 78 per cent, whereas for women the rate rose from 53 per cent to 64 per cent. Correspondingly, the proportion of women looking after the home full-time fell from one in three to one in 12. Further data from the Labour Force Survey, cited in *Scottish Social Statistics* (Scottish Executive 2001a: Table 4.3), show that in 1999 over 70 per cent of women with no children, or whose youngest child was over five, were economically active compared with 60 per cent where the youngest child was under five. Most women are now in formal employment (55 per cent), the first time that a majority of women have been so recorded (Figure 4.2 and Table 4.1); a majority (59 per cent) of men are, too, but this is a drop from 64 per cent in 1981 (Figure 4.1 and Table 4.1).

Figure 4.1 Economic activity among men aged 16–74, 1981–2001

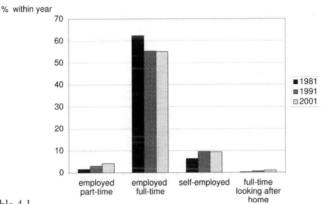

Source: Table 4.1.

Figure 4.2 Economic activity among women aged 16–74, 1981–2001

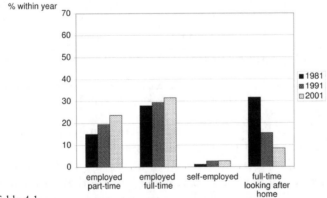

Source: Table 4.1.

Much of the increase for women results from more of them working part-time, up from one-sixth in 1981 to one-quarter twenty years later. Women work part-time, by and large, in order to accommodate their domestic responsibilities (Table A4.1). Three out of four women cite family reasons for working part-time, either because they choose to spend more time with their family or because their domestic commitments prevent them from

Table 4.1 Economic activity, by gender, among people aged 16–74, 1981–2001

% in columns within sex	Year		
	1981	1991	2001
Males			
Employed, part-time	1.6	3.0	4.2
Employed, full-time	62.4	55.4	55.1
Self-employed, part-time[1]	6.3	0.2	0.9
Self-employed, full-time[1]		9.3	8.4
Unemployed[2]	10.2	7.4	5.2
Student	4.6	3.4	3.8
Retired	11.1	10.2	10.4
Full-time looking after home	0.2	0.6	1.0
Long-term sick or disabled	3.2	6.7	8.0
Other	0.3	3.8	3.0
Sample size	7463	4914	4256
Females			
Employed, part-time	15.0	19.5	23.6
Employed, full-time	27.9	29.4	31.5
Self-employed, part-time[1]	1.1	1.0	1.2
Self-employed, full-time[1]		1.6	1.5
Unemployed[2]	4.2	4.2	2.6
Student	4.8	2.7	3.9
Retired	13.6	16.7	16.7
Full-time looking after home	31.6	15.5	8.5
Long-term sick or disabled	1.5	4.8	7.3
Other	0.3	4.8	3.3
Sample size	7933	5442	4750

Sources: Labour Force Survey March–May 2001, 1991, 1981, weighted (sample sizes unweighted).
1. Separate figures not available for 1981 for full-time and part-time self-employment.
2. ILO definition in 2001, 'unemployed and seeking work' in 1981 and 1991.

working full-time. Part-time working is overwhelmingly a female activity, for only 15 per cent of part-time workers are male (Table 4.1) and their reasons for working part-time are different. Such men are far more likely than women to say that they do so either because they earn enough part-time or because they are financially secure. Similarly, a greater proportion of women than of men is in temporary work (Table A4.2), and, again, for many this seems to be a matter of preference, probably constrained by domestic circumstances (Table A4.3). In 2001, 44 per cent of men in temporary employment said that they did so because they could not find permanent work (compared with 31 per cent of women who gave this response); 29 per cent of women said they did not want a permanent job (compared with 17 per cent of men). Indeed, there appears to have been a rise in the number of women not wanting a permanent job in recent years. In general, then, there have been significant changes in the pattern of women's economic activity over the last 20 years.

Let us continue to explore this theme of gender and economic activity. To what extent do women in Scotland have different employment trajectories compared with men? This introduces the key variable of age, for the nature of employment for both genders changes as people get older: see Figures 4.3 and 4.4. In very broad terms, men and women are not dissimilar as regards how their employment statuses change as people age.[1] Thus, the vast majority of both genders are in paid work during the ages 25–54, with almost nine out of ten men, and more than seven out of ten women, in paid employment or seeking work. More men than women are economically active in all age groups but noticeably between the ages of 16–19, and over 60, reflecting the current earlier retirement age for women and young women's greater propensity to stay on in initial education (see Chapter 7). Nevertheless, most young people, men and women, are still in education until age 18, just as at the other end of the age distribution virtually identical proportions of both genders – eight out of ten – are retired by the age of 65. Some of the interesting differences between the genders relate to the 'other economically inactive' category, where the peak for women comes between the ages of 55 and 59 (38 per cent), and for men between 60 and 64 (32 per cent), suggesting that for some men at least long-term sickness and disablement is a prelude to formal retirement at age 65. In any event, both genders have seen a significant increase in the numbers registered as long-term sick and disabled: a 150 per cent increase for men, and a 387 per cent increase for women (Table 4.1).

THE CHANGING CHARACTER OF EMPLOYMENT

How has the nature of work in Scotland changed over our recent history? There are two key components: the sectors in which people are employed (what is called the Standard Industrial Classification) – agriculture, manufacturing, hotels and restaurants, education, public administration, and so on – and the occupations they perform, whether they are, for example, managers, administrative staff, manual workers. How these map on to each other is interesting but complicated, and will be developed more in Chapter 6 when we discuss social class. Nevertheless, it is a vital part of our story of Scotland's changing social structure, and it merits some elaboration here.

As we can see from Figure 4.5 and Table 4.2, there have been significant changes as well as stability over the past twenty years. The number of people working in manufacturing has fallen, from around one in four in 1981, to

Figure 4.3 Economic activity of men by age, 2001

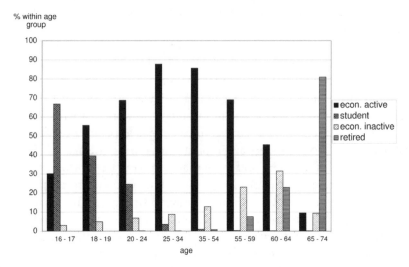

Source: Census 2001 (Table CAS028).

Figure 4.4 Economic activity of women by age, 2001

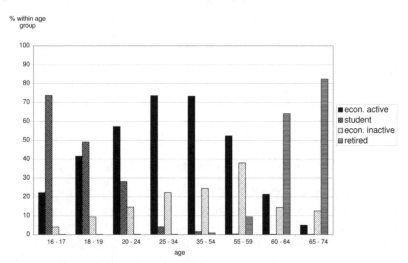

Source: Census 2001 (Table CAS028).

around one in seven today. It is interesting that the decline in what used to be called 'primary' industries – agriculture, fishing, mining and quarrying – has not been at anything like this rate in recent years, but that is because employment in these industries, as a proportion of all employment, had been in steady decline for much of the second half of the twentieth century. By 1981, only 5.4 per cent worked in these industries, and by 2001 only 3.6 per cent.

Figure 4.5 Broad industrial sector of people in employment, 1981–2001

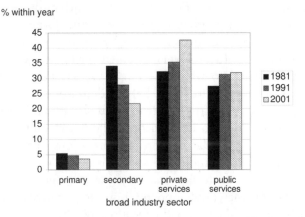

Source: Table 4.2: 'primary' is the first three categories in that table; 'secondary' is the next three; 'private services' is all the categories from 'wholesale' to 'real estate'; 'public services' is all the categories from 'public administration' to 'other community' etc.

Table 4.2 Industry section,[1] of people in employment aged 16 or older,[2] 1981–2001

% in columns	Year		
Section	1981	1991	2001
Agriculture, hunting and forestry	2.9	2.5	2.1
Fishing	0.4	0.5	0.3
Mining, quarrying	2.1	1.7	1.2
Manufacturing	24.1	18.5	13.2
Electricity, gas and water supply	1.4	1.2	1.0
Construction	8.6	8.2	7.5
Wholesale, retail and motor trade	14.5	14.6	14.4
Hotels and restaurants	4.5	4.5	5.7
Transport, storage and communication	6.9	6.6	6.7
Financial intermediation	2.7	3.5	4.6
Real estate, renting and business activity	3.7	6.2	11.2
Public administration and defence	7.0	7.9	7.0
Education	7.2	7.6	7.3
Health and social work	9.5	11.5	12.4
Other community, social and personal	3.8	4.4	5.2
Private households with employees	0.4	0.4	0.1
Outside UK	0.3	0.2	0.0

Sources: Registrar General for Scotland (1983b: Table 9); Registrar General for Scotland (1994b: Table 8); Census 2001(Table UV34).
1. Standard Industrial Classification 1992; for 1981 and 1991, the 1980 classification has been converted to the 1992 classification by means of an approximation derived using the table on p. 37 of volume 5 of the user guide for the Labour Force Survey of June–August 2002.
2. 16 or older in 1981 and 1901 censuses; 16–74 in 2001 census; March–May 2001 Labour Force Survey shows very similar pattern for 16 or older.

If manufacturing is no longer the important employer it once was, which sectors are the growth points? Finance, together with business and property management, are major growth areas, with the former increasing its proportion of employment over 20 years by more than 70 per cent, and the latter growing threefold to over one in ten of all people employed (Table 4.2). Perhaps contrary to what one might expect, not all public sector employment has increased its share. Public administration, and education, are virtually static in proportional terms, while health and social work has risen by nearly one third to 12 per cent, and other community, social and personal services by a similar proportion from a lower base.

The gendering of these industrial sectors is quite distinctive (Figure 4.6 and Table 4.3). Manufacturing and construction employed one-third of men (and, unsurprisingly, only one in ten women), whereas wholesale and retail, health and social work, and education together employed half of all women (compared with just over one in five men).

Figure 4.6 Broad industrial sector of people in employment, by sex, 2001

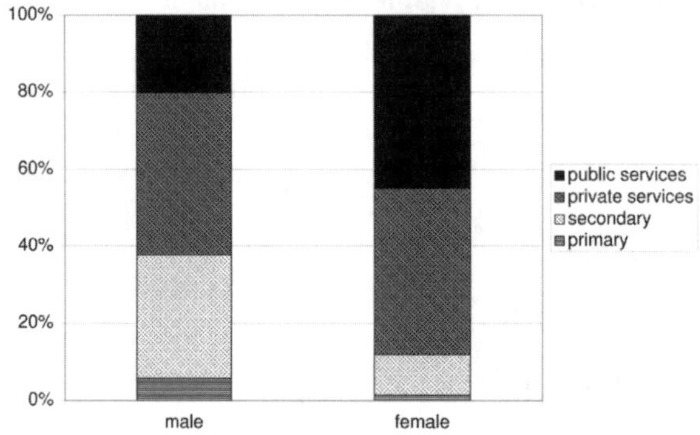

Source: Table 4.3; for meaning of broad categories, see note to Figure 4.5.

In large part, the uneven growth in public sector employment reflects the shift away from the public to the private sector. Whereas, for example, the private/public split in employment terms in 1979 was 58/43, by 2001 it stood at 68/32 in favour of the private sector (Table A4.4). The virtual demise of nationalised industries and public companies nowadays concentrates public sector employment in health, in education at both the school and post-school level, and in the various other services administered by local government.

Employment is but one measure of value, and we can be misled if we assume that diminishing employment equates with diminishing value. The gross value added (GVA) index neatly indicates just how uneven GVA is

Table 4.3 Industry section, of people in employment aged 16–74, by sex, 2001

% in columns	Male	Female
Section		
Agriculture, hunting and forestry	3.2	0.9
Fishing	0.5	0.1
Mining, quarrying	2.0	0.4
Manufacturing	17.6	8.4
Electricity, gas and water supply	1.4	0.6
Construction	12.9	1.5
Wholesale, retail and motor trade	13.1	15.8
Hotels and restaurants	4.3	7.4
Transport, storage and communication	9.3	3.8
Financial intermediation	3.6	5.8
Real estate, renting and business activity	11.8	10.5
Public administration and defence	7.0	6.9
Education	4.3	10.6
Health and social work	4.3	21.4
Other	4.6	6.1

Source: Census 2001 (Table S36).

over time. (This is shown for all industry sectors in Table A4.5, and for selected sectors in Figure 4.7.) Mining, for example, has seen a sharp reduction in employment since the index year of 1975, and yet its GVA had risen by 79 per cent by the end of the century. Other sectors which have done significantly better than the average include some with broadly stable shares of employment – distribution and hotels (92 per cent growth) and electricity (87 per cent) – and some with growing employment, such as financial and public services (90 per cent).

Figure 4.7 Gross Value Added index, by selected industry sector, 1975–99

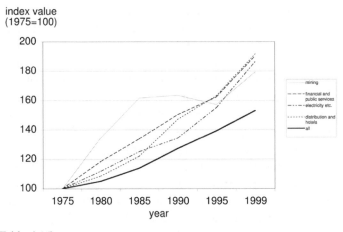

Source: Table A4.5.

We can also measure the economic value of industrial sectors by the value of exports. Table A4.6 also allows us to assess the domestic value added ('domestic content'). One of the interesting features of this table is that while computer manufacture is the major exporter (14 per cent), it appears to have low levels of domestic value added (only 8 per cent), suggesting that the Scottish computer industry acts largely as a staging post for product value generated elsewhere. In simple terms, it appears to confirm the status of much of 'silicon glen' as 'screwdriver' – that is, assembly – territory, lacking significant research and development. This appears to be confirmed by Table A4.7 which concentrates on the manufacturing sector, and shows that, unlike virtually all other such industries, around three-quarters of gross value added, gross output, and net capital expenditure in electrical/ instrument engineering comes from outwith the UK. (No up-to-date information is available on patterns of ownership from the different parts of the UK.)

INDUSTRIAL AND OCCUPATIONAL CHANGE

Let us now explore the relationship between industry and occupational structures in a little more depth. To anticipate the argument which we will develop in Chapter 6, occupational change overall is driven by two sets of forces: what happens to industrial sectors as such; and how occupations are organised and re-organised *within* these sectors. Thus, to take one example, a decline in the number of coal miners at the coal face may be the result of (1) fewer people employed in the coal industry, or (2) changes in the skill mix required in the industry, perhaps a process of re-skilling, as automation replaces labour. Both processes are likely to be at work, and mining (with quarrying) is a good example. There has been a fall in the number and output of coal mines in Scotland, the last deep mine, Longannet, having been closed in 2002, though drift mining continues across the old Scottish coalfields of the Lowlands. This industry is nowadays quite evenly split in terms of employment between manual trades (process operatives, skilled trades and 'elementary' workers) at 45 per cent, and non-manual occupations (managers, science and technology professionals, and associated professionals) at 39 per cent (Census 2001: Table S39). The 'pick and shovel' image of mining and quarrying is long gone.

Lest we think that this is true of all 'primary' industries, it is useful to inspect the occupational structure of both agriculture (with hunting and forestry) and fishing (Census 2001: Table S39). What distinguishes these industries is their continuing reliance on skilled trades specific to their needs. Thus, more than half of agricultural employment (53 per cent) is in skilled trades, and a further 26 per cent in 'elementary' occupations. In short, almost three-quarters of employment in agriculture is employed in 'manual' occupations, despite (or because of) the continual replacement of labour by technology. Agriculture is a good example of a fairly closed industry with quite specific occupational trades not readily transferable to other industries. It could be that, as employment has shrunk in this industry, so it has become more specialised occupationally. Fishing too is quite specific in its occupational requirements, and like agriculture has more than half (59 per cent) of its labour force in 'skilled trades' specific to fishing. With a further 14 per cent in 'elementary' occupations, this means that about two-thirds of employment in fishing is in manual trades, despite, once more, rapid technological development. Concomitantly, in both agriculture and fishing, there are relatively few non-manual workers: managers and senior officials, professionals and associated professionals make up only 10 per cent and 16 per cent respectively.

The old mainstream industries of manufacturing and construction have also undergone fundamental transformation in terms of occupational structures. The image of masses of semi- and unskilled workers, typified by the traditional navvy, is certainly a redundant one. Fifty per cent of construction workers are defined as being in skilled trades, and only 10 per cent are in elementary (labouring) occupations. Likewise, the manual base of manufacturing which makes up six in ten of the workforce consists of process operatives (29 per cent) and skilled trades (20 per cent), with elementary workers numbering only 11 per cent. On the other hand, 30 per cent of manufacturing employment in Scotland is now in managerial, professional and associated professional posts.

Does this mean that unskilled – elementary – workers are a thing of the past, replaced either by technology or by more skilled workers? The answer is that around one in eight (12.7 per cent) of both male and female workers are still in elementary occupations (Census 2001: Table CAS 33) but that such workers are now, more than ever, concentrated in service occupations. For example, almost half (48 per cent) of all workers in the hotel and restaurant industry are now in 'elementary' occupations – such as porters, waiters and cleaners – and indeed 22 per cent of all workers in elementary occupations generally are now concentrated in hotel and catering alone. Relatively poorly paid and unskilled workers are now mainly in these industries, as well as in the retail and wholesale trades where 65 per cent of all sales and customer service occupations are now to be found. We shall discuss some of the implications of these employment patterns for people's earnings in Chapter 5.

What of public sector employment? This sector has developed its own specific trades and specialisations such that, for example, two-thirds (65 per cent) of workers in public administration, defence and social security are to be found in either associated professional and technical trades, or administrative and secretarial occupations. An even greater degree of occupational specialisation is to be found in education, where as many as 54 per cent are in teaching or research posts, and, likewise, 33 per cent of people employed in health and social work are health or social work professionals or associated professionals.

Both industrial and occupational structures are heavily gendered. Women are significantly more likely than men to work in wholesale and retail trades (16 per cent of all female workers), in health and social work (21 per cent), in education (11 per cent) and in hotels and restaurants (7.4 per cent) (Table 4.3 above). Men are significantly more likely than women to be found in manufacturing (18 per cent), construction (13 per cent) and transport (9.3 per cent). In terms of occupations, 49 per cent of men are still in manual jobs, and women are still concentrated in administrative, secretarial, and personal services (34 per cent). This gendering of work clearly has implications in terms of social class, and we will explore this aspect in Chapter 6.

Three broad conclusions may be drawn about occupational and industrial change; these are also amplified in greater detail in Chapter 6.

- There is little evidence of a de-skilling process; we are seeing the disappearance of unskilled work, notably in sectors such as manufacturing and construction.
- There are many more managerial and administrative jobs in such industries, while manual employment dominates the likes of agriculture and fishing which have very little by way of managerial cadres.
- Many sectors, public and private, have developed occupational skills specific to their needs, such as in education and health or social work, as well as in manual trades related to processing. Occupational skills are tied to the particular needs of an industrial sector, rather than a generic labour force which moves between sectors. Most elementary 'unskilled' employment is now found in service industries such as hotel and catering, or in retail trades.

We can also draw broad conclusions about where we are likely to find particular occupations (Census 2001: Table S39):

- The largest number of managers and senior officials (23 per cent of all such workers) are to found in retail and wholesale trades.

- Six in every ten professionals work in education (38 per cent of all professionals), or in real estate/business (22 per cent).
- Associate professionals and technical occupations appear mainly in health and social work (27 per cent), and public administration (17 per cent).
- Administrative and secretarial staff are spread more thinly through most sectors, with public administration (17 per cent), finance (14 per cent) and real estate/business (15 per cent) being their biggest employers.
- Skilled manual trades are to be found mainly in construction (31 per cent) and manufacturing (22 per cent).
- Personal services are to be found mainly in health and social work (53 per cent).
- Sales and customers services employment is, not surprisingly, largely concentrated in retail and wholesale sectors (65 per cent), while process, plant and machine operatives are in manufacturing (40 per cent) and transport, storage and communications (21 per cent).
- Workers in 'elementary' occupations are mainly in hotels and catering (22 per cent), as well as in real estate/business (13 per cent).

CONDITIONS OF WORK

What about people's working conditions? The UK generally has a long-hours working culture, and Scotland is no exception. Figures in *Scottish Social Statistics* (Scottish Executive 2001a: 58) show that in 1998 the average hours worked per week by full-time male employees were 10 per cent higher than the EU average. In 2001, the median number of hours worked for men was 42, and for women 35, despite the fact that around two in every five working women work part-time (Tables A4.8 and 4.1). Three-quarters of all men are working more than 37 hours per week, and even one-third of all women (Table A4.9). Men aged 30–44, the group most likely to have families, are working on average 45 hours per week, and 80 per cent of them more than 37 hours per week. Women in child-bearing and child-rearing age groups are also working long hours (on average about 35 hours per week). The Scottish Household Survey (Scottish Executive 2003c: Table 5.17) shows that, among women of working age with children in the household, 27 per cent work full-time compared with 45 per cent of those without children. Only those over 60 years of age are down to, on average, just over 20 hours. Women employees working part-time work a median of 20 hours, and those working full-time marginally fewer hours than men, 38 as against 43 (Figure 4.8).

Figure 4.8 Median hours worked, by gender, 2001

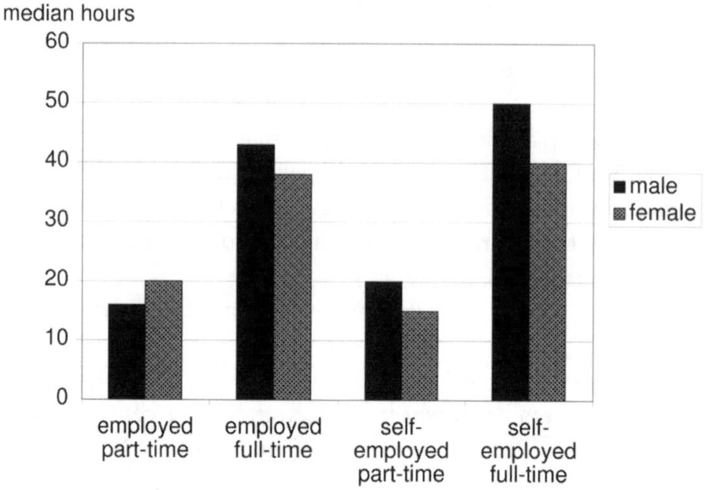

median hours

Source: Table A4.10.

Only in retail and wholesale trades, and in hotels and catering, do women work on average less than 30 hours per week (Table A4.11), and even there the median is upwards of half-time working. In virtually all other industrial sectors, women work well over 30 hours, and in the case of manufacturing they work on average only four hours less per week than men. Men in all sectors work around 40 hours or longer, and in agriculture, and mining and quarrying, they work in excess of 50 hours per week.

Fitting these lengthy hours of work into lives with many other commitments, especially for women, is made easier for some workers by flexible working patterns. In 1999, nearly one in five Scottish employees, and one in four women workers, worked some kind of flexible working pattern (Scottish Executive 2001a: 58).

Accidents at work are not directly attributable to long working hours, but they continue to be a feature of industry in Scotland, notably among lower supervisory and technical workers, 7 per cent of whom indicate that they have been off work as a result of a work-related accident in the past 12 months; in their case, the absence was usually for two days or more (Table A4.12). Routine workers too have an above-average accident rate, with 6.5 per cent recently off work. Fatalities among Scottish workers fell from 37 to 27 between 1997 and 2001, while the number of 'major' injuries remained virtually the same (Table A4.13).[2] Indeed, the level of industrial injuries among the self-employed rose significantly between 1997 and 2001, and major incidents more than doubled.

The capacity of trade unions to secure better working conditions has, in most industries, declined with their membership. In the decade between 1991 and 2001, the numbers belonging to trade unions fell from four out of ten to just over three out of ten. The most highly unionised industries are education (67 per cent), electricity, gas and water (63 per cent), and public administration (62 per cent) (Table A4.14). The lowest levels of union-isation are in the hotel and catering trades (7 per cent), fishing (10 per cent), and mining and quarrying (11 per cent). The low figure for the latter industry is a reflection of the virtual demise of deep mining in Scotland with its strong traditions of union activism: unionisation there has fallen further by two-thirds in a decade, from the already low 30 per cent that had resulted from the defeat of the previously dominant miners' union in the strike of 1984–5. The decline in union membership, however, occurs in all industrial sectors, and only education has seen a modest decline, of less than 1 percentage point. Unionisation in manufacturing fell by one-third in ten years, from 42 per cent to 29 per cent. By and large, there are now above-average levels of unionisation only in sectors where a large share of employment is in the public sector (such as education and health), or where former nationalised industries remain strongly regulated by the state (such as electricity and transport). Nevertheless, in most sectors, the proportion who are union members is smaller than the proportion who are in work-places where unions are recognised, and, in that sense, the working conditions of 44 per cent of all workers are probably affected indirectly or directly by union activity.

Ethnicity and economic activity

Two per cent of Scotland's population are from a minority (non-white) ethnic group, compared with 1.3 per cent in 1991. The largest minorities are in Pakistani, Indian and Chinese ethnic groups, and self-employment is relatively high among these (13 per cent, 13 per cent and 12 per cent respectively), and twice that of the white population (Table A4.15). If we treat 'in employment' as employees and self-employed, then more than one-third of employed people of Pakistani origin, and one-quarter of both Indian and Chinese, are self-employed, compared to only one in ten of whites. A much higher proportion of women in ethnic groups than in the white population are full-time looking after the home, most notably among people of Pakistani and South Asian origin, with (at 30 per cent) a rate of three times that in the white population; some explanations of this are discussed in Chapter 6.

The largest proportions of ethnic minorities in Scotland work in retail and wholesale, notably people of Pakistani origin (38 per cent) and Indian origin (22 per cent), while more than half of Chinese people work in the hotel and restaurant business (Table A4.16). In terms of the types of work done, Pakistanis and other South Asians are mainly to be found in the managerial and senior official category (26 per cent), as well as in sales and customer service (22 per cent): see Table A4.17. People of Indian origin work in professional occupations (30 per cent), or as managers and senior officials (20 per cent). Chinese people are mainly in 'skilled trades' (for example, in the catering industry), or managers and professionals. In contrast to people of Chinese origin who are strongly linked to the restaurant trade, the bulk of the Indian and Pakistani population do not work in 'manual' occupations. For example, while 46 per cent of the Chinese population are in skilled trades, process operatives and elementary occupations, the figure for the white population is 35 per cent, for the Pakistani population 22 per cent, and for the Indian population just 18 per cent. Levels of reported unemployment do not vary much among ethnic groups, with people of Pakistani origin marginally above, and those of Indian and Chinese origin marginally below, the white rate (Table A4.15).

These patterns relate to the social class distribution of the various ethnic groups, and so are discussed more fully in Chapter 6. All in all, Scotland's small ethnic minority population is occupationally specialised, to be found in small businesses, much as immigrant groups such as Italians and Jews were in the nineteenth century. If Scotland actively encourages inward migration to offset its falling birth rate, it will be interesting to see what impact this has on patterns of employment.

RELIGION AND EMPLOYMENT

In recent years there has been something of a controversy as to whether Catholics in Scotland are discriminated against in terms of employment. The 2001 census was the first since the nineteenth century to ask about religious affiliation, much for this reason, although data here come from the Scottish Household Survey because it allows for fuller analysis. Catholics make up around one in six of Scotland's population and, as we can see from Table 4.4, their unemployment rate is not substantially out of line with the rest of the population. Catholics have a higher than average level of long-term sickness and disability, possibly reflecting age and occupational effects, as well as possibly deriving from long-term lineage effects going back more than a century (see Chapter 2 and Abbotts et al. (1997)). Catholics are no longer under-represented among managers, senior officials or professionals (Table A4.18): 23 per cent of them were in those groups, compared with 25 per cent of those with no religion and 24 per cent of Church of Scotland members. Only in the small religious groups described here as 'other Christian' or 'other religion' is the proportion much higher, at 33 per cent and 36 per cent respectively. The latter reflects the relatively high proportions in these occupations among people from minority ethnic groups (as noted above). The former reflects the mainly middle class nature of the Scottish Episcopal Church (as discussed more fully in Chapters 6 and 7). Likewise, there is very little difference in the sectors of industry in which Catholics and non-Catholics work (Table A4.19): no longer, as in the nineteenth century, are Catholics concentrated in construction, for example. It seems safe to conclude that Catholics in Scotland are not discriminated against in terms of employment.

Table 4.4 Economic activity, by religious group, among people aged 16–74, 2001

% in columns	Religious group				
	None	Church of Scotland	Roman Catholic	Other Christian	Other religion
Employed, part-time	12.0	12.2	10.6	12.9	12.3
Employed, full-time	45.3	38.1	37.7	35.5	33.1
Self-employed, part-time or full-time	6.0	4.2	3.3	7.9	6.6
Unemployed	5.0	2.9	4.7	2.1	3.2
Student	6.2	4.4	6.0	6.4	12.8
Retired	9.6	24.1	16.8	22.4	12.0
Full-time looking after home	9.3	7.5	10.6	8.4	14.2
Long-term sick or disabled	4.9	5.8	8.4	3.3	3.5
Other	1.5	0.9	1.8	1.1	2.2
Sample size	3,570	6,097	1,900	992	273

Source: Scottish Household Survey 2001, weighted (sample sizes unweighted).

CONCLUSION

How can we sum up Scotland's employment structure? The shift from manufacturing to services has been confirmed, and with it a move to non-manual work. As we shall see in Chapter 6, this does not imply that such people have automatically become 'middle class', or indeed think of themselves as such. Most obviously this applies to women, a much higher proportion of whom are working than ever before, and overwhelmingly in non-manual jobs. Even for those working part-time (23.6 per cent), for most women this is a substantial commitment of hours over and above their family commitments – on average some 20 hours per week. Those in full-time employment (31.5 per cent), some of whom will also have family commitments, work on average 38 hours per week. As the working population shifts from manual to non-manual employment, there is also a concomitant shift to skilled manual work and away from unskilled or 'elementary' occupations.

NOTES

1. These data are cross-sectional, and do not refer to the same cohorts of people over the life course. Nevertheless, they give some indication of how people move into and out of employment statuses as they age.
2. Whether a major injury is only potentially fatal or becomes a fatality is often a matter of good or bad luck.

CHAPTER 5

Income, Wealth and Poverty

The previous chapters have described the population of Scotland, the structure of families and households, and the nature of the work people in Scotland do. They show that, structurally, Scotland is a very different place in which to live and work in the early years of the twenty-first century compared with twenty years ago. As we concluded in Chapter 4, the labour force is increasingly to be found in service industries, and in non-manual and more skilled jobs. More women are working, and working considerable numbers of hours. How then are these changes reflected in people's incomes, their savings and their wealth? In Chapter 8, we shall explore some aspects of the lived experience, the goods people own, what they buy and eat, and their leisure activities. Up to a point, the differences we shall find in consumption and lifestyle are of course the result of differing choices, influenced by age, stage in the family cycle, social class and individual preference. Some of these choices are to a considerable extent not directly affected by income; it is true that money isn't everything. It is also true that the lifestyle and opportunities open to high income earners and the wealthy are very different from the experience of the majority of Scotland's citizens.

In this chapter we shall examine how income and wealth are distributed, though it must be said at the outset that data on the distribution of wealth are limited even at the United Kingdom level, let alone for Scotland. It is true that there are formidable technical difficulties in making even moderately reliable estimates of wealth but the extensive publications of the Royal Commission on the Distribution of Income and Wealth (1977) showed that it is not impossible. However, with the arrival of the years of the Thatcher governments, willingness to invest in detailed research on the distribution of wealth waned, though in recent years the Inland Revenue has taken the task forward.

The extent to which the unequal distribution of income, and of wealth from savings, property and other investments, is seen as significant (or even to be deplored) is to a considerable extent a matter of political and social opinion about the appropriate balance between equality, redistribution, and rewarding talent and effort in a society. The inheritance of wealth is self-evidently not about rewarding the receiver's efforts, but raises issues about redistribution versus individuals' right to pass on what they have created or themselves inherited to their children and other individuals. These are controversial issues and it is not our task to explore them here. There is, however, rather more consensus that very low incomes and high levels of poverty are unacceptable, especially when children are adversely affected.

So the subject of this chapter is whether people as a whole have become better off in the last twenty years, and how resources are distributed.

THE RISE IN INCOME

The average weekly gross income per household in Scotland, allowing for inflation, increased by just over a fifth between 1979 and 1997. The year-on-year increase and the three-year moving average of income (indexed to 1979) in Figure 5.1 show how income after a period of relative stagnation rose steadily in the second half of the 1980s, and after a brief dip in the early 1990s continued to rise. The mean weekly household income in 1997 was £367.40 (Table A5.1). Wages and salaries were the source of three-quarters of the total in 1980 but only two-thirds by 1997, with the proportion coming from self-employment and other income rising by just over a half from 11.7 per cent at the start of the period to 17.9 per cent by the end. Social security benefits rose by over a quarter from 12.7 per cent to 16.1 per cent.

Figure 5.1 Average weekly household income, 1979–97

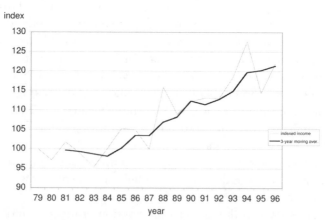

Source: same as Table A5.1 (but in more detail than the table).

INCOME DISTRIBUTION

This rise in real income over the last couple of decades has not, however, been accompanied by a decrease in inequality. Figure 5.2, which shows the distribution of average weekly income in 1988 and 1997, makes the point well: the gradient is similar in the two years.

Figure 5.2 Distribution of average weekly household income, 1988 and 1997

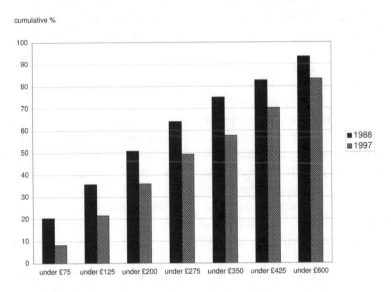

Source: Table A5.2.

The published report of the 2001 Scottish Household Survey (Scottish Executive 2002c: 123) shows that 'a third of Scottish households (33%) have a net annual household income of £10,000 or less while almost a third (31%) have a net annual income of £20,000 or more'. The report goes on to say, as one might expect, that 'income is closely related to the number of people in the household'. Thus, in order to compare different kinds of household controlling for size, it is necessary to 'equivalise' the income figures: that is, adjust them to take account of the number of people in the household. When this is done, inequality can be seen to be distributed very unevenly across family types (Table A5.3).

While approximately half of the individuals living in single households without children are in a household with an income which falls below the median equivalised income,[1] nine out of every ten individuals in single households with children are in this position, as are just under two-thirds of pensioners.

An income below 60 per cent of the median is frequently regarded as indicating poverty, especially since the Labour government adopted it in setting specific targets for reduction of child poverty (Hills 2001: 1). Across all family types, over one-fifth (22 per cent) of individuals are in a household with an income below this putative poverty level. Once again, single people with children are in the most disadvantageous circumstances, with fully 55 per cent of such individuals living in a household with income below 60 per cent of the median. Sampling error makes precision impossible but between one in five and one in three pensioner households are in the same plight. In sharp contrast, only around one in ten couples without children fall into this category.

Thus, despite rising prosperity over the last twenty years, a considerable proportion of Scotland's citizens are not sharing the benefits, and around one in five are in real poverty, if one adopts a relative definition. Hills (2001: 1–10) reviews the evidence on and attitudes to poverty in Britain as a whole and infers that 'the public do have some form of relative definition of poverty in mind'. He concludes (2001: 26) that the British Social Attitudes Survey 'shows that the majority believe that there is a significant amount of poverty, and that the government should be doing something to reduce it'. In March 1999, Tony Blair in his Beveridge lecture made a pledge to eliminate child poverty in Britain in twenty years, a goal which resonates with many people presumably because children are seen as suffering through no fault of their own. Re-analysing the same survey as used by Hills, we find that people in Scotland were rather more likely than people in the rest of Britain to attribute adult poverty to injustice: in Scotland, 32 per cent chose the explanation 'injustice in our society', as compared to 21 per cent in Britain as a whole.[2] Similar proportions in Scotland and Britain chose the option 'inevitable part of modern life' (35 per cent and 34 per cent respectively), and in Scotland even fewer than in Britain as a whole chose 'unlucky' (10 per cent compared to 15 per cent) or 'laziness or lack of willpower' (18 per cent compared to 23 per cent).

How then do Scotland's children fare? The figures are stark (Table A5.4), with 59 per cent of dependent children in 1998–9 living in households with equivalised income below the median and nearly one in three (30 per cent) in households with equivalised income below 60 per cent of the median, and thus living in poverty as it is frequently defined. The economic status and the size of the family are, unsurprisingly, crucial here. Where there are one or more full-time employees in the family, and no more than two dependent children, 38 per cent of children are in households with equivalised income below the median, and 7 per cent are in households with equivalised income below 60 per cent of the median. Where there are three or more children in such economic circumstances, the proportions rise to, respectively, 56 per cent and 27 per cent. Where there are no full-time workers, the proportions are around 95 per cent and around two-thirds.

If we look at the economic status of individuals as shown in Table 5.1, a similar picture emerges in finer detail. Single persons or couples in full-time work are structurally in the best situation, with couples where one is in full-time and one in part-time work not far behind. Interestingly, while the latter group fares less well generally, only one in twenty in either group fall below the 'poverty line' we have been using. The unemployed are in the worst situation, followed by those aged 60 or over. The self-employed are close to the average on both measures, reflecting the wide range of economic situations that the status encompasses, from highly paid professionals to struggling small shopkeepers.

Table 5.1 Percentage of individuals below median[1] and 60% median equivalised[2] income, by economic status, 1998–9

%	Below median	Below 60% median
Self-employed	42	19
Single or couple, in full-time work	19	5
One in full-time work, one in part-time work	35	5
One in full-time work, one not working	(50)	22
One or more in part-time work	64	(22)
Head or spouse aged 60+	67	28
Head or spouse unemployed	92	76
Other	87	55
All economic statuses	50	22

Source: Scottish Executive (2001d: Table 3.4). Figures in brackets are particularly uncertain because of sampling error.
1. Median is for all of Britain.
2. Household income is equivalised to take account of the number of individuals living in the household. After housing costs.

The overall picture is, then, one of rising real incomes over the past twenty years but with some groups, especially those in full-time employment, benefiting disproportionately. Figure 5.3 shows how full-time employees have fared and reveals a familiar picture of two other kinds of structured inequality, by occupational class and gender; the full details are in Table A5.5.

Whether male or female, in manual or non-manual employment, for those in full-time employment average gross weekly earnings at current prices have increased steadily. Female non-manual workers have been steadily catching up with male manual workers and their average weekly earnings are identical in 2000. However, across the board, non-manual workers earn considerably more than manual, and male workers more than female.

Figure 5.3 Average gross weekly earnings of full-time employees, 1980–2000

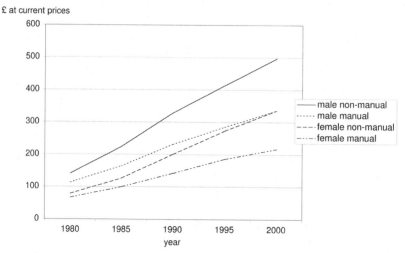

Source: Table A5.5.

Full-time non-manual workers in 2000 earned on average around one and half times as much as manual workers; the ratio is 1.48 for males and 1.54 for females. The advantage accruing to non-manual workers has increased steadily and considerably since 1980 when the corresponding figures were 1.25 for males and 1.18 for females. At the same time, for full-time workers, the gender differential *within* the two broad occupational classes has decreased. In 1980, males earned roughly one and three-quarters times as much as females; the ratio was 1.69 for manual workers and 1.79 for non-manual workers. By the year 2000 the differential was closer to one and a half, the ratio being 1.54 for manual workers and 1.48 for non-manual. Nevertheless, that difference remains substantial.

A complex set of factors leads to this gender differential. Direct gender discrimination takes place where men and women with the same labour market characteristics – be they educational qualifications, training, time in the labour market, or working in similar firms – are differently rewarded. But the detailed occupational distributions *within* the genders differ somewhat, and women are much more likely to spend time out of the labour market. The question is, then, how much of the differential is the result of factors such as these, as opposed to gender discrimination and a continuing failure to achieve the aims of the Equal Pay Act of 1970. Joanna Swaffield, of the Centre for Economic Performance at the London School of Economics, has examined this using data from the British Household Panel Survey, which collects detailed lifetime market histories of workers. After allowing for qualifications and labour market experience, and taking into account time in full-time and part-time work, she concludes that '41.5 per cent of the gap between women's and men's pay is a result of direct gender discrimination' (Swaffield 2000: 23). For full-time employees the gap rises to 50 per cent. There is a long way to go before gender discrimination is a thing of the past.

We earlier quoted the report of the 2001 Scottish Household Survey as saying that 'income is closely related to the number of people in the household'. This can be seen clearly in Table 5.2 which also reveals other aspects of inequality.

Table 5.2 Net annual household income, by sex of highest income householder and household type, 2001

% of households in rows		Income band[1] (£)					Sample size
Household type[2]	Sex of highest income householder	0–6,000	6,000–10,000	10,000–15,000	15,000–20,000	20,000+	
Single adult	Male	21.2	25.9	27.3	13.8	11.8	1225
	Female	18.1	30.1	30.3	14.3	7.2	968
Small adult	Male	3.3	7.8	15.7	19.3	53.9	1843
	Female	6.9	16.5	19.4	16.0	41.1	718
Lone parent	Male	6.5	23.7	21.5	18.3	30.1	91
	Female	6.7	39.9	35.9	12.6	4.9	765
Small family	Male	1.2	2.8	10.0	20.1	65.8	1799
	Female	3.1	10.7	24.5	16.7	45.0	407
Large family	Male	1.7	2.8	9.1	20.4	66.1	909
	Female	2.3	11.9	27.8	17.6	40.3	178
Large adult	Male	4.0	8.6	15.2	20.5	51.7	1125
	Female	8.0	16.3	21.3	15.9	38.5	291
Older smaller	Male	7.1	29.8	32.4	17.6	13.1	1807
	Female	13.6	30.8	29.3	15.4	10.9	412
Lone pensioner	Male	27.7	45.6	19.8	4.0	3.0	631
	Female	31.3	47.4	17.3	2.9	1.1	1792
All	Male	7.6	15.8	19.0	17.6	40.0	9430
	Female	16.8	32.6	24.4	11.1	15.1	5531

Source: Scottish Household Survey 2001, weighted (sample sizes unweighted).
1. Net income after taxation and other deductions from employment, benefits and other sources, brought into the household by the highest income earner, their spouse, and any contribution from other household member.
2. Definition of household types: see Table 3.1.

Where the highest income earner is male, net annual household incomes of over £20,000 are obtained by over half the households in four household types – small adult (54 per cent), small family (66 per cent) large family

(66 per cent) and large adult (52 per cent). The same groups also fare best if the highest income earner is female but, unsurprisingly in the light of our discussion above, the proportion with net incomes over £20,000 falls and the figures for these same four household types are 41, 45, 40, and 39 per cent. Only if we reduce the bottom of the net income band by a quarter, and look at households with net annual household incomes over £15,000, do the households where the highest income earner is female achieve similar proportions to those where the highest income earner is male. Despite this considerable gender inequality, however, none of the other family types, even with male highest income earners, matches these figures. At the other end of the income distribution, with net incomes of £6,000 or less, we find a slightly different picture. To be sure, overall one in six (17 per cent) of households with a female highest income earner are in this income bracket and only half as many (8 per cent) of those with male highest income earners. However, two family types have the highest proportions – single adults (around one in five) and lone pensioners (around three in ten) – and here the gender differentials are both smaller and in the case of single adult households reversed.

The data in Table 5.3, showing net annual household income by economic activity of the highest income earner, reinforce these findings, highlighting the relative deprivation of those poorly placed in the labour market. Where the highest income earner is retired, a fifth of households have net annual income of £6,000 or less; only one in nine of all households are in this position. The proportion of households with net annual income of £6,000 or less rises further to 44 per cent where the highest income earner is unemployed, and further still to over half (52 per cent) where this person is a student. If we look at the next higher income bracket of £10,000 or less, the overall proportion rises to one-third (33 per cent). The retired at 62 per cent, the unemployed (78 per cent) and students (75 per cent) are still heavily over-represented.

Relatively few (11 per cent) of the households where the highest income earner is part-time fall into the £6,000 or less bracket because even with part-time work these households are on the whole relatively better off than the retired, unemployed and students. When we move up to the £10,000 or less bracket, the problems of these households, with the highest income earner maybe working relatively few hours or for poor pay, start to become more apparent, with 37 per cent of such households in this income bracket, slightly higher than the overall proportion of one-third. If we raise the top limit yet again and look at households with net income below £15,000, we find 71 per cent in this range where the highest income earner is part-time compared to 54 per cent overall.

Table 5.3 Net annual household income, by economic activity of highest income householder, 2001

% of households in rows	Income band[1] (£)					Sample size
Economic activity of highest income householder	0–6,000	6,000–10,000	10,000–15,000	15,000–20,000	20,000 +	
Employed, part-time	10.6	25.6	34.9	16.5	12.4	775
Employed, full-time	0.8	5.4	16.7	21.3	55.8	6656
Self-employed, part-time or full-time	3.2	4.6	15.4	22.7	54.1	996
Unemployed	44.4	33.7	17.3	3.1	1.4	413
Student	52.4	22.5	15.9	6.6	2.6	208
Retired	21.6	40.7	24.4	8.1	5.2	4350
Full-time looking after home	14.3	50.5	29.0	5.5	0.7	547
Long-term sick or disabled	14.2	44.8	28.9	9.1	3.0	860
Other	25.3	36.3	21.9	10.3	6.2	156
All	11.1	22.1	21.0	15.1	30.7	14961

Source: Scottish Household Survey 2001, weighted (sample sizes unweighted).
1. Net income after taxation and other deductions from employment, benefits and other sources, brought into the household by the highest income earner, their spouse, and any contribution from other household member.

Finally at this bottom end of the distribution, it is striking that households where the highest income earner is either full-time looking after the home, or is long-term sick or disabled, make up around one in seven in the lowest income bracket compared to one in nine overall. However, this rises dramatically to nearly two-thirds (65 per cent) and six in ten (59 per cent) respectively in the below £10,000 group compared to one-third (33 per cent) overall.

The social impact of deprivation of various kinds is exacerbated where individuals or households are multiply deprived or are in relative poverty for long periods. It is those in long-term unemployment and the long-term sick or disabled who are probably most affected, because students will eventually cease their studies and may indeed, as a result of the qualifications gained, become relatively well paid (as we discuss in Chapter 7). Moreover, for a good many unemployed, this is not a long-term status. Those in part-time employment because of family responsibilities may also be able to move into full-time work at a later date.

We have seen how crucial it is for households to have someone in employment, especially full-time employment. Where the highest income earner is employed full-time or is self-employed, few households fall into the lowest income bracket of £6,000 or less (1 per cent and 3 per cent respectively). Similarly, the income bracket over £20,000 holds few surprises. Nearly one third (31 per cent) of all households fall into this group, but where the highest income earner is full-time the proportion is 56 per cent and where self-employed 54 per cent. Reducing the lower limit, we find that a household income over £15,000 is achieved by 46 per cent of all households but by over three-quarters of those with a full-time or self-employed highest income earner (77 per cent in both groups).

The data we presented earlier on occupational class differences in full-time earnings can be refined further if we continue to look at net annual household income but do so now by the socio-economic group of the highest income earner (Table A5.6). Because the data are restricted to those with a socio-economic group classification, the household incomes are somewhat higher, with an overall median of close to £20,000 compared to under £15,000 in the previous set of data. Overall, 4 per cent of households fall into the lowest category, below £6,000 income, and the data are clearly stratified by class. Under-represented in this category are households whose highest income earner is an employer or manager whether in large or small establishments, a professional whether self-employed or employee, or in an intermediate non-manual occupation. Those in the junior non-manual, the semi-skilled manual and the non-professional self-employed categories are slightly over-represented at 6 per cent, but it is those in personal service (10 per cent) or unskilled manual occupations (12 per cent) who stand out. It is noteworthy that in these data, where we can separate out the professional from the rest of the self-employed, the wide range of activity covered by this group becomes apparent. At the other end of the distribution, with household income over £20,000, just above the median, we find in this bracket four in five (82 per cent) of households with a professional self-employed highest income earner compared to 39 per cent for the other self-employed. Employers and managers in large establishments (79 per cent) and professional employees (78 per cent) are prominent, with employers and managers in small establishments (60 per cent), the intermediate non-manual, and foremen and supervisors (both 58 per cent) somewhat over-represented.

What then of other possible stratifying factors? The religious group to which the highest income holder belongs has no pronounced effect (Table A5.7), although those of no religion do slightly better, and adherents to the Church of Scotland slightly worse, than average. There are also small differences by region (Table A5.8). In the highest income brackets (whether over £20,000 or over £15,000), households in the West of Scotland (42.5 per cent over £15,000) do worst, followed by Central and Tayside (45.2 per cent), East (49.5 per cent) and the North and the Islands at 50.4 per cent. The same ordering holds at the bottom end of the distribution. We shall, however, see shortly that if one looks at multiple deprivation across much smaller geographical units than regions, it occurs much more frequently in some areas than others. As can be seen from Figure 5.4, the pattern by broad ethnic group is unusual. The proportions in the lowest category with household incomes below £6,000 might lead one to imagine that the non-white groups fare much worse than the white ones, because the proportion where the highest income earner is non-white is more than 1.5 times the proportion where that person is white. However, in the next two bands the households with white highest income earners predominate, and if we take the first two groups together the proportions are exactly the same: 33 per cent. In the highest bracket there is no difference. The pattern probably reflects the differing fortunes of different ethnic groups but unfortunately the non-white grouping is too small even in this large survey to divide into its constituent parts. From the point of view of the discussion earlier, however, it is significant that a much higher proportion of the households with non-white highest income earners are below the poverty line we have been using. Some further indirect light is cast on income inequalities among ethnic groups when, in Chapter 6, we use census data to examine their social class distributions.

Figure 5.4 Net annual household income, by broad ethnic group, 2001

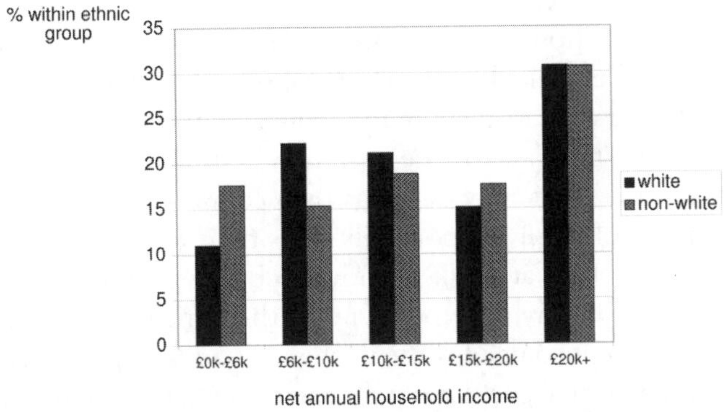

Source: Table A5.9.

RELATIVE POVERTY AND DEPRIVATION

A picture is emerging of Scotland in the early twenty-first century as a society in which both individuals and households have become considerably more affluent over the last twenty years, with large increases registered by those in full-time employment. Scotland remains stratified by occupational class and gender, and to some extent by ethnic group and age with some retired persons and their households in the lowest income brackets. As with many of the issues we discuss in this book, it is important to bear in mind that what we have been describing in the last few pages is a snapshot of a dynamic situation. Specific households in the income categories which we have been discussing may move up or down as their situation changes. Most obviously, as we have noted, few people remain students for more than a few years, and most people eventually find themselves in the retired category where their financial situation will depend heavily on the generosity and security of their occupational pension scheme, and how successfully they have prepared for their retirement in other ways.[3] Hills (2001: 5) cites data published by the Department of Social Security (1999) from the first seven years of the British Household Panel Survey which make this point well.[4] Only 55 per cent of the sample had *never* had annual incomes falling into the poorest fifth; thus 45 per cent had been in this category for anything from one to seven years. Twelve per cent had income in this category for five or more years, and 4 per cent were in the poorest fifth for all seven years. Thus, even over a relatively short period of seven years there are considerable flows in and out of the poorest group, but more than one in ten spent from five to seven years in this category and it is likely that in the years in which they 'escaped' it was by no great margin. Undoubtedly, the circumstances of some of this 'trapped' group will have improved as time went on but some will have spent most years in the poorest section of the community.

Retired people whose income after retirement is low, the long-term unemployed, the unskilled and others who are on balance unlikely to escape from the lowest brackets of individual or household incomes must, then, be distinguished from those who may well leave the disadvantaged category over time. This may occur as they complete their tertiary education, are relieved of family responsibilities as their families grow up, or are able to gain promotion at work or move to better-paying larger establishments. This is not in any way to downplay the difficulties they encounter, but to emphasise that some of those in the least-advantaged situations may improve their lot as time goes by. By the same token, this further emphasises the problems faced by those with little or no hope of escape.

It is important to appreciate that one cannot infer from these data that households in the lowest income groups are failing to make ends meet although this is undoubtedly true for some. The vast majority do cope. The Scottish Household Survey asks respondents which of six phrases 'best describes how you and your household manage financially these days'. The options offered are: Manage very well; Manage quite well; Get by alright; Don't manage very well; Have some financial difficulties; and Are in deep financial trouble. The report on this aspect of the survey combines data from 2001 and 2002 (Scottish Executive 2003c: Table 6.39). Overall, 6 per cent of the sample fall into the last two categories, and as one moves up through the same five household income groups that we used in Tables 5.2 and 5.3 the proportions are 11, 10, 7, 6, and 2 per cent. On the other hand, one-third of the lowest income category say that they Manage very well (8 per cent) or Manage quite well (24 per cent). Nearly half (47 per cent) say that they 'Get by alright', bringing the proportion in those top three groups to roughly four in five (79 per cent). The corresponding percentages for the whole population are 15, 33 and 41, making 89 per cent in total, only ten points higher than in the lowest-income group. How households manage and perceive themselves as managing is heavily dependent on expectations, and a range of skills.

The fundamental issue, however, is that these poorer groups in Scottish society are relatively deprived, and to a considerable extent socially excluded, as we shall see in Chapter 8, from many of the goods and services which the majority of the population have come to take for granted. This has consequences which go beyond aspects of life style and content-ment, and impact upon civic involvement, health and longevity.

The problems flowing from low income which households face are exacerbated if this is combined with other aspects of deprivation. In Chapter 2 we used the detailed work on social deprivation undertaken for the Scottish Executive by the Social Disadvantage Research Centre at Oxford University (Social Disadvantage Research Centre 2003), which examined deprivation in five 'domains': income; employment; health and disability; education, skills and training; and access to services. The data reflect the social policy purposes for which the work was carried out. Thus, for example, the income domain assesses deprivation in terms of the number of adults and children in income support households, and in households with job seeker's allowances and tax credits, and the employ-ment domain uses data on unemployment, compulsory New Deal partici-pants and so on to assess the exclusion from the world of work of those who wish to work. The geographical access to services index is very differently distributed to the first four. The local authority divisions (referred to in the report as 'wards') which are deprived on the first four indices tend to be considerably less deprived in terms of geographical access to services, partly because services tend to be better in urban areas and urban areas tend to have higher levels of deprivation, and partly because efforts are made to provide certain services in deprived areas.

These data are somewhat different from those we have considered thus far in this chapter in so far as, in general, they are ecological: they identify the most deprived areas in Scotland, not the most deprived individuals or households. The five domains are combined into an overall index, the Scottish Index of Multiple Deprivation.[5] There are 122 wards in the most multiply deprived 10 per cent of all such divisions in Scotland. Of these nearly three-quarters (73 per cent) fall within the most deprived 10 per cent on three domains, and nearly half (46 per cent) in the most deprived 10 per cent on four or more. There are nearly 700,000 people living in the most multiply deprived 10 per cent of wards, around one in seven (13.7 per cent) of Scotland's population. At the other end of the spectrum are to be found nearly 600,000 people, more than one in eight (11.7 per cent) of the population, who enjoy the advantages of living in the least deprived 10 per cent of wards. The report says that 'the most deprived wards are strongly concentrated in a strip from Fife and East Lothian in the east, to North and East Ayrshire in the west', and that 'Glasgow has the highest number of wards in the most deprived decile (44) and Dundee the second highest (15)' (Social Disadvantage Research Centre 2003: 44).

Although these data in general are descriptive of small areas, two of the indices – those relating to income deprivation and employment deprivation – are scores which *can* be interpreted in terms of individuals because they are rates. An income deprivation score of 30.1 means that 30.1 per cent of the ward's population are income deprived in the terms of this study. Across the 122 wards in the most income deprived 10 per cent, the proportion runs from half the population (48.4 per cent) being income deprived in Parkhead ward in Glasgow to a quarter (25.1 per cent) in Whinhall ward in North Lanarkshire. Parkhead also ranks first on employment deprivation with 41.9 per cent of the population deprived in this way, 27th on the education domain, 2nd on health, but 1146th on geographical access. Whinhall ward ranks 132nd on employment, with 25 per cent of the population employment deprived, and 112th, 158th and 1,095th in the other domains. On the overall index of multiple deprivation they rank 3rd and 124th respectively. By way of contrast, in the least income deprived ward, Westhill Central Ward in Aberdeenshire, one in 100 individuals are income deprived and around one in 60 are employment deprived. The ward ranks 1,212th on education; 1,221th on health and 1,218th overall. Because these are ecological data, there will be people in very difficult circumstances in the most privileged of wards and vice versa, but these data show clearly how there are areas of Scotland where, in general, people are deprived or reasonably well off in every sense.

Wealth

As we said at the beginning of this chapter, extensive, reliable data on wealth are hard to come by. There are forms of wealth which have an iconic significance for those who would like to see a more equal society in Scotland, and the ownership of land ranks high in this respect.

Virtually all the land in Scotland (97 per cent) can be regarded as rural, and only 12 per cent of that rural land is publicly owned. In 1999, the remaining 88 per cent was owned and controlled by a tiny group of landowners, as can be seen from Table 5.4, taken from research by Andy Wightman. Half the land was owned by 343 people and one-quarter of it was owned by 66 people. What is more, the situation in these respects has barely changed since 1970. A very similar pattern is apparent if we consider all land in Scotland, and these figures can be found in Table A5.10.

Table 5.4 Ownership of privately owned rural land, 1970 and 1999

Proportion of land	Number of owners	
	1970	1999
one-quarter	62	66
one-third	110	120
one-half	300	343
two-thirds	867	1,252

Source: Andy Wightman (personal communication; see also Table A5.10).

The capital value of this land, much of it in the form of estates, is often considerable but unlike some forms of wealth its capacity to generate income is less impressive. Many sporting estates provide an opportunity for social display rather than economic return. Wightman (1996: 173) writes about the estates in general that:

> Not only do they fail to make economic sense but the hundred years of their existence have perpetuated a state of affairs whereby no real investment has been made which by now might be expected to have secured some more economic return. Such money that has been poured in is better categorised as conspicuous consumption which has little local multiplier effect and is entirely dependent for its generation on a continuing stream of wealthy external interests.

Elsewhere Wightman and Higgins (2000: 25) comment appositely that, 'owning a sporting estate is on a par with conspicuous consumption of, for example, a yacht or a classic car'.

Can anything be gleaned about the *general* distribution of wealth rather than this somewhat special case? The Inland Revenue provide estimates of the distribution of personal wealth, based on inheritance tax, capital transfer tax and other data (Inland Revenue web site), but these are only for the UK as a whole. It is difficult to say how the distribution in Scotland will differ from that for the UK. In the absence of any detailed evidence on wealth distribution in Scotland, we present the UK data as the best information that is available. It is *a priori* improbable that the distribution differs to such an extent as to change the general picture. (We report below some evidence from the Family Resources Survey that would support this claim.) The estimates use improved versions of the techniques thought most appropriate by the Royal Commission on the Distribution of Income and Wealth. The estates of all those dying in a year are treated as a sample, stratified by age, sex and marital status, of the estates of the living. The data are then adjusted to take into account the steadily increasing death rates by age (because the unadjusted data relate far more to older people than younger) and the differential mortality of men and women, the married and unmarried.[6] This distribution is further adjusted to compensate for un-recorded or under-recorded information and some valuation differences. The major problem with this technique is that it is based on a sample of estates reported to Inland Revenue Capital Taxes (formerly known as the Capital Taxes Office) and thus excludes the majority of smaller estates.[7] As a result these estimates of what is known as 'identified' wealth cover only about 40 per cent of the total population aged 18 or over.

No individual asset can exceed £5,000 if an estate is to be excluded, and the Inland Revenue state that the total assets of an excluded estate would rarely exceed £25,000. The Inland Revenue therefore makes estimates of the distribution of this 'excluded wealth' and combines it with the previous adjusted estimates of 'identified wealth' to produce a distribution of what is known as 'marketable wealth'. These estimates do not include rights to occupational and state pensions but these, unlike the other assets included, can not be realised at will.[8]

It is important to appreciate both that what follows must be treated with proper caution, and that the disparities revealed are so large that we can be confident that wealth is very unequally distributed.[9] We shall present first (Figure 5.5) material based on the distribution of identified wealth because these data are published in greater detail.

The unequal distribution of wealth in 2000, even among this group, is dramatic. Figure 5.5 shows clearly how the gross value of the estates rises much more slowly than the number of estates making up this value. Within the roughly four in ten of the population covered by the estimates, 30 per cent have gross capital value of less than £25,000. Just over two-thirds of these (21 per cent) have wealth of less than £10,000. We have already stated that the excluded 60 per cent of estates rarely have assets exceeding £25,000. Thus, these figures for identified wealth considerably underestimate the degree of inequality. Let us, then, make the not unreasonable, and probably generous, assumption that two-thirds of the excluded estates have wealth less than £10,000 and one-third have between that and £25,000. This would

Figure 5.5 Cumulative percentages: estate numbers and gross values, UK, 2000

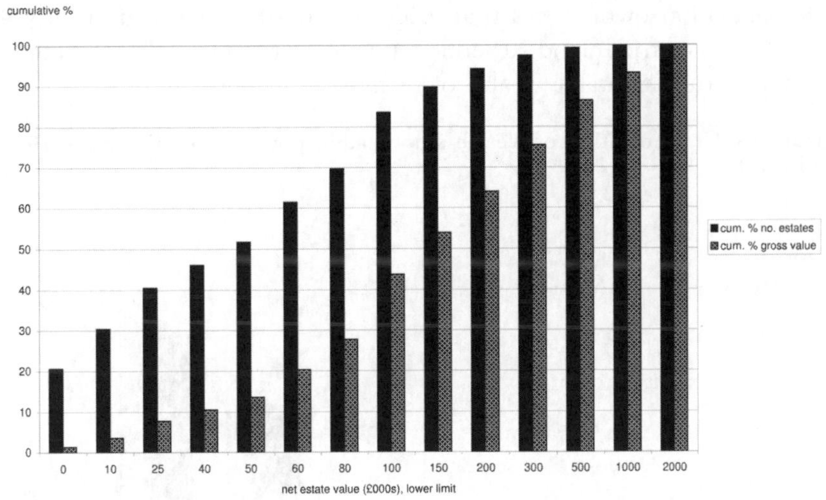

Source: Table A5.11.

mean that around half of the UK population (48 per cent) have wealth less than £10,000 and another quarter (24 per cent) have between £10,000 and £25,000.

Returning to the more wealthy 40 per cent covered by the estimates, 70 per cent own gross wealth less than £100,000, amounting to only 28 per cent of the cumulative gross value; 83 per cent have less than £150,000, still amounting to well under half (44 per cent) of the cumulative gross value. One quarter (25 per cent) of the total gross wealth is owned by the 2.5 per cent of the population with estates of gross value over £300,000.

The estimates of 'marketable wealth' covering the whole population are equally striking, especially when it is remembered that they do include domestic property, the biggest source of wealth for most people. Additionally they provide estimates of change over time (Figure 5.6). The most wealthy 1 per cent of the population owned 18 per cent of the wealth in 1986; this figure rose by the late 1990s but has been fairly flat since then (22 per cent in 1997, 23 per cent in 1998 and 1999, 22 per cent in 2000).[10] Perhaps even more indicative of how unequally wealth is distributed is that the wealthiest 50 per cent owned 90 per cent of the wealth in 1986, 93 per cent in 1997, and 94 per cent in 1998, 1999, and 2000. It follows, of course, that the poorest half now own around 6 per cent of the wealth, a proportion that has fallen from about 10 per cent in the mid-1980s but has remained stable since 1997. Indeed in 2000, it is estimated that over a quarter of the population (28 per cent) had wealth of less than £5,000, and 37 per cent less than £15,000 (Inland Revenue web site: Table 13.5). The 86 per cent of the UK population owning less than £100,000 in 2000 represents nearly 40 million people; the Inland Revenue estimate there to be 220,000 adults in the UK with marketable wealth of £1 million or more.

Figure 5.6 Concentration of wealth among adult population, UK, 1986, 1997 and 2000

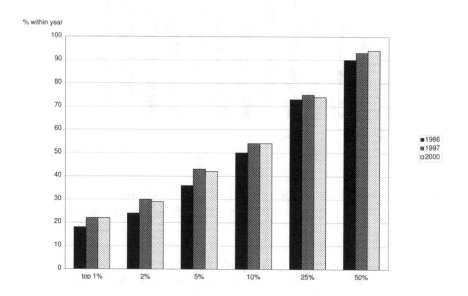

Source: Table A5.12.

However cautiously we treat these figures, it seems indisputable that there has been no equalisation of wealth in the fifteen years covered by these estimates. Nevertheless, the growing inequality of the period up to 1997 seems to have been brought to an end, and it may well be that the Labour government's policies on taxation – especially tax allowances – and the minimum wage have helped: Gordon Brown's annual budgets during the period covered by these figures were consistently redistributive in their effects (Clark et al. 2001: 7).

The Scottish Household Surveys of 2001–2 provide data on the amount of savings and investment owned by households: see Figure 5.7 (Scottish Executive 2003c: Table 6.36). Unlike the material just outlined, the data do not include the value of buildings or land, for many people a major component of their wealth. Overall, slightly over one-fifth of households

(22 per cent) have savings and investments of less than £1,000 and one-quarter (26 per cent) have between £1,000 and £4,999, so that just under half (48 per cent) of households have savings and investments of less than £5,000. Figure 5.7 gives these data and also the distribution for three groups of household income: £0–£6,000; £10,001–£15,000; and over £20,000. There is, as one would expect, a broad association between household income and savings and investments. In the lowest income group, 30 per cent have savings of less than £1,000, a figure which falls to 14 per cent in the highest income group. Just over a fifth (21 per cent) in the highest group have savings of over £30,000, double the proportion in the lowest group (11 per cent).

Figure 5.7 Savings and investments by net annual household income, 2001

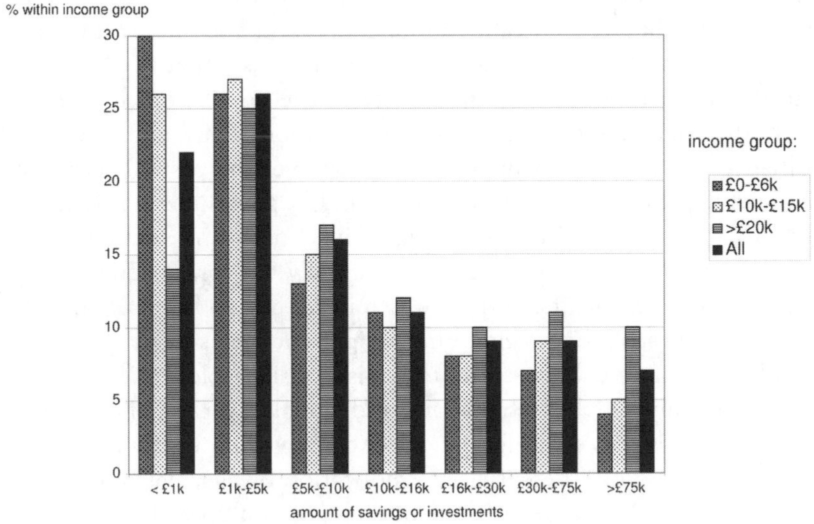

Source: Table A5.13.

Roughly comparable data on assets and savings are collected for Great Britain by the Family Resources Survey of 2001–2, and the figures we have given for Scotland do not differ greatly from these figures (Department of Work and Pensions 2003: Table 5.12). The Family Resources Survey shows that only 15 per cent of households in the Great Britain have savings of more than £20,000. Half of the households (49 per cent) have savings of less than £1,500, with 28 per cent having no savings at all. The survey is thought to somewhat underestimate savings and assets, which include such holdings as bank or building society accounts and stocks and shares. A breakdown is given (Department of Work and Pensions 2003: Table 5.1) by government office region, which shows that the percentage of households in Scotland owning the various types of asset tends to be slightly lower than for Great Britain as a whole, and that 9 per cent have no accounts at all compared to 7 per cent for Britain. This comparison increases the confidence with which we can use the Inland Revenue data on wealth discussed earlier as broadly applying to Scotland.

Conclusions

These data on wealth certainly do not weaken the conclusion we came to earlier that Scotland in the early twenty-first century is a considerably more affluent society than it was in the 1980s, especially for those in full-time employment. However, they serve to further reinforce the observation that Scotland remains an unequal society in terms of both income and wealth. In the case of the latter, the wealth of individuals and households at the upper end of the distribution is dramatically greater than that of those at the bottom end or indeed the vast majority of the population. It is unfortunately difficult enough to estimate the situation today and it would be foolhardy to make statements about change over the past 20 years. What can be said is that policy since the change of UK government in 1997 has at best brought to an end the widening of inequality that had been taking place since 1979. To go further and actually narrow inequality would require that governments, both at Westminster and in Edinburgh, embark on a more redistributive regime than at present seems likely.

Although, as we have seen, there is considerable variation in the financial fortunes of households and individuals over the life cycle, and variation also as they move in and out of employment, or from part to full-time work and so on, there is clear stratification by age, class and, to some extent, gender. Some areas of Scotland are multiply deprived and a considerable proportion of Scotland's people, probably around one in seven, are severely disadvantaged and unlikely to escape from this situation into better circumstances. It is not our task in this book to comment on the moral and political implications of the picture presented in this chapter or indeed elsewhere; it is for the reader to draw her or his own conclusions.

Notes

1. The median here is the median for Great Britain as a whole, and income is after housing costs.
2. Sample sizes were 325 in Scotland and 3,426 in Britain as a whole.
3. At the time of writing of this book (Autumn 2003), there is growing concern as occupational pension schemes come under pressure or are closed, as the state pension is seen to be inadequate, and as the government is placing more emphasis on self-provision.

4. The data are for Britain but there is no reason to believe that figures for Scotland would differ greatly.
5. This was done using weights determined on theoretical grounds. The income and employment domains each have a weight of 30 per cent, health and education of 15 per cent and geographical access 10 per cent.
6. Expressed simply, the technique used is to multiply the figures for each stratum by the reciprocal of the mortality rate for that stratum. A further correction makes an adjustment by size of estate taking this as a proxy for social class and some related variables. The web site gives detailed notes on the methods used.
7. A less serious weakness, among others, is that some forms of wealth such as lottery winnings and some forms of 'windfall' gain are not accurately reflected.
8. It should be noted for completeness, should the reader be interested, that estimates are also made of the value of pension rights to produce further series of statistics: see the Inland Revenue web site.
9. It must be borne in mind that although the data refer to 'estates', the distribution is of the estates of the *living* – essentially the estate which would be reported to the Inland Revenue were they to die.
10. All estimates for 1999 and 2000 for 'marketable wealth' are provisional.

CHAPTER 6

Social Class and Social Opportunity

(chapter written jointly with Cristina Iannelli)

Social class has appeared intermittently throughout the earlier chapters, and could in fact have provided an organising principle for much of the story which they have told. Smaller families, greater longevity, better health, changing patterns of work and growing affluence are all linked in some way to the changing nature of class. A society dominated neither by primary or secondary producers, nor by manual jobs, is not, on the whole, a working class society. The new service industries are run by professionals and semi-professionals, who got there – as we will see in the next chapter – by means of the massively expanded systems of secondary and higher education. The old image of the male manual worker as a metaphor for a particular kind of Scotland has lost its potency also for gender reasons: women, as we have seen, occupy different niches in the labour market from men, and so their increasing participation in it has been another force changing the class structure.

This chapter looks at the changing nature of class in Scotland, dealing with four large issues. The first develops further the question of the decline in size of the manual working class. How extensive has that been, and what classes have taken its place? Is Scotland really now a professional society? Has the decline been because – as is often supposed – the characteristic industrial sectors of the working class have declined, the manufacturing industries on which Scotland's second industrial revolution was built? Or is it because, regardless of this indisputable decline, all sectors of the economy have now become more professionalised, as the routine tasks have been increasingly transferred to machines?

The second issue has to do with the intersection between social class and other forms of social stratification, notably gender, age, ethnicity and religion. Has the change in the class structure affected men and women in similar ways? Are the remnants of the old kind of working class only to be found in ageing pockets of society? Where in the class structure do

Scotland's recent immigrants and their sons and daughters fit in: are they the equivalent of the so-called 'guest workers' of Germany, confined to a marginalised ghetto of low-status work? That was the experience of their Irish Catholic predecessors a century ago, but how have their descendants fared as they have gained access to educational opportunities generally unavailable to their grandparents?

Third, it is important to bear in mind that class is not just about social structure: it is also about individual biography, set within changing family circumstances. A change in the occupational class structure always means a change in the opportunities open to people as they grow up. The second half of the twentieth century was a period of probably unprecedented openness in the class structure, in the sense that it became normal for people to move into a better kind of job than that of their parents. The main reason for this was that professional and semi-professional jobs were expanding their share, while manual jobs were contracting theirs. But what has happened as the middle class has, in this occupational sense, grown inexorably? Have the sons and daughters of the new middle class continued to rise ever higher, or has the process of upward movement come to an end?

Finally, class is not only a matter of the objective measurement of occupational status and rewards. It is also a matter of consciousness, which brings us back to the question of class and the identities of Scotland. Does this increasingly professional society see itself as middle class? How do people view the relationship between the classes: as one of continuing conflict or as a matter of harmony? How does the changing nature of class and of class consciousness relate to Scotland's increasingly diverse political system, where the traditional party of the working class – Labour – commands no more than about one-third of the vote in elections?

Our definition of 'class' in this chapter is based primarily on the classification of occupations, apart from some discussion of class consciousness in the final section. Using occupation to measure class is the most common approach, both in the academic literature and in official publications. Simply put, social class refers to the structuring of power, mainly but not exclusively economic power, power in the marketplace, which differentiates people according to the skills and resources they are able to bring to the market, and the rewards they derive from it (Runciman 1978: 43–56).[1] For most people their life chances are determined largely by what they work at, what they do for a living, because that is the source of income for most people. It characterises their life security, gives them access to housing, education, social capital and so on.

CLASS STRUCTURE

The statistical description even of occupational class is bedevilled by problems of definition. Are changing definitions necessary to cope with the changing reality of the occupational structure, or are they a source of confusion in trying to assess change? Since the population census of 2001, this has been exacerbated by the wholesale revision of the various class schema that are employed by government statisticians in the UK and the abandonment by them of all the previous schema. Therefore, in order to be able to look at changes over time, we have had to use three measures of occupational class in the book. These are explained in detail in Appendix 2, but in brief they are:

- Socio-economic group (SEG): for many decades, this was the basis of official measures of class, for example in the decennial census of population.
- National Statistics socio-economic classification: this is the scheme that has replaced the SEG classification, and is the only source of information about social class in the 2001 population census, and in government surveys after 2000, such as the Labour Force Survey. It was devised by the Office of National Statistics in consultation with sociologists.
- Goldthorpe classes:[2] this scheme was developed over many years by John Goldthorpe and colleagues at Nuffield College, Oxford, partly in an attempt to deal with some of the conceptual inadequacies of official measures of class. We use it here mainly to measure social mobility (the movement of people from the class in which they grew up to the class they occupy as an adult), because versions of the Goldthorpe scheme have become the standard measure used internationally for this purpose.

First, we look at change in the class structure since 1991 using the new socio-economic classification; the census report of 2001 helpfully reclassifies the 1991 data to allow for this comparison to be made. The results are shown in Figure 6.1 (and also in detail in Table A6.1). All three of the groups at the professional and managerial end of the distribution have increased their share: in the decade, the total proportion in these jobs rose from just over a quarter (27 per cent) to over a third (36 per cent). Concomitantly, the groups which have fallen in relative size are mainly the intermediate non-manual (from 17 per cent to 13 per cent) and the routine manual (from 19 per cent to 12 per cent). Thus Scotland has become more professional, and the more routine jobs – whether non-manual or manual – have declined in importance.

Figure 6.1 Socio-economic classification of economically active people aged 16–74, 1991 and 2001

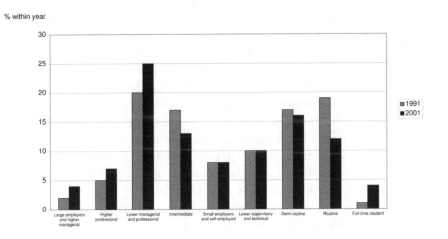

Source: Table A6.1.

Scotland is by no means unusual in this respect, and similar trends have been noted in other European countries (Gallie 2000: 285–6; Marshall et al. 1997: 42; Mueller and Pollak 2001: Table 1; Vallet 2001: Table 1). The Scottish occupational class structure is very similar to that in the other countries of the UK, with the partial exception of Northern Ireland. The Labour Force Survey of March–May 2001 shows that the proportion of economically active people aged 16 to 74 who were in higher or lower managerial or professional jobs (the three categories at the left-hand end of Figure 6.1) in the four countries was 39 per cent in England, 34 per cent in Wales, 36 per cent in Scotland, and 30 per cent in Northern Ireland. Correspondingly, the proportion in semi-routine or routine jobs was 25 per cent in England, 28 per cent in Wales, 28 per cent in Scotland, and 32 per cent in Northern Ireland. The absence of much difference in the class structure of Scotland and the rest of Britain is longstanding, contrary to the popular belief that Scotland is more working class. For example, in the 1981 census, the Scottish proportion in the working class socio-economic groups (as defined in Appendix 3) was 51.8 per cent, while the proportion in England and Wales combined was 48.9 per cent (McCrone 1992: 85). The broad similarity stretches back at least to the 1921 census, when 74 per cent of people in Scotland and 75 per cent of people in England and Wales were in the working class socio-economic groups (McCrone 1992: 79).

Nevertheless, in 2001, within England there was a heavy concentration of professional and managerial jobs among those resident in London and the south-east: inner London had 53 per cent in such occupations, outer London 47 per cent, and the south-east 42 per cent. The concentration was even more pronounced when we use people's place of usual work rather than where they live: most notably, central London (defined as the area bounded by the main railway termini of the city) had 66 per cent in these occupations, compared, for example, to 37 per cent in Scotland. We return to the question of regional variation within Scotland later in this chapter.

Using socio-economic group allows the trends in Scotland to be taken back further, to 1981, as is shown in Table 6.1, and allows us to ascertain which occupations have grown and which declined over a 20-year period.[3] There has been a striking growth in the proportion of managers – from 9 to 16 per cent – and of professionals, from 3 to 6 per cent. The intermediate non-manual sector has increased somewhat from 10 to 16 per cent, while there has been at best stagnation in the junior non-manual category. Farm owners and managers have continued their long-term decline, from 1.2 per cent to 0.7 per cent. Skilled manual jobs have declined from 19 per cent in 1981 to 11 per cent in 2000, although there was also a slight increase in the proportion of people who *supervised* manual work (from 3 to 4 per cent). If we look at the wider picture, the total in all the manual categories – that is everything in the table from 'personal service' to 'agricultural workers', excluding agricultural owners and managers – fell from 52 per cent to 41 per cent, and, in the sense that this group of workers no longer forms the majority, Scotland can no longer be described as a working class country. The level of manual work was far higher earlier in the twentieth century: for example, in the 1961 census it was 63 per cent and in the 1921 census it was 74 per cent, as we have seen (McCrone 1992: 138).

The statistics confirm changes that are widely acknowledged, and that are evident to anyone who has lived in Scotland through the last couple of decades. They are also changes that are found in all western European societies. In the public debate about the decline of the Scottish working class, de-industrialisation is often cited as an explanation of the decline of the size of the working class, and it is undoubtedly the case that the sectors of the economy which have most sharply contracted are the ones that tend to have the greatest proportion of manual jobs. For example, as we saw in Chapter 4, the manufacturing sector's share of employment fell from 24 per cent to 13 per cent between 1981 and 2001, and – using the 1981 Labour Force Survey – we can calculate that manufacturing in 1981 had 34 per cent of all manual jobs, nearly three times as great as the next largest (construction with 12 per cent). Thus, a decline in the manufacturing sector would certainly tend to remove manual jobs from the economy.

Table 6.1 Socio-economic group of economically active population aged 16 or older, 1981–2000

% in columns	Year		
Socio-economic group	1981	1991	2000
Employers and managers, large establishments	4.4	4.2	9.3
Employers and managers, small establishments	4.4	8.5	7.1
Professionals, self-employed	0.5	0.8	1.1
Professionals, employees	2.9	3.9	5.1
Intermediate non-manual	10.2	14.5	16.2
Junior non-manual	19.3	21.0	18.9
Personal service	6.1	4.7	6.1
Foremen and supervisors	2.6	2.4	4.4
Skilled manual	19.3	14.2	10.5
Semi-skilled manual	12.4	10.8	9.6
Unskilled manual	7.7	7.0	5.1
Other self employed	2.3	4.0	3.8
Farmers (employers, managers and self-employed)	1.2	1.1	0.7
Agricultural workers	1.4	1.1	1.1
Armed forces	0.9	0.8	0.5
Inadequately classified	4.5	0.9	0.5
Sample size	240135	207378	5733

Sources: Registrar General for Scotland (1983b: Table 17); Registrar General for Scotland (1994b: Table 14); Labour Force Survey March–May 2000, weighted (sample sizes unweighted).

Matters are not, however, as straightforward as this plausible argument would lead us to believe. The reason is that change is taking place in two ways. As we have just seen, the proportion of the labour force employed in the various sectors of the economy is changing; this is sectoral change. But at the same time the distribution of the types of job which make up the sectors is also changing; this is structural change.

The full details of changes within industrial sectors are in Table A6.2, which uses the Labour Force Surveys of 1981, 1991 and 2000 to show the broad socio-economic groups to which employees in each sector belonged. Inspection of individual sectors shows that there was a great deal of structural shift within them, and not just in the manufacturing sector. Most notably, between 1981 and 2000 the proportion in the professional and managerial category of the broad SEG rose sharply in *every* sector, even the declining ones: for example, it rose from 10 to 22 per cent in manufacturing, from 27 to 40 per cent in real estate, from 14 to 28 per cent in financial intermediation, from 11 to 27 per cent in education and from 10 to 18 per cent in health and social work.

We have, then, to find a way of assessing whether sectoral change (the decline of manufacturing, for example) or structural change (such as the growth of managerial posts within sectors) is the main explanation for the decline of the working class. One relatively simple way to do this is to estimate what the class structure would have looked like if there had *only* been sectoral change – the relative growth and decline of the various industrial sectors. In other words, we are looking to see what the structure would have been if there had been no structural change in occupations within sectors. This can then be compared with the structure as it actually is, enabling us to assess the influence of sectoral change. Table 6.2 shows the results of this process using broad socio-economic groups.[4] The first column shows the actual distribution in 2000. The second column shows the actual change between 1981 and 2000. For example, the professional and managerial group increased by 9.9 percentage points while the skilled manual group declined by 5.5 points. The third column is the crucial one. It shows what the changes would have been had only sectoral change taken place. It is immediately apparent that sectoral change is not the important factor leading to the growth of the professional and managerial class or the decline in the manual classes.

Table 6.2 Components of change in socio-economic groups, 1981–2000

Socio-economic group	2000 actual (from Table 6.1)	Actual change 1981–2000 (from Table 6.1)	Change 1981–2000 if wholly due to sectoral change[1]
Professional and managerial	23.3	9.9	1.0
Intermediate non-manual	16.2	6.0	2.4
Junior non-manual	18.9	–0.4	3.9
Skilled manual	18.7	–5.5	–2.6
Semi-skilled manual	15.7	–2.8	0.0
Unskilled manual	6.2	–2.9	–0.3
Unclassified or armed forces	1.0	–4.4	–4.5

Source: Tables 6.1 and A6.2.
1. This is the SEG distribution if the 1981 SEG distributions within industry sections (from Table A6.2) are applied to the actual distribution of 2000 industry section (from Table A6.2).

Let us look at this in more detail. First, consider the top two classes in Table 6.2. Sectoral change explains only 1 percentage point out of the 9.9 point growth in the professional and managerial class, and explains only 2.4 points out of the 6.0 point growth in the intermediate non-manual class. This confirms the observation we have already made from Table A6.2, that there was a growth in the first class within all sectors. From that same table, we can see that there was also a growth in the intermediate class in all sectors apart from education and health and social work.

Second, there also seems to have been some upward regrading of junior non-manual posts within sectors. If sectoral change had been the only source of change, then the share of these jobs would have grown in size by 3.9 percentage points, whereas they at best held their share (a fall of 0.4 points). The lack of growth of junior non-manual employment seems particularly to have been the case in the finance sector as we can see from Table A6.2. Their share in that sector fell from 77 per cent to 43 per cent, while the proportion in intermediate non-manual posts rose from 3 per cent to 22 per cent, and in professional and managerial posts from 14 per cent to 28 per cent. Similar trends are evident in the utilities sector (electricity, for example) and in real estate. There are two reasons to believe that any regrading of junior non-manual jobs has probably been mainly a matter of upgrading. The first is again the point that the manual categories below the junior non-manual level have mostly been contracting whereas the levels above it have been expanding, as in finance and so on. The second is direct evidence on the skills that people report as being required in their jobs. For the UK as a whole, Gallie (2000: 289–90) describes surveys which have found that most people reported in the 1980s and 1990s an increase in the skills that they needed for their work. Less specifically, but pointing in the same direction, is the evidence from the Labour Force Surveys used in Table A6.2. The proportion of people in the professional and managerial category who possessed a degree rose from 26 per cent in 1981 to 32 per cent in 1991 and to 41 per cent in 2000; those holding a higher education qualification below the level of degree (but nothing better than that) rose from 5 per cent to 9 per cent and then to 14 per cent.

We can also see from Table 6.2 that manual jobs have declined within each sector. If the only source of the fall had been the sharp decline of manufacturing and similar industries, the skilled manual class would have fallen in size by 2.6 percentage points, whereas it actually fell by twice that. Over all the three manual categories, the fall resulting from sectoral change was only 2.9 points, in contrast to the actual fall of 11.2 points. Again, we can see this by looking at particular industrial sectors in Table A6.2. For example, the skilled working class fell from 41 per cent to 35 per cent of employment in manufacturing, and the manual classes as a whole declined in this sector from 73 per cent to 60 per cent.

In short, the fall in the size of the working class, and the growth of professional and managerial employment, is due mainly to change in the nature of the work processes within nearly all sectors – more automation, more supervision and more professional autonomy. Sectoral change, such as the decline in manufacturing, has played a much less significant role.

CLASS AND OTHER SOCIAL DIVISIONS

How, then, does this changing class structure relate to some of the other main ways in which Scottish society is organised? So far as gender is concerned, the changes have been experienced almost equally by women and men, even though their class distribution is quite different. Both these points are illustrated in Table A6.3, using the new socio-economic classification from the censuses of 1991 and 2001. There has been growth in managerial and professional posts for both sexes, and a decline in routine jobs. Women in 2001 have a lower share than men in the higher managerial and higher professional posts (6 per cent compared with 14 per cent), and a larger share in the lower-status versions of these (28 per cent as against 22 per cent); nevertheless, the proportion of women who worked in the highest-status managerial and professional jobs did double in the decade (from 3 to 6 per cent). Women also have large clusters of jobs in the intermediate non-manual category (20 per cent) and in what is the main concentration of female industrial employment, the semi-routine category (20 per cent). Women are also much less likely than men to be self-employed, as we have seen in Chapter 4.

It is indeed the case as we suggested earlier that the declining working class is now concentrated in the older age groups, as Table A6.4 shows,[5] again using the socio-economic classification from the 2001 census. For example, among people aged over 60, 47 per cent were in the lower three classes, in contrast to 35 per cent in the 30–44 age group; the corresponding figures in the first three classes were 38 per cent and 52 per cent. Furthermore, the age group between these two resembles the younger one more than the older one, even though most of its members would have entered the labour force more than two decades ago. It follows that some of the growth of professional and managerial jobs in this period must have been due to the promotion and retraining of people already in work, and not only to the replacement of an older workforce. We must also bear in mind that, among the retired people who have been excluded from the table, there is likely to be a disproportionate number of former middle-class employees, who tend to have a fixed retirement age in the public sector, and so it is likely that some of the oldest age group benefited from such promotion as well.

Assessing the class position of people in the main ethnic groups is complicated by the relatively large proportion of the non-white groups who are full-time students for example 19 per cent of all Indians, 18 per cent of Pakistanis or other south Asians, and 30 per cent of Chinese (2001 Census: Table S213). By contrast, only 7 per cent of white people are full-time students. So Table A6.5 shows only those people who were classified, but including people who have never worked or who have been unemployed for a long time (defined by the census to be not having worked in 1999 or later). Three features stand out. The first is that Indians in Scotland are likely to be in professional or managerial positions, and in fact most of them are professionals, not managers: 42 per cent are in the first two categories, compared to 33 per cent of white people, 20 per cent of Pakistanis and other south Asians, and 25 per cent of Chinese. As we will see in Chapter 7, this is due to the high level of educational qualifications held by Indians.

Second, all three of the non-white groups have substantial minorities in the self-employed category, a point we have already noted in Chapter 4. Nevertheless, contrary to what is probably the popular image in Scotland that Chinese and Pakistani people are primarily self-employed and work in the family shop or restaurant, four-fifths of them are not in the self-employed category. The image may nevertheless be partly correct. There is evidence that these two very broad ethnic groups are concentrated in three quite distinct kinds of employment. One is as *employees* in semi-routine jobs and some of these may be staff employed in businesses owned by other Pakistani or Chinese people. As well as in self-employment, these ethnic groups are also to be found working as employees in professional occupations (as with Indians).

The final point concerning ethnic group concerns the interaction with gender. The proportion of people who have never worked is much higher in the non-white groups than among whites (Table A6.5). This is almost entirely because of different patterns of white and non-white female work. As many as 49 per cent of women in the Pakistani and other south Asian group have never been in paid employment; the proportion for Indian women is 25 per cent, for Chinese women is 19 per cent, but for white women is only 6 per cent. This may partly be due to the difficulty which people who are not fluent in English may experience in gaining employment, partly because of cultural differences in attitudes to paid work, and partly because of under-reporting of paid work being done from home (Modood 1997: 87–8). In other respects, however, the gender differences in the minority groups are similar to those in the white group – there are fewer women than men in the professional and managerial class, and in the self-employed class, and more in the intermediate class.

There are, then, large interactions between class and ethnicity. However, there are almost no such interactions with the largest religious groups, as Table A6.6 shows for socio-economic group (although if we had detailed information on the non-Christian religions, then we would almost certainly get a picture similar to that for ethnic group in Table A6.5). Roman Catholics in Scotland have, historically, been disadvantaged socially, insofar as most of them have their family origins in migration from Ireland in search of poorly paid labouring work in the nineteenth and early-twentieth centuries. In the light of that history, the most striking feature of this table is the size of the Catholic middle class. The proportion of both Catholics and Church of Scotland adherents in the first four categories is 18 per cent, not much different from that of people with no religion (20 per cent), especially if sample size is taken into account. The only Christian group with a substantially larger professional and managerial class is 'other Christian' (28 per cent), which, according to the 2002 Scottish Social Attitudes Survey is about one-third Episcopal church, one-half no denomi-nation, and the remainder mostly dispersed among a variety of small Presbyterian groupings. The same is true in reverse of the combined working class groups (all between 'personal service' and 'other self-em-ployed'), which make up 35–6 per cent of each of the Catholic, Church of Scotland and no religion columns, but only 26 per cent of the other Christian column.

The spatial segregation of class at the level of broad regions has almost vanished, as the economies of the various regions of Scotland have converged on a common norm. The 2001 Census (Table KS14a) reports the distribution of socio-economic category across the 32 local government areas. The proportions in the various managerial or professional occupa-tions (the three categories at the left-hand end of Figure 6.1 above) mostly lie between 20 per cent and 28 per cent: below 20 per cent are Dumfries and Galloway (18 per cent) and East Ayrshire (19 per cent), and above 28 per cent are East Renfrewshire (35 per cent), East Dunbartonshire (34 per cent), and Edinburgh (33 per cent). At a more local level, class remains highly segregated, as the data on the social deprivation of neighbourhoods in Chapter 2 show.

One other spatial aspect is important to class: migration (Table A6.7). Migrants, especially from outwith Scotland, are more likely to be in managerial and professional jobs than people who have been less geogra-phically mobile: for example, fully 32 per cent of people who were born outwith Scotland were in managerial or professional posts in 1999 (the first four socio-economic groups, along with farm owners or managers). The proportion for those born in a different region of Scotland from where they were living was slightly less, at 28 per cent, but the proportion among those who had not moved region was only 18 per cent. The patterns were the reverse of this for the manual classes.

SOCIAL MOBILITY

That last point about geographical mobility brings us to the question of class as biography – the trajectories through which people move to their present class. We investigate this here by using the Scottish component of the British Household Panel Survey, which allows us to look at the relationship among people's current class, the class they were in when they first entered the labour force, and the class in which they grew up. In the normal parlance of studies of social mobility,[6] we refer to respondents' current class, where they have thus far arrived, as their 'destination class', and to the class of their father when they were aged 14 as their 'origin class', the place where they started. We use the Goldthorpe classes, the rationale for which is summarised in Appendix 4 and developed fully in the sources cited there. The reason for recording only the father's class is that a large proportion of the mothers were not themselves in the paid labour force when the respondents in 1999 were aged 14, and so could not be classified by means of an occupational schema. Age 14 is taken to be the final point at which the oldest members of the survey sample stopped being children: for example, it was the school leaving age until 1947.

Social mobility is, then, the extent to which people change classes in these various transitions. To investigate change over time, we calculate rates of mobility in four cohorts, defined as those born respectively in the decades 1937–46, 1947–56, 1957–66 and 1967–76. The choice of decades is somewhat arbitrary, but we have tried to make the boundaries correspond to important changes in the economy, the labour market and the structure of secondary schooling (because, as we will see in Chapter 7, gaining educational credentials is one means by which people can be socially mobile). Thus the first two cohorts mostly attended secondary school (in the 1940s until the early 1970s) before the stabilisation of comprehensive schooling, while the second two attended a mostly comprehensive system (in the early 1970s until the 1990s). The first cohort finished that schooling during the period of post-war economic reconstruction (until the early 1960s), the second during the first post-war boom (1960s to early 1970s), the third during the breakdown of that boom (1970s to early 1980s), and the fourth during the de-industrialisation of the 1980s and early 1990s.

The cohort approach has its flaws: it takes no account of migration into and out of Scotland, nor of differential mortality, but there are reasons to believe that, if anything, these would tend to lead us to under-estimate the extent to which inequalities of opportunity have fallen over the past half century (Paterson 2001). This is an approach that, in the absence of a series of cross-sectional surveys, has been used by social historians quite extensively (Heath 2000).

We look first at the origin and destination classes of people in the four cohorts in 1999. The table showing the origin classes (Table 6.3) is the distribution of the occupations of respondents' fathers when the respondents were aged 14.[7] Table 6.4 shows, for men and women separately, the destination classes, which are simply the classes in which people currently work.[8] We can see in Table 6.4 the longer-term versions of the trends we have noted already for the last 20 years: the growth of professional employment for men, the growth of routine non-manual employment for women, the decline of unskilled manual employment for both men and women. Note also that in all the tables on social mobility it is, of course, necessary to omit people whose occupation could not be classified. That explains, for example, why the proportion of older women (born between 1937 and 1946) in service-class jobs is quite high (36 per cent): 59 per cent of all women in that age group were unclassified, in contrast to 44 per cent of men in the age group, and to no more than 30 per cent of women in younger age groups.

Table 6.3 Father's class by birth cohort, among people aged 23–62 in 1999

% in columns	Birth cohort			
Father's class when respondent was aged 14[1]	1937–46	1947–56	1957–66	1967–76
Service class (I, II)	12.7	19.5	21.5	27.2
Routine non-manual (III)	4.9	6.2	5.1	4.3
Self-employed (IV)	11.9	11.5	13.5	14.7
Skilled manual (V, VI)	35.7	31.2	36.1	35.1
Semi- and unskilled (VII)	34.9	31.6	23.8	18.6
Sample size	334	485	627	469

Source: British Household Panel Survey, waves 1 and 9, weighted (sample sizes unweighted).
1. Condensed version of Goldthorpe classes; the Goldthorpe classes represented in each row are indicated by Roman numerals.

Leaving aside the effects of cohort and sex for the moment, we are able to explore the overall pattern of how the class of origin relates to people's current class. Table 6.5 shows what are known as outflows and inflows. The outflow is the proportion of people from a specific origin class who end up in

Table 6.4 Respondent's class, by birth cohort and sex, among people aged 23–62 in 1999

% in columns within sex	Birth cohort			
Class[1]	1937–46	1947–56	1957–66	1967–76
Male				
Service class (I, II)	29.5	43.2	42.7	38.0
Routine non-manual (III)	7.4	11.2	5.1	12.2
Self-employed (IV)	20.5	12.1	13.9	6.6
Skilled manual (V, VI)	18.9	22.3	22.6	24.9
Semi- and unskilled (VII)	23.8	11.2	15.7	18.3
Sample size	104	200	287	227
Female				
Service class (I, II)	36.0	40.8	37.5	38.8
Routine non-manual (III)	28.1	30.0	36.6	37.4
Self-employed (IV)	6.7	5.2	5.2	1.9
Skilled manual (V, VI)	2.2	4.7	4.3	9.7
Semi- and unskilled (VII)	27.0	19.2	16.4	12.1
Sample size	86	218	277	254

Source: see notes to Table 6.3.
1. Condensed version of Goldthorpe classes; the Goldthorpe classes represented in each row are indicated by Roman numerals.

each destination class; it shows where people end up from each starting point. It is, then, the percentage calculated across rows. In the table, it is the figure in the upper row of each of the five pairs of percentages. For example, of all those people whose father was in a semi-skilled or unskilled occupation when they were aged 14, 30 per cent were in the service class, 20 per cent were in a routine non-manual job, 10 per cent were self-employed, 17 per cent were in a skilled manual job, and 23 per cent were – like their fathers – in a semi-skilled or unskilled job. The inflow percentage, by contrast, is the percentage by column: that is, the proportion of people in a specific destination class who started off in each origin class: it shows where people came from to reach that destination.[9] For example, among all those respondents who were in service-class jobs (the first column), 32 per cent of the fathers had been in the service class themselves, 8 per cent had been in routine non-manual jobs, 14 per cent had been self-employed, 27 per cent had been in skilled manual jobs, and 19 per cent had been in semi-skilled or unskilled manual jobs.

Table 6.5 Class outflows[1] and inflows,[1] 1999

Origin class[2]	Destination class[2]					Sample size
	Service class (I, II)	Routine non-manual (III)	Self-employed (IV)	Skilled manual (V, VI)	Semi- and unskilled (VII)	
Service class	59.3	17.3	4.1	10.2	9.2	300
(I, II)	32.4	18.4	9.4	14.9	12.2	
Routine non-manual	52.6	20.5	2.6	6.4	17.9	79
(III)	7.6	5.8	1.6	2.5	6.3	
Self-employed	39.0	16.6	20.3	13.4	10.7	190
(IV)	13.5	11.2	29.9	12.4	9.0	
Skilled manual	32.0	23.5	8.6	18.1	17.7	473
(V, VI)	27.4	39.4	31.5	41.8	37.1	
Semi- and unskilled	30.0	20.4	10.2	16.6	22.7	358
(VII)	19.1	25.3	27.6	28.4	35.3	
Sample size	546	300	124	201	229	

Source: see notes to Table 6.3.
1. The upper number in each cell is the outflow percentage, and the lower number is the inflow percentage. The outflow is the percentage within a row: that is, the proportion of people from a specific origin class who end up in each destination class. The inflow percentage is the percentage within a column: that is, the proportion of people in a specific destination class who started off in each origin class.
2. Condensed version of Goldthorpe classes; the Goldthorpe classes represented in each row are indicated by Roman numerals.

Because the professional classes were growing throughout the period, these classes I and II were the main destination for all origin classes, even the semi-skilled and unskilled working class: that is, in each row, the largest row percentage (upper number in each cell) is always in the first column. This illustrates the way in which structural change in the pattern of classes can itself induce social mobility. If the lower classes are contracting and the upper classes expanding, there is bound to be upward mobility. This will be experienced by the individuals concerned as real gains compared to their fathers, even though we might judge that it was inevitable given the changing structure. In consequence, the professional classes today draw on very diverse class origins (the column percentages in the first column):

only one-third came from a professional background (the lower figure in the first cell in the first column), and 47 per cent came from a working class background (the sum of the lower figures in the bottom two cells in the first column). The idea that society is socially open is sustained by the high proportion of the service class who have come from lower down the social scale, even though it is partly a result of changed class structure rather than of openness itself. In other words, there are simply more service class jobs, and expanded opportunity because of that, rather than greater opportunity for people to move up the occupational ladder at the expense of other people who move down. Despite all that, it is important to note that over a third of the working class stay in the working class. That is, for people whose father was in a skilled manual job, the proportion who were themselves in a manual job was about 36 per cent, made up of 18.1 per cent in the skilled manual class plus 17.7 per cent in the semi-skilled or unskilled manual class. Likewise, for people whose father was in a semi-skilled or unskilled manual job, the proportion in a manual job was 39 per cent (16.6 per cent plus 22.7 per cent). Looking at this differently, there is little downward mobility, with fewer than one in five of the working class coming from middle class families. For example, among respondents who were in skilled manual jobs, the proportion whose father was in the service class or in a routine non-manual job was 17 per cent (14.9 per cent plus 2.5 per cent). The analogous figure for respondents who were in semi-skilled or unskilled jobs was 19 per cent (12.2 per cent plus 6.3 per cent).

Table 6.5 does not, however, show us how mobility might be changing, because it describes the sample as a whole, taking no account of age. This is done in Table 6.6.[10]

The most striking point to note first is that most people in each cohort, and for each sex, were upwardly mobile. Indeed, in all but the youngest cohort of men, a majority of the whole sample had been upwardly mobile. For example, among people born between 1957 and 1966, 55 per cent of men had been upwardly mobile, and 63 per cent of women. Even the 46 per cent of men in the youngest cohort who had been upwardly mobile still constituted the largest single group, because the proportion of men in that cohort who had been downwardly mobile was 36 per cent and the proportion who had been immobile was 18 per cent. More detailed statistical modelling shows that, in line with our previous discussion, this upward mobility was largely because the professional classes were expanding their share, rather than because of any changes in the relative chances of mobility from a given starting point (Iannelli and Paterson 2003). For example, for all cohorts, people who had a service class origin were more likely to end up in a service class job than people who had a skilled-manual origin. But for both these origin groups the proportion in a service-class job had risen across the cohorts. So the inequality in opportunities for mobility associated with class of origin had remained fairly stable, but all classes had benefited from a higher level of overall opportunity.

Table 6.6 Social mobility, by birth cohort and sex, among people aged 23–62 in 1999

% in columns within sex	Birth cohort			
Mobility	1937–46	1947–56	1957–66	1967–76
		Male		
Downwards	25.2	15.9	27.9	35.5
Immobile	15.7	20.9	16.8	18.3
Upwards	59.1	63.2	55.3	46.2
Sample size	93	172	246	192
		Female		
Downwards	18.1	29.0	23.1	28.8
Immobile	25.0	15.6	13.9	15.3
Upwards	56.9	55.4	63.0	55.8
Sample size	70	187	243	197

Source: see notes to Table 6.3.
Uses 11-class version of Goldthorpe scheme, not the condensed versions in Tables 6.3 to 6.5.

The second important point to be observed from Table 6.6 is the apparent beginnings of a decline again in the upward mobility of the youngest cohort. We might be tempted to surmise that this had something to do with the economic recession of the 1980s, when these people were entering the labour market, but that is not really plausible because, as we have already noted, this period was accompanied by a rapid increase in the proportion of the labour force who were in professional and other middle class jobs. If anything, the largest effect of the recession would have been to destroy working class jobs, and hence to encourage working class people to gain the educational qualifications that would enable them to move into a middle class job. Nor can the pattern in Table 6.6 be attributed to this youngest cohort's not yet having reached the peak of their careers: the same pattern is evident if we look at first jobs rather than current job (Table A6.8). The most likely explanation is that the middle class is reaching what we might call saturation: as the middle class gets larger, the opportunity to move further upwards is reduced, essentially because there is nowhere else to go. We can see, by comparing Tables 6.3 and 6.4, that, because the same even longer-term trends were applying to fathers too (the fathers of the oldest cohort having themselves been born roughly between about 1890 and the end of the First World War), the discrepancy between men and their fathers became less as time went on: thus, in the oldest cohort the proportions in the professional classes were 13 per cent of fathers but 30 per cent of sons, whereas in the youngest cohort these proportions were 27 per cent and 38 per cent. Eventually, upward mobility has to stop or go into reverse if the supply of new middle class jobs is less than the increase in middle class origins.

Women in the two youngest cohorts have experienced rather greater levels of upward mobility than men (Table 6.6), mainly because of women of working class origins entering routine non-manual jobs (Iannelli and Paterson 2003): for example, in the cohort born between 1957 and 1966, the proportion of women who were upwardly mobile was 63 per cent, but the proportion of men was 55 per cent. The whole process of women entering the labour market has been discussed more fully in Chapter 4, and part of that story has to do with women postponing or rejecting becoming a parent. There is, however, a question as to whether legislation to outlaw invidious discrimination against mothers in the workplace might have helped their careers. Some evidence relating to this is in Table 6.7, which shows movement between first job and current job by sex and by parental status. To get adequate sample sizes, we have had to condense the cohorts into two: 1937–56 and 1957–76.

First, looking only at people who are not parents, we can see some difference between men and women. In the older cohort here (born between 1937 and 1956), 54 per cent of the males and 41 per cent of the females had been upwardly mobile. In the younger cohort, the corresponding proportions were 49 per cent and 47 per cent. The patterns are, moreover, quite similar to those for the younger male parents: the proportions of them who had been upwardly mobile were 61 per cent in the older cohort and 52 per cent in the younger one. In other words, for men, being a parent does not seem to be any impediment to career mobility.

Female parents of both cohorts, however, experience less upward mobility, and more downward mobility, than any of the other groups, and so in that sense being a mother still does have an impact on occupational opportunity. For example, in the younger cohort, only 38 per cent of female parents had been upwardly mobile, compared to 52 per cent, 49 per cent and 47 per cent in the other groups. Nevertheless, it is also notable that the change in upward mobility (from 31 per cent to 38 per cent) between the older and the younger cohort is less unfavourable for female parents than for any of the other three groups, with the result that the gap in upward mobility between female and male parents fell from 30 percentage points in the older cohort (61 minus 31 per cent) to 14 percentage points in the younger (52 minus 38 per cent). This may perhaps indicate that the position of mothers may be better protected now than it was, as legislation on equal rights prevents their position from deteriorating as rapidly as that of men when the supply of professional and managerial jobs starts to dry up. However, it might also simply reflect the fact that mothers are more likely to be in low-status jobs than women who are not mothers: for example, 19 per cent of mothers were in semi-skilled or unskilled jobs, compared to 10 per cent of women who are not mothers, and 14 per cent of mothers were in personal service jobs compared to 10 per cent of women who were not mothers. The corresponding figures for men are 15 per cent in semi-skilled or unskilled jobs and 2 per cent in personal service jobs. Because of that, a reduction in the availability of new non-manual jobs has proportionately less of an effect on mothers than on men or on women who are not mothers.

Table 6.7 Career mobility, by condensed birth cohort, sex and whether a parent,[1] among people aged 23–62 in 1999

% in columns within sex	Birth cohort			
Mobility between first and current job	1937–56	1957–76	1937–56	1957–76
	Male parent		Male non-parent	
Downwards	17.4	14.9	25.7	17.9
Immobile	21.7	33.2	20.0	33.3
Upwards	60.9	51.9	54.3	48.8
Sample size	187	219	34	168
	Female parent		Female non-parent	
Downwards	31.1	25.6	18.2	17.8
Immobile	37.7	36.0	40.9	35.7
Upwards	31.1	38.4	40.9	46.5
Sample size	184	251	26	154

Source: see notes to Table 6.3.
Uses 11-class version of Goldthorpe scheme, not the condensed versions in Tables 6.3 to 6.5.
1. Natural parent of any children. Thus ignores step-parenthood and adoption.

CLASS IDENTITY AND CONSCIOUSNESS

How do these structural changes relate to people's feelings about class as expressed in surveys? In the Scottish Election Surveys of 1979 and 1999, people were asked to assign themselves to labels 'working class' or 'middle class'. Most did so, and the results for each broad socio-economic group are shown in Table 6.8. By 1999, every class showed a majority of people calling themselves 'working class', even the professionals. Even in 1979 only a slight majority even of professionals and managers called themselves 'middle class'. Working class identity has always been strong, and has not become weaker. As may be seen from the totals, the explanation of the rise is a greater willingness to express a class identity in answer to the question. In 1999, over the sample as a whole, 95 per cent were willing to choose a class identity, some 11 percentage points higher than in 1979. But what demands explanation is not that rise but the continuing dominance of the working class identity in 1999.

Table 6.8 Self-perceived class,[1] by broad socio-economic group, 1979 and 1999

% in rows within year	Year				Sample sizes	
	1979		1999		1979	1999
Self-perceived class	working class	middle class	working class	middle class		
Broad socio-economic group[2]						
Professional and managerial	42.2	50.0	51.8	43.5	90	292
Intermediate non-manual	52.8	30.3	56.1	38.8	89	189
Junior non-manual	71.6	19.3	72.6	26.1	88	237
Skilled manual	78.4	10.8	82.8	14.6	139	274
Semi-skilled manual	84.2	10.5	79.1	15.7	95	239
Unskilled manual	81.3	6.3	79.6	15.3	32	113
All	62.8	20.9	69.2	26.9	533	1344

Source: Scottish Election Survey 1979 and Scottish Social Attitudes Survey 1999, weighted (sample sizes unweighted).
1. Balance in each year is percentage not acknowledging a class identity.
2. Omitting armed forces and inadequately classified.

The key to this lies in the different views held by people who had or had not been upwardly mobile. The election survey of 1997 asked the same question, and also collected information analogous to that which we have used to calculate rates of mobility. Among those who had remained in the working class (Goldthorpe classes V, VI and VII), 86 per cent called themselves working class, as did 76 per cent of the small group who had been downwardly mobile from the middle class (classes I, II, III and IV) to the working class. At the other end of the spectrum, only 44 per cent of those who remained in the middle class called themselves working class. But the most significant group numerically, around a third of the whole sample as we have seen earlier in this chapter, are those who moved up from the working class to the middle class. Fully 80 per cent of this upwardly mobile group still called themselves working class. It seems that the continuing working class consciousness of the increasingly middle class society is probably because of upward social mobility.

By contrast, in other countries, notably the USA but also England, a middle class identity is to be found across the occupational structure, often associated with a feeling that class conflict has declined. A 'classless' society has not usually meant the utopia that might have been hoped for by Marxists in the nineteenth century, with the proletariat subsuming all other classes; it has, rather, tended to mean that, in a society of greater choice and individuality, an increasing majority of people were able to live in ways that only the middle class could enjoy in the past.[11] Scotland has undoubtedly shared in these processes, as we have seen earlier in the book, and as is explained more fully in Chapters 7 and 8. All occupational classes have come increasingly to believe that there is little class conflict, as is shown in detail in Table A6.9. Yet its citizens do not interpret that as meaning that everyone has become middle class.

Of course, the meaning of a 'middle class' identity varies between countries too: being 'middle class' in the USA connotes quite different things from the same label in Scotland. But that may be the whole point, because this national foible in Scotland has had rather important political consequences, helping to explain the collapse of the Conservative vote and the conversion of the Labour party to supporting the setting-up of a Scottish Parliament. The Conservative party has declined in Scotland over the past 20 years because it declined in all classes, but the most numerically important decline was in the expanding middle class. Almost certainly, that is because of the insistence of large numbers of people in the new middle class on calling themselves working class: when we calculate party support by class identity, we find that in 1999 the Conservatives could capture the allegiance of only 11 per cent of those who call themselves working class, down from 21 per cent in 1979 (Table A6.10). Their share of those with a middle class identity fell too, from 60 per cent, but remained moderately high at 30 per cent: the problem for the party was not this but the unpopularity of a middle class identity itself. Labour's success, by contrast, has been due to its capacity to attract the votes of people who call themselves middle class as well as retaining the support of those who call themselves working class. From Table A6.10, we see that Labour had an unwavering 46 per cent of the allegiance of those who called themselves working class, and its share of those with a middle class identity rose from 14 per cent to 30 per cent. The main challenger to Labour for its working-class base was the SNP. Out of this competition with the SNP and increasing electoral weakness of the Conservatives came the conversion of the Labour party to supporting self-government, and the belief that Scotland is an anti-

Conservative country. More recently, the same suspicion of a middle class identity may have played a part in preventing any revival of the Conservatives' share of the vote – still only 16 per cent in the 2003 election to the Scottish Parliament; it may also have underpinned some of the increasing pluralism of Scottish voting around an essentially left-of-centre position: diversity on the left is perhaps what you get when a more affluent, more middle class and (we will see in the next chapter) much better-educated electorate tries to find means of expressing its persisting sense of being working class.

CONCLUSIONS

If there is one dominant conclusion, it is that Scotland is becoming a professional society in a much more thorough way than it was even in the 30 years after the Second World War, when the professions came to dominate social policy and public life but still from their inherited position as a relatively small elite. The class of professionals and managers now makes up over one-third of the population. This has happened at a time when Scotland has resumed some democratic control of its own politics, and the two processes may in fact not be unconnected. The professional class came to support an elected parliament during the 1980s and the 1990s, as they became alienated from the policies of the Conservative government. Their openness to these new ideas may be partly due to their own diverse origins in the upward social mobility of the post-war years. Now that the parliament is in place, they are the leaders of the civic institutions with which it has to negotiate if it is to achieve anything in the way of policy or of public debate

The diversity of the new middle class is not only a matter of its own class origins. It now contains a greater proportion of women than ever before, although still less than half. For the first time, it contains Catholics more or less in proportion to their share of the population. It also has a significant minority from the Asian ethnic groups, whose younger members especially are taking part in education and hence professional careers to such an extent that they are bound to rise into influential positions in Scottish society over the next half century: Asians are very likely to become as prominent in the leadership of Scotland as people of Jewish, Italian or Irish family origins were in the second half of the twentieth century.

Yet, middle class though it has become, Scotland still thinks of itself as being a working class country. These new professionals acquire their sense of identity, and their social democratic political views, from a resultant belief in the public provision of social welfare, and public responsibility for economic and social development. This conjunction of middle class economic position and left-of-centre politics makes the direction in which Scotland is going rather different from its southern neighbour, and perhaps, in the long term, more akin to that of the Scandinavian countries than it has been for many centuries.

TECHNICAL NOTE: SHIFT-SHARE ANALYSIS

In what follows we are referring to the construction of Table 6.2 in the text; it also involves the use of the data in Table 6.1 and Table A6.2.

The first column of Table 6.2 shows the actual distribution of people into the various broad socio-economic groups in 2000. It is mostly derived directly from Table 6.1 (using the correspondence between full SEG and broad SEG outlined in Appendix 3). For example, the figure of 23.3 against the category 'professional and managerial' is calculated by adding the percentages in Table 6.1 corresponding to the first four categories plus those 'farmers' who were not self-employed. The second column then shows the actual change in this distribution from 1981 (again mostly derived from Table 6.1): for example, the size of the professional and managerial group rose by 9.9 percentage points, from 13.4 per cent in 1981 to 23.3 per cent in 2000. Thus far, then, Table 6.2 is simply a summary of information that has already been presented.

The final column of Table 6.2 is the key one. It is calculated in three steps. What we do first is to calculate, for each sector, an estimate of the number of people there would have been in each broad SEG if the occupational structure *within* each sector had remained the same between 1981 and 2000. This involves the use of the data in Table A6.2. We take the 1981 distribution of SEG *within* each sector from Table A6.2 and apply it, sector by sector, to the sample size of each sector in 2000, which is also given in the same table. For example, consider the sector 'manufacturing'. We see from the relevant part of Table A6.2 that, *in 1981*, the proportion of people working in manufacturing who were in the 'professional and managerial' category was 9.7 per cent. Reading along that row in that table, we then find 3.8 per cent in 'intermediate non-manual', and so on up to 0.3 per cent unclassified or in the armed forces. Table A6.2 also shows us that, *in 2000*, there were 807 sample members in the manufacturing sector. So, if the distribution of SEGs in the manufacturing sector in 2000 had been the same as in 1981, 9.7 per cent of these 807 would have been professionals and managers (that is about 78), 3.8 per cent would have been intermediate non-manual posts (about 31), and so on for the rest of the sector. We repeat this calculation for each industrial sector, thus getting estimates of the number of people in each broad SEG in each sector, under the supposition that the distribution of SEG within sector was the same in 2000 as in 1981.

The second step is to sum these estimated numbers across the sectors to give an estimated total number in each broad SEG. For example, for the professional and managerial category, we have estimated that there would have been about 78 people in the manufacturing sector. Likewise, we can calculate that there would have been about 60 professionals and managers in the construction sector (13.3 per cent of 451), and so on. Adding up our estimates across all the sectors, we obtain an estimate of the total number of professionals and managers there would have been in 2000 had there been only sectoral change between 1981 and 2000. We can then express this total as a percentage of the sample as a whole which gives us a figure of 14.4 per cent in the professional and managerial group. We repeat this process for each of the SEGs.

We now have a complete distribution of the SEGs in 2000 as they would be had there been only sectoral change between 1981 and 2000. The final step is to record for each SEG the change that this represents from the distribution in 1981, thus obtaining column three of Table 6.2. For instance, the figure of 14.4 per cent for the professional and managerial group represents an increase of 1.0 percentage points on 1981.

NOTES

1. In this book we do not directly examine the other aspects of power which Weber identified – social status and what he called 'party', power conferred by social organisation – because these aspects of power do not lend themselves to enquiry using large-scale aggregate data of the kind on which we focus here.
2. Strictly, these should be called Hope-Goldthorpe classes because Keith Hope was heavily involved in their original development (Goldthorpe and Hope 1974). However, the schema has subsequently been so extensively used and revised by Goldthorpe that we follow the normal convention here. See also Appendix 3.
3. Note that the trends between 1991 and 2000 in Table 6.1 – using socio-economic group – are very similar to those shown for 1991 and 2001 in Figure 6.1 using the new National Statistics Socio-Economic Classification.
4. The way in which Table 6.2 is calculated is explained in a brief note on shift-share analysis, as the process is called, at the end of this chapter.
5. The table excludes people who had never worked, were unemployed long-term, or had retired. This covers 34 per cent of those aged 16–29, 13 per cent of the 30–44 group, 18 per cent of the 45–59 group, and 73 per cent of the group aged 60 and older .
6. Strictly speaking, what is being discussed is occupational mobility, or at any rate mobility between classes defined by occupation, but it has become customary to speak of social mobility and we follow the practice here.
7. The origin classes were, not surprisingly, almost identical for men and women.
8. It is worth noting that Table 6.4 is an amplification of Table A6.3, allowing for different ways of measuring class, a slightly different age range, different surveys, and slightly different dates. For example, in Table A6.3, the proportion of women aged 16 to 74 in

the first three categories of the new socio-economic classification in 2001 was 34 per cent. Since these categories cover employers, managers, and higher and lower professionals, this is broadly consistent with Table 6.4, which shows, for 1999, between 36 per cent and 41 per cent of women aged 23 to 62 in Goldthorpe's 'service class'.

9. The relevant percentages are the figures in the lower row of each of the five pairs of percentages.

10. The calculations underlying this table are in principle as follows (although the actual calculations use the 11-class version of the Goldthorpe schema, not the condensed version shown in Table 6.5). First, for each of the four cohorts, and for each sex, a table analogous to Table 6.5 is constructed, showing the number of people in each combination of origin class and destination class. For each cohort and each sex, we can thereby add up the number of people who were in a higher class than their father, the number who were in a lower class, and the number who were in the same class. For example, for those whose father was in the service class, no-one could be in a higher class, some were in the service class, and the rest had been downwardly mobile. Similarly, for people whose father was in the skilled manual class, upward mobility would mean the respondent's being in the professional, routine non-manual, or self-employed classes. Immobility would mean the respondent's being in the skilled manual class, and downward mobility would mean the respondent's being in the semi-skilled or unskilled manual class. After obtaining in this way the total number of each cohort who had moved upwards, stayed the same, or moved downwards, these numbers can be expressed as a percentage of the whole cohort for that sex. It is these percentages that are recorded in Table 6.6: for example, of male respondents who were born between 1937 and 1946, 25.2 per cent had been *downwardly* mobile (from whatever class of origin they started in), 15.7 per cent had stayed in the same class, and 59.1 per cent had been *upwardly* mobile.

11. The emphasis placed on lifestyle indicates clearly the extent to which in many societies social class has come to be equated with status situation, in Weber's terms, and the extent of the decline in the 'classic' Marxist sense of class as meaning the relationship to the means of production.

CHAPTER 7

Education and Life Chances

In Scotland as in many other countries, there were several educational revolutions in the twentieth century; we deal here with the tail end of one – in secondary schooling – and with the full throes of the other – in higher education – and assess some of the effects of both of them. Although full participation in the elementary stages from ages five to 12 had more or less been achieved by the 1920s, secondary education was then only in its infancy. No more than about one third of the age group took part in the five-year course that could lead to the Leaving Certificate, and about the same proportion entered shorter courses that lasted no longer than three years, and usually only one or two. The remaining third never entered any kind of post-elementary schooling at all, and left at age 14 (Paterson 2003: 65). Even these figures overstate the significance of a full secondary education, since only about one in 20 of the age cohort actually gained the Leaving Certificate (ibid.: 68).

The most profound changes in secondary schooling therefore happened after the Second World War. By the 1950s it had been accepted that everyone should take part in some kind of secondary course, and after 1965 all secondary schools in the public sector were organised along comprehensive lines: that is, they were intended to educate all the children in their local community, no longer selecting their pupils according to measures of academic attainment. These comprehensive public schools educated about 95 per cent of all secondary-age pupils, a proportion that remained stable between the 1970s and the end of the century. The remainder were in selective private schools which charged fees. In the public schools, the main consequences of ending selection (and of raising the school leaving age to 16 in 1973) were the reform of courses and certification at age 16 to cater for a much wider range of ability than hitherto. This resulted in an increase in the proportion staying on for at least five or six years of secondary schooling, and an increase in the proportion gaining significant numbers of passes in the Higher Grade examinations at ages 17–18 (the successors to the Leaving Certificate, universally known in Scotland as the Highers). This latter part of the revolution in secondary schooling is, then, the first topic of this chapter.

The consequences did not end with the expansion of secondary schooling, however, because, by the 1990s, it was also encouraging a large growth in post-school education, to such an extent that, by the end of the century, Scotland had a mass system of higher education. Scotland is still going through this second educational revolution. As secondary and higher education both expanded, moreover, some of the most intractable social inequalities in access to education and in levels of attainment started to diminish. The consequences for people's access to further learning, to good jobs, to social status, and to social influence have been profound. The significance of education for individual opportunity has never been as great as it is now. Even if it is no more than the means by which relative advantage is passed from one generation to the next, a substantial period of initial education is the only route into adulthood for almost everyone. Insofar as educational advantage is now one of the most valuable legacies which parents can pass on to their children, education is itself – as we will see – becoming the most important element in the system of stratification in Scotland. Determining, as it does to a large extent, access to occupational advantage, its importance exceeds in magnitude the inequalities stemming from gender, ethnic origin and religion. In maintaining class-based inequality in Scotland, the transfer of educational advantage from parents to children may now be more important than the direct transfer of material wealth.

EXPANSION

For school education, the expansion of the last two decades is clear from Figure 7.1. This shows the proportion of school students who stayed on voluntarily into the fifth year of secondary school. For male and female combined, it rose from under half in 1980 to over two-thirds in 1999. The rise was sharper for female students, from 48 per cent to 72 per cent. By the end of the century, it had become normal to stay on, and indeed as high a proportion of the age group was experiencing at least five years of secondary schooling in the 1990s as were experiencing any kind or length of post-elementary education in the 1920s and 1930s. Secondary schooling has therefore gone through an enormous transformation: from providing the first step in the ladder towards the high-status professions, it has become, in effect, a necessary condition of citizenship.

Figure 7.1 Staying-on rates in school, by sex, 1979–80 to 1998–9

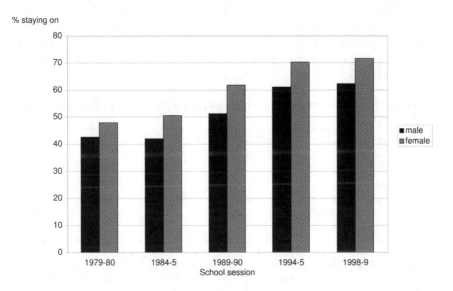

Source: Table A7.1.

Table 7.1 records the same process differently, not as the proportion of the age cohort staying on, but as the proportion of people of a particular age taking part in any kind of education, in five broad categories.[1] Although this series can be taken back only to 1985, it does allow us to set the rise in school participation in the context of a parallel rise in all kinds of full-time education, up to age 21. So this table starts to move us on from the expansion of secondary schooling to the current rapid expansion of higher education. In a statistical sense, the most notable sector other than school was full-time higher education, participation in this age group rising from one in ten to one-quarter between 1985 and 2000. Recorded differently, as the proportions of the age group entering full-time higher education by age 21, the trends are similar (Table 7.2). In 2000 the symbolically important threshold of 50 per cent participation was exceeded for the first time. As with staying on at school, the expansion has been most striking among women, who shifted from having lower rates of participation than men in the 1980s (16 per cent compared to 19 per cent in 1980, for example) to having much higher rates from the early 1990s (56 per cent compared to 45 per cent by the end of the century).

We can also observe a growth (from 3 per cent to 7 per cent) in the proportion taking full-time courses of non-advanced study, mainly vocational further education (Table 7.1). As the post-school sectors expanded, participation in such courses also became more formal, in the sense that proportionately fewer students studied part-time: indeed for further education, the proportion in part-time courses fell from the clear majority of students (15 per cent part-time compared to 3 per cent full-time) to just about a half of students (8 per cent part-time compared to 7 per cent full-time).

Table 7.1 Participation rates in education, among people aged 16–21, 1985–6 to 2000–1

% of all aged 16–21	1985–6	1990–1	1995–6	2000–1
School	12	13	18	18
Further education: full-time	3	4	5	7
Further education: part-time	15	11	11	8
Higher education: full-time	11	14	23	26
Higher education: part-time	3	3	2	2
All education	44	45	59	62

Sources: For 1985–86 and 1995–96: Scottish Office (1997b). For school participation, recalculated from Tables 2–8 on base of 16–21 year olds. FE information is from Table 9 and HE information from Table 10. For 1990–91 and 2000–1: Scottish Executive (2003d: Table 1).

Table 7.2 Entry to full-time higher education by age 21, by sex, 1980–1 to 2000–1

Year	Male		Female		All	
	old series	new series	old series	new series	old series	new series
1980–81	19.2		16.3		17.8	
1985–86	19.5		18.8		19.1	
1990–91	25.4	27.1	26.5	28.7	25.9	27.9
1995–96	39.1	37.7	46.5	44.8	42.7	41.2
2000–1		44.9		56.1		50.4

The Age Participation Index is the number of Scots aged under 21 who entered full-time higher education courses anywhere in the UK for the first time, as a percentage of the population in Scotland aged 17. The series has a discontinuity in 1994–95 when the Higher Education Statistics Agency took over the compilation of the statistics on participation in the older universities from the Universities Statistical Record.

Sources: for old series 1980–81: Scottish Office (1996a: Table 11); for old series 1985–86 to 1995–96: Scottish Office (1997c: Table 10, as corrected on 13 March 1998); for new series 1990–91 to 2000-1: Scottish Executive (2002d: Table 6).

Taken together, all these figures sum up the broad effects of the two educational revolutions which we mentioned in the introduction to this chapter. They show the mature effects of the expansion of secondary schooling that started much earlier in the twentieth century, and they show also the continuing massive change in rates of participation in higher education.

All the statistics we have looked at so far relate to people aged under 21. Scots have never participated widely in lifelong formal education: even among those who do well educationally, the belief has probably been that a good initial education is all that is needed to allow independent learning later (Schuller and Bamford 1998). The recent expansion has not made substantial inroads into this pattern: in 2000, the proportions taking part in any kind of organised education were 15 per cent among those aged 25–9, 12 per cent for 30–9, 9 per cent for 40–9 and 3 per cent for 50 and over (Table A7.2). In all these age groups, the most common type of education was part-time further education. There would also have been quite widespread use of adult education, of libraries and other sources of books, and – increasingly – the educational aspects of the internet (Paterson 2003: 183–7). But after their mid-20s people have tended to leave formal education behind.

Formal institutions were, nevertheless, providing a diverse range of educational experiences, with post-school courses mainly provided by the higher education institutions and the further education colleges. The higher education institutions were themselves of various origins and types (Scottish Executive 2002a: Table 3). By 2000, there were the four old universities dating in some form from the fifteenth and sixteenth centuries, four more created in the 1960s (although three of them had much older origins as providers of higher education since the nineteenth century), and five created after 1992 from former technological institutions that had mostly been created in the first few decades of the twentieth century. There were also six specialist colleges, fewer than 20 years ago because several such colleges – including all the teacher-education institutions – had merged with neighbouring universities. The 47 further education colleges in 2000 were of more recent origin, mostly dating from the 1950s when they were founded as local technical colleges; they were therefore much more geographically dispersed than the higher education institutions (Scottish Executive 2002a: Table 4).

There are essentially three levels of higher education in Scotland: postgraduate (almost exclusively in the higher education institutions), first-degree study (also mainly in these institutions), and non-degree study (mainly in the further education colleges). Cutting across this is the mode of study: most first degree courses are followed full-time, whereas most non-degree and postgraduate courses are followed part-time, although with large minorities studying full-time. The numbers on each of these types and levels of course are shown in Table A7.3. For undergraduate courses, colleges provided a large and growing share: they had 27 per cent of all undergraduates in 1990 and 34 per cent in 2000. They dominated part-time undergraduate courses, their share being 69 per cent in 1990 and 61 per cent in 2000, and also courses at higher education level but below degrees (71 per cent in both years). Overall, the growth at undergraduate level in the decade was nearly twice as great in the colleges as in the higher education institutions (120 per cent compared to 63 per cent), and was also about twice as great in non-degree courses as in first-degree courses (118 per cent compared to 55 per cent). Not shown in Table A7.3 is that, among *entrants* to undergraduate courses, over one half (52 per cent) enter further education colleges; the proportion of full-time higher education students entering a college is about 36 per cent (Gallacher 2002: 125).

Having said that, however, the growth was greatest in what might be called the non-core activities of each sector at undergraduate level. Thus, for example, part-time non-degree numbers grew by 72 per cent in the colleges, compared with a 226 per cent growth in full-time non-degree numbers. Full-time first degree numbers in higher education institutions grew by 48 per cent, but part-time first degree numbers there grew by 165 per cent. The consequence was that the two sectors – colleges and higher education institutions – were less distinct in 2000 than they had been a decade earlier. Moreover, over half of those who left the colleges with a higher education diploma then proceeded to take a degree at a university (Gallacher 2002: 128).

Postgraduate study, in contrast, remained almost the exclusive preserve of the higher education institutions. The growth in part-time study at this level was not as large as appears from Table A7.3,[2] but nevertheless, even allowing for the redefinition of some of the statistics, it is clear that more postgraduates were studying part-time than before: 45 per cent compared to 39 per cent.

To these figures may be added the statistics of participation in the Open University. The total numbers of students there grew from 5,994 in 1980–1 to 10,717 in 1990–1 and 13,775 in 2000–1 (Scottish Office 1995a: Table 13; Scottish Executive 2002b, Table 8). Nearly all of these were undergraduates, although the proportion of postgraduates did rise slowly: there were 45 in 1980–1, 352 in 1990–1 and 1,466 in 2000–1.

Although we have presented detailed data on various aspects of educational expansion, it is important to bear in mind that the underlying processes are, in principle, quite simple. By the end of the twentieth century, secondary education had become universal for four years and the clear majority experience for at least five years. And, in the wake of that expansion, higher education of some sort had also become the majority experience in the first few years of the new century.

RISING ATTAINMENT

What then has led to this rise in participation in higher education? The main explanation has been rising attainment in school education at ages 17–18, itself mainly a consequence of rising attainment at age 16 and hence ultimately a consequence of the ending of selection for secondary education (Paterson and Raffe 1995). Some key trends are illustrated in Figure 7.2, and more fully in Table A7.4. The very striking fall in the proportion gaining 'no awards' resulted from the redefinition of certification that happened in the early 1980s, in an attempt to recognise the work being done by almost all pupils. The old Ordinary Grade courses, inaugurated in 1962, had been intended for students in roughly the top 30 per cent of the range of ability in any particular subject, but by the mid-1970s they were being taken by around three-quarters of pupils (Paterson 2003: 133). There was thus a tension between their broadly academic style and the interests and aptitudes of most of the candidates. Furthermore, the students who did not attempt any Ordinary Grades left school without any record of the work they had done. The policy response was to replace these examinations by Standard Grades, which attempted to provide courses and assessment that would be suitable for the full range of ability. In most subjects, there were three levels of examination, the highest being more demanding than the Ordinary Grade, and the lowest being aimed at people who would never have sat an Ordinary Grade. The relative success of this reform is clear when it is seen (Table A7.4) that, by 1999, 96 per cent of all school leavers had had some kind of recognition of the work they had done.

These changes were a redefinition of attainment at age 16, not a raising of most students to levels or types of attainment that would previously have been reached only by a minority. Nevertheless, there had been increases also in the proportions reaching the Higher Grade, although they were still only a minority. Thus the rate of passing three or more Highers rose from 20 per cent in 1981 to 32 per cent in 1999; that for five or more rose from 10 per cent to 18 per cent. Passing three or more Highers is usually interpreted as the minimum required for entry to higher education, although that has not been formally the case since the late-1980s. Girls overtook boys in the late 1970s and, on both these measures, were quite far ahead by 1999: for example, 21 per cent as against 16 per cent passing five or more Highers. The question of standards of examination always arises when comparing attainment over time, and over long time-scales is so difficult to address as to be in effect impossible (Goldstein and Heath 2000). Nevertheless, in a 20-year period the regular quality-control mechanisms of the authorities who

Figure 7.2 Highest attainment of school leavers, by sex, 1981–99

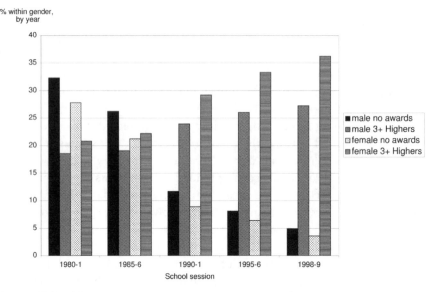

% within gender, by year

Legend:
- male no awards
- male 3+ Highers
- female no awards
- female 3+ Highers

School session: 1980-1, 1985-6, 1990-1, 1995-6, 1998-9

Source: Table A7.4.

run the public examinations do provide reasonably reliable assurance that the standards have remained much the same (Devine et al. 1996; SQA 2003). The gradual rather than abrupt rise in the proportions illustrated in Figure 7.2 is another reason to accept that there has been real change, and it has been one reason why Scotland has not suffered from the same crisis of public confidence in standards that is sometimes evident in England (Paterson 2000).

There are no comparable cohort data to measure rising attainment in higher education. However, we can estimate very roughly that at least 40 per cent of the age group are now graduating by their early 20s. This conclusion is reached by piecing together information from various sources on participation and drop-out. As we have seen, around 50 per cent enter full-time higher education (32 per cent entering higher education institutions and 18 per cent further education colleges). In the higher education institutions, approximately 84 per cent of entrants gain a qualification (Scottish Higher Education Funding Council 2001: Table 8), and so the proportion of the *age group* gaining an award from a higher education institution is probably around 27 per cent (84 per cent of 32 per cent). The completion rates from higher education courses in further education colleges are not so easy to calculate, because the only published figure (86 per cent) relates only to successful completion of each year and also does not distinguish between full-time and part-time students (Scottish Further Education Funding Council 2003: 17). However, we can get a rough estimate of the overall completion rate if we apply the 86 per cent to full-time courses only, and assume that it holds also for the second year of a two-year course.[3] In that case, the completion rate would be about 74 per cent (86 per cent of 86 per cent), and so the proportion of the age group gaining a higher education award from a further education college would be around 13 per cent (74 per cent of 18 per cent). Adding this to the proportion from the higher education institutions estimated above (27 per cent) gives 40 per cent. Part-time students would add an unknown further amount to this percentage. That 40 per cent is more than the 35 per cent or so who completed even *part* of a full secondary course in the late 1950s (Paterson 2003: 131). This is a remarkable extension of the period of initial education for the most academically able 35–40 per cent of young people. As a result, higher education is becoming as important a route to citizenship as secondary schooling was only half a century ago.

These data on rising attainment relate to achievements of people leaving formal education, and so do not in themselves tell us about the social distribution of educational experience among the adult population as a whole. Not surprisingly, however, we find clear evidence that a rising proportion of all adults have more than minimal amounts of education, and indeed also that a rising proportion has quite advanced levels. The data in Table 7.3 come from the Labour Force Survey, and so relate only to people of working age (defined here as 15 to 59). The effects of educational expansion and rising attainment are clear: the proportion with some kind of higher education certificate rose from one in ten in 1981 to over a quarter in 2001, the sharpest rise being in the 1990s. The increase was much the same for women and men, although in every year men were slightly less likely to have degrees than women and more likely to have higher education diplomas.[4] Although we have to be cautious about interpreting the apparent fall in the proportion with no qualifications at all – because respondents to the 2001 survey were offered a much fuller list of qualifications to jog their memories than the respondents to earlier surveys – it seems reasonable to conclude that most of the qualifications which people might have forgotten in these earlier surveys would have fallen into the category second from the bottom. Grouping these two lowest categories, we then find that the proportion with low or no qualifications fell from 52 per cent in 1981 to 44 per cent in 1991 and 27 per cent in 2001. This reflects not only the widening conception of attainment in the compulsory period of schooling but also the growth of vocational qualifications for adults already in the workforce.

Table 7.3 Highest educational attainment, among people aged 16–59, 1981–2001

% in columns		Year	
Highest educational attainment:	1981	1991	2001
First degree, higher degree, professional qualification	8.9	10.6	17.3
HND, HNC, etc	1.3	3.9	9.6
Higher Grade, A level, etc	9.0	23.6	20.2
O Grade, Standard Grade, etc	28.5	17.6	26.0
Scotvec modules, CSE, etc	5.1	5.7	10.1
None of these or no answer	47.2	38.7	16.8
Sample size	12559	8188	7422

Source: Labour Force Surveys 1981, 1991, March–May 2001, weighted (sample sizes unweighted).

Gender was not the only dimension in which inequality has diminished or even been transformed (insofar as women are now reaching higher levels of attainment than men): a weaker trend in the same direction has been evident in relation to social class. Unfortunately, for this purpose, the best source stops in 1993 at present, because the data from the Scottish School Leavers Surveys of the late 1990s are not yet available for independent analysis.[5] Nevertheless, even in the period 1980–93, there was some narrowing of socio-economic inequality, as Table A7.6 shows in relation to four measures of school attainment. The general pattern applying to all four measures is illustrated also in Figure 7.3, showing the proportion passing three or more Higher Grades. All groups showed improvement in respect of all four of the measures, but the rise was greatest for the working class groups (the three on the right-hand of the graph). For example, for the criterion of passing three or more Highers, the increases in the three non-manual groups were, respectively, 37 per cent, 39 per cent and 22 per cent, whereas those for the manual groups were between 2.5 and 11 times higher: 145 per cent, 102 per cent and 247 per cent. These latter were from a much lower base, and as we explain in Appendix 4, this makes straightforward comparison somewhat misleading. We can, however, show that the effect was to reduce inequality if we use the measure known as the odds ratio. This is explained more fully in Appendix 4, but here it can be thought of as an index of the inequality between two social groups in their chances of reaching a certain level of educational attainment. Between 1980 and 1993 the odds ratios for passing three or more Highers, comparing other social classes to the professional and managerial group, moved from 12.1 to 5.5 for the unskilled manual group, 6.8 to 5.6 for the semi-skilled manual, and 6.1 to 3.8 for the skilled manual, all indicating a decline in inequality. These are still larger than the odds ratios for the intermediate and junior non-manual groups (in

1993, 2.8 and 0.9 respectively) indicating less inequality between these groups and the professional and managerial group, but the overall picture is of less differentiated attainment than previously. There is no reason to believe that this trend will have gone into reverse since 1993; indeed, because the Labour government in 1997 and then the coalition of Labour and the Liberal Democrats in the Scottish Executive after 1999 have concentrated on improving the examination performance of children in the most disadvantaged social groups, it is likely that the narrowing of inequality will have continued.

Figure 7.3 School leavers passing three or more Highers, by socio-economic group, 1980–93

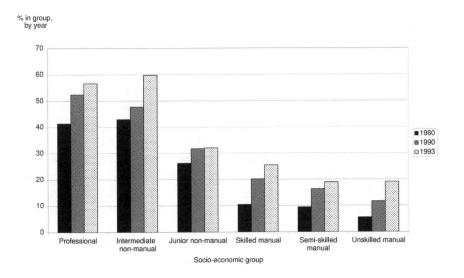

Source: Table A7.6.

For the same groups of students, this reduction in inequality of attainment at school then translated into a reduction in the inequality of direct entry to full-time higher education upon leaving school. Between 1980 and 1993, entry rates from the three manual groups rose respectively by 259 per cent, 266 per cent and 272 per cent; for the three non-manual groups the rise was by 90 per cent, 71 per cent and 74 per cent (Table A7.7). Thus the odds ratios fell too. Compared to the professional and managerial group, these moved from 10.4 to 7.6 in the unskilled class, from 6.9 to 4.8 in the semi-skilled class, and from 5.2 to 3.5 in the skilled class. The changes for the other two non-manual groups were, respectively, from 0.9 to 1.1 (the intermediate group having already more or less reached parity with the professional group by 1980), and from 1.8 to 2.6. One important source of this widening of access to higher education has been the further education colleges, which are much better at attracting working class entrants than the old universities especially (Raab 1998; Raab and Storkey 2001).

The truncation of the series from the School Leavers Survey may be partly compensated for by using surveys of the adult population and relating attainment to birth cohort, just as we did for social mobility in Chapter 6. Table 7.4 shows attainment by cohort for three broad social-class groups describing the household in which the respondent grew up. The bottom line gives the proportions for the whole population, and shows the effects of educational expansion over a long time period: of those born between 1927 and 1936, only 21 per cent had at least a Higher Grade pass, and only 11 per cent had any kind of higher education qualification. For those born between 1967 and 1976 the proportions had more than tripled, to 64 per cent and 38 per cent. The rise was greater for those whose father was in a working class occupation than for those whose father was in a professional occupation: for example, for the criterion Higher Grade or better, there was a rise of 417 per cent in the unskilled group, but of 43 per cent in the professional group. Part of this is due to what is often called a 'ceiling effect' (explained more fully in Appendix 4): the more disadvantaged social groups begin to narrow the gap with the most advantaged only when the most advantaged group reaches a plateau above which it is unlikely or impossible to improve (Raftery and Hout 1993). Thus, since it seems unlikely that the proportion of any social group with at least a Higher Grade qualification could rise much above the 84 per cent reached by the sons and daughters of professional fathers in the youngest cohort, any further expansion is almost certain to result in reduced inequality. But that is not the whole story, because there has been a narrowing also in relation to the more stringent criterion of gaining a higher education qualification, a change less likely to be purely a ceiling effect. Compared to the professional class, the odds ratios went from 20.1 to 3.8 in the skilled class, and from 33.2 to 5.6 in the unskilled class. Nevertheless, even if inequality reduces only when the middle class reach a plateau of attainment, that may still be seen as a success for the social democratic programme of educational expansion, for which the universal provision of public goods, to all classes equally, was seen as the best way of including the working class in a common citizenship. It is a success also because the working class has shrunk in size (as we saw in Chapter 6), so that the remaining educational disadvantage is experienced by a smaller proportion of the total population than before.

Table 7.4 Highest educational attainment, by selected[1] father's class and birth cohort, among people aged 23–74 in 1999

%		Birth cohort				
Father's class when respondent was aged 14[2]	Criterion[3]	1927–36	1937–46	1947–56	1957–66	1967–76
Professional	H Grade or HE qual.	58.8	73.4	67.4	72.5	84.2
(I,II)	HE qual.	53.9	51.4	44.9	45.9	59.8
	Sample size	37	40	87	135	124
Skilled manual	H Grade or HE qual.	19.9	26.7	37.8	50.0	53.1
(V,VI)	HE qual.	5.5	16.1	22.8	23.6	28.1
	Sample size	133	119	152	218	168
Unskilled	H Grade or HE qual.	10.3	17.4	28.9	38.5	53.2
(VII)	HE qual.	3.4	9.0	9.7	16.3	20.9
	Sample size	130	121	162	159	87
All[4]	H Grade or HE qual.	21.2	31.6	43.7	53.5	63.5
	HE qual.	10.9	18.1	23.6	28.6	37.5
	Sample size	355	334	485	627	469

Source: British Household Panel Survey 1999, weighted (sample sizes unweighted in brackets).
1. Other classes had some sample sizes too small to be reliable (all sample sizes within cohort less than 100).
2. Condensed version of Goldthorpe classes, as indicated.
3. H grade is Higher Grade; HE is higher education (diploma, first degree, postgraduate degree or professional qualification).
4. Including those classes omitted.

Using this same birth-cohort approach, we can also examine the changing educational attainment of people in minority ethnic groups. No national survey in Scotland is large enough to do justice to this, because there are not enough people in the non-white groups to allow a statistically reliable division into cohorts. So we have to resort to the population census of 2001, the published information from which does not allow us to analyse its broad tables further. The results are in Table 7.5. The most striking point to note is, again, convergence: indeed, for the youngest cohort, all three of the broad minority groups noted here have higher proportions with a higher education qualification than the white group, whereas in most of the earlier cohorts the white group is ahead of the Chinese and the Pakistani and south Asian groups. Nevertheless, the rather different trajectory of the Indian group reminds us that data on people who are immigrants or whose parents were immigrants are not easy to interpret. From the 2001 census (Table S236) we know that, whereas 96 per cent of the whole Scottish population was born in the UK, the proportions were only 49 per cent for Indians, 59 per cent for the Pakistanis and 34 per cent for Chinese; unfortunately in the census tables this is not broken down by birth cohort. If we allow ourselves to speculate a bit from these two tables, we might then imagine that many Indians came to the UK and to Scotland as professional migrants – for example, working in the health-care professions (as is noted in greater detail in Chapter 4). That kind of origin would account for the fairly high levels of higher education qualifications even among older Indians. By contrast, although large groups of Pakistani and of Chinese people in Scotland also were born outside the UK, the oldest among them may have come to Scotland with few educational certificates: that would account for the low proportions with higher education qualifications among the older Pakistani and Chinese people. The strikingly higher rates of higher education qualification among younger Pakistani or Chinese people might indicate that the (UK-born) children of these original immigrants have made impressive progress. This would certainly be consistent with other evidence that young people of Pakistani and Chinese origin in the 1990s were participating in higher education at roughly twice the rate of white people (Paterson 2003: 171; Raab 1998; Raab and Storkey 2001). The younger Indians, to the extent that they are indeed the children of older professional migrants, would tend to have high attainment for that very reason: in other words, their high attainment may be explained by the influence on them of their father's own professional education, rather than only as the striving by a marginalised immigrant group to use education to escape invidious discrimination in the labour market.

Table 7.5 Highest educational attainment, by ethnic group and birth cohort, among people aged 23–74 in 2001

%		Birth cohort				
Ethnic group	Criterion[1]	1927–36	1937–46	1947–56	1957–66	1967–76
White	H Grade or HE qual.	21.6	27.9	41.4	46.8	53.2
	HE qual.	15.9	20.3	28.6	31.5	35.9
Indian	H Grade or HE qual.	41.6	51.4	47.8	54.2	69.9
	HE qual.	38.7	47.9	41.1	44.8	62.8
Pakistani or other	H Grade or HE qual.	15.2	24.6	31.5	34.2	46.9
South Asian	HE qual.	12.8	21.3	25.1	26.3	37.6
Chinese	H Grade or HE qual.	10.3	14.9	26.4	39.3	64.6
	HE qual.	7.7	13.0	22.3	33.5	56.0
Other	H Grade or HE qual.	31.9	47.9	60.7	64.0	67.0
	HE qual.	26.6	41.7	53.4	55.7	57.1

Source: Census 2001 (Table S216).
1. H grade is Higher Grade; HE is higher education (diploma, first degree, postgraduate degree or professional qualification).

A not dissimilar interpretation may be offered of the patterns of educational attainment by religion (Table A7.8). Older Catholics, being themselves mainly immigrants from Ireland or immediate descendants of them, had relatively low educational attainment. The publicly funded Catholic schools then provided educational opportunities that increased the average level of attainment among Catholics much more sharply than attainment was rising in most other religious groups, so that, by the youngest cohort, Catholics were ahead of all other groups apart from the small group of 'other Christians'. This group, as we noted in Chapter 6, is quite strongly middle class, comprising mainly the adherents of the Episcopal church and Christians of no denomination.

By contrast with other inequalities, and with other countries, Scotland has remarkably little variation in educational attainment among broad regions. For example, grouping region in terms of the former local government areas,[6] the survey of school leavers in 1993 showed that in all these regions, around one-third of leavers had passed three or more Highers, and that, also in all regions, this represented approximately a doubling since 1980 (Table A7.9). The same general absence of broad regional variation is found in surveys of the educational attainment of the adult population, for example the Scottish Household Survey of 2001 (Table A7.10). The uniformity of Scottish educational provision and attainment was already being remarked on by researchers in the 1930s and in the 1950s (Paterson 2003: 49 and 113), and has not diminished since. Various waves of reform have been achieved with remarkable uniformity, from the introduction of a standard type of comprehensive schooling in the 1960s and 1970s to the standardising influence of a single examination board, as certification was extended to almost the whole school population in the 1980s and 1990s. It is true that, at a more local level, there is variation insofar as there is social-class segregation among neighbourhoods, especially in the cities (Paterson 1997a: 15). Nevertheless, according to the results of the 2000 survey of secondary school students known as the PISA study, even that segregation is lower than in most European Union countries, although on most measures not as low as in Scandinavia (Smith and Gorard 2002).

So the expansion of formal education which we summarised near the beginning of the chapter, and the rising attainment which we summarised at the beginning of the present section, may best be explained as a dynamic process over time. Each wave of expansion creates the conditions in which the next wave will happen, because students become adults, have children, and encourage them in turn to aspire higher. The expansion has also led to some very striking changes in the social distribution of formal educational attainment. There has been a reduction or even a reversal in gender inequality. There has been an ending of the educational disadvantage faced by Catholics. There have, more recently, been some very impressive educational advances by students in minority ethnic groups. And even occupational class is now a weaker source of inequality than it once was, although – unlike these other dimensions – it remains a significant source of inequality.

THE EFFECTS OF EDUCATION

We have been commenting on some of the results of increasing participation and rising attainment throughout this chapter, especially in movement between stages, such as from secondary to higher education. For most people, however, education remains a means to a job, whatever else it may also be. Table 7.6 shows how necessary it is to have succeeded in education in order to get a good job. Well over half of people in professional or intermediate non-manual jobs hold a higher education qualification, and only around a quarter do not have at least a Higher Grade. In that sense, a secondary education has become the minimum required to enter the professions, even the lower-level professions. For the higher-level professions – those recorded in the new Socio-Economic Classification as class I – fully 73 per cent have a degree (from the Labour Force Survey of March–May 2001). At the other end of the distribution in Table 7.6, around three-quarters or more of people in the manual occupations left school with nothing better than Ordinary Grades or Standard Grades.

Table 7.6 Highest educational qualification by socio-economic group, among people aged 16–59, 2000

% in rows	Highest educational attainment						Sample size
Socio-economic group	First degree, higher degree, professional qualification	HND, HNC, etc	Higher Grade, A level, etc	O Grade, Standard Grade, etc	Scotvec modules, CSE, etc	None or no answer	
Professional and managerial	41.3	14.2	18.5	15.6	5.1	5.3	1268
Intermediate non-manual	44.0	15.0	16.3	13.6	5.4	5.8	891
Junior non-manual	7.0	11.8	31.3	28.9	8.2	12.8	1063
Skilled manual	2.6	6.2	25.7	41.2	12.8	11.5	1017
Semi-skilled manual	3.3	6.7	17.1	32.8	16.6	23.5	842
Unskilled manual	1.1	1.6	11.7	26.7	20.6	38.2	325
Unclassified or armed forces	6.7	4.9	16.5	25.6	12.2	34.0	2303

Source: Labour Force Survey March–May 2000, weighted (sample sizes unweighted).

So there is no evidence at all that, as education expands, it becomes worthless. If anything, the importance of education in gaining a good job may have been increasing over time (Table A7.11). By looking at the Labour Force Surveys of 1981, 1991 and 2000, we can calculate the occupational distribution (in terms of socio-economic group) of people of working age holding each particular level of educational attainment. Among those with degrees, a growing proportion was in professional or managerial jobs: 28 per cent in 1981, 42 per cent in 1991, 44 per cent in 2000. By contrast, among those with Ordinary Grades or Standard Grades, the proportion who were not economically active at all – mainly being unemployed, or looking after a family, or having taken early retirement – grew from 24 per cent to 27 per cent, and the proportion in semi-skilled or unskilled jobs grew from 16 per cent to 19 per cent. In between, the possession of Highers, but nothing better, was decreasingly likely to lead to a junior non-manual job, the proportion in this attainment group who were in such occupations falling from 30 per cent to 22 per cent. Nevertheless, higher education is not the only route into management: among people with only Highers, the proportion in professional or managerial posts was 11 per cent in 1981 and 16 per cent in 2000.

Education is also a means by which people are socially mobile. Table A7.12 shows the rate of mobility at current job, first job, and between first and current job, according to the level of educational attainment.[7] It enables us to examine the role of education in the processes by which people's current or first job differs from that of their father, and also in the process of career mobility by which people's current job may differ from their first job. As may be seen from the first part of the table, people with higher levels of education are more likely to have been upwardly mobile at their current job, and less likely to have been downwardly mobile, than people with lower levels of education. For example, comparing those who have a degree with those who have minimal or no qualifications, the proportions who have been upwardly mobile were 62 per cent and 50 per cent, and the proportions who have been downwardly mobile were 21 per cent and 26 per cent. This finding is hardly surprising, confirming simply that education has been a means by which people have improved their position. But the process is not simple, because there is no association between education and mobility at first job (second segment of the table): for example, the proportion who had been upwardly mobile at their first job was 47 per cent among those with a degree, not much more than the 38 per cent among those who had low or no qualifications. What matters is the different rates of mobility between the first job and the current job, as shown in the final part of the table. Education of the kind recorded here did not in itself necessarily lead to promotion. What is more likely is that possessing a degree, for example, enables people to enter jobs where promotion prospects are better. Possessing a degree may also be an indicator of a capacity to learn on the job and to be effective in that job, which in turn may be more likely to lead to moving to a higher-status job. Nevertheless, it is also clear that there is substantial upward movement at all levels of education: a degree may facilitate mobility, but it is not essential to it.

One of the means by which occupational mobility comes about is through geographical mobility, and people with a great deal of education are much more likely to be geographically mobile than those with little education (Table A7.13). Immigrants to Scotland tend to be well-educated: 31 per cent of people with degrees were born outwith Scotland, compared to only 13 per cent of those with no higher qualification than an Ordinary Grade or a Standard Grade. Some of that may be because people move to Scotland in order to go to higher education, because about 16 per cent of undergraduate students are from outwith Scotland, and around one-third of them remain in Scotland if they enter employment upon graduation (Paterson 1997b: 37–40; Scottish Executive 2002b: Table 17; Scottish Executive 2003b: Table 6). But that is not the only explanation, because the gradient across education categories is seen also at higher education levels below degree, even though movement into Scotland for such types of course is minimal: in 2000, it was just 4 per cent (Scottish Executive 2002b: Table 17). It seems likely, then, that there is a direct link between educational attainment, moving to a better job, and geographical mobility in order to find such a job. (Such topics are discussed in detail for migrants from England by Watson (2003).)

These processes may not work symmetrically, however. The propensity to leave Scotland for employment among graduates who originally came from Scotland is much less than the propensity to stay in Scotland among graduates who came from elsewhere. The third of the latter who stay is much greater than the approximately 15 per cent of the former who leave (Scottish Executive 2003b: Table 6). Commentators on the needs of the Scottish economy often point accusingly to the quarter of all graduates of Scottish higher education institutions who leave the country to gain employment, and insist that more of them be enticed to stay. But if as few as 15 per cent of Scottish students leave, and as many as one-third of non-Scottish students stay, the scope for persuading more to stay may be much more limited than is sometimes supposed.

We have seen, then, that education confers occupational benefits, and we have presented some evidence that the benefit is growing. This is consistent with research showing that there is an increasing financial return to gaining a degree, not because the salaries of graduates have risen strongly, but more because the salaries of people who have not been to higher education have stagnated (Bell 1999: 366–8). What is perhaps rather surprising, then, is that, within education itself, the relative 'return' to a high level of attainment has not been rising. This is because the expansion of higher education has been so rapid that it has mainly happened by drawing in people whose school attainment would not previously have given them access. The trends are in Table A7.14, from the surveys of schools leavers between 1980 and 1993. People with many Highers had always been very likely to enter higher education, and this was maintained. But a greater proportion of people with moderate numbers of Highers were also now entering higher education, so that 61 per cent of people with three Highers entered in 1993, compared with only 38 per cent in 1980. It was even the case, by 1993, that substantial minorities of people with just one or two Highers were entering, partly because other forms of attainment – for example in vocational courses – were being recognised, especially in the further education colleges as they began to take a growing share of higher education students.

These trends then give no evidence for the theory of 'credential inflation', according to which it becomes necessary to reach ever higher levels of attainment in order to gain a place in higher education. This should not be confused with what is sometimes called 'credentialism', by which it becomes increasingly important to hold qualifications in order to gain a job. There is, as we have seen, firm evidence of credentialism. But this greater demand for qualifications has not led to devaluing of particular types of qualification because the supply of places in higher education has grown more rapidly than the rise in attainment. In other words, the 'demand' (attainment at school) has not out-stripped the 'supply' (of places in higher education), and so there is little scope for credential inflation to operate.

The effects of education at which we have been looking so far have been for the individual – gaining a job, or making further educational progress. Perhaps the most important effect sociologically, however, is between generations. Because educational expansion has been happening at the school level for a long time, especially since the 1960s, the school leavers of the 1990s tended to have better-educated parents than the leavers of 1980 (Table A7.15). For example, in 1980 only 12 per cent of leavers had at least one parent who had stayed on in education to age 17 or older. By 1993, this had risen to 28 per cent. Correspondingly, the proportion where no parent had stayed on beyond age 15 fell from 64 per cent to 30 per cent. This increase in what has been called the 'cultural capital' of parents is one of the main explanations of expansion, as parents – especially, according to some evidence, mothers – who had a good experience of education encourage their children to seek the same (Burnhill et al. 1988).

The new cultural capital may even be coming to form the basis of a new form of stratification. Table 7.7 shows the proportions of school leavers entering higher education at each level of parental education. Participation has risen at all levels, but – in contrast to the slow reduction of inequality which we saw in relation to social class (Table A7.7) – there is no more than a weak trend towards any narrowing of inequality in relation to parental education. Calculating odds ratios for the comparison with people with two parents educated to 17 years or older, the change between 1980 and 1993 was from 1.7 to 2.5 among those with one such parent, from 4.6 to 5.5 among those with one parent educated to 16 years, and from 10.8 to 8.5 among those where no parent was educated beyond 15 years. Having educated parents continued to confer much the same advantage as it did at the beginning of the 1980s.

Table 7.7 Direct entry to higher education by school leavers, by ages at which parents left school, 1980, 1990 and 1993

Ages at which parents left school	Year of leaving school		
	1980	1990	1993
Both 17 or older	47.1	47.9	68.1
Sample size	1112	351	376
One 17 or older, not both	34.4	38.3	46.5
Sample size	1975	568	658
One 16, neither 17 or older	16.2	15.9	27.8
Sample size	3401	914	958
One or both 15, neither older	7.6	9.6	20.0
Sample size	14330	1266	989
Both no information	12.0	14.4	21.8
Sample size	2340	487	488

Source: Scottish School Leavers Surveys, weighted (sample sizes unweighted).

What is more, this cultural capital operates over and above the effects of social class as measured by occupation. Table A7.16 shows the proportion of school leavers entering higher education according to their father's class and the combined educational level of their parents. At every level of class, in each year, people with better-educated parents were more likely to enter higher education than people with less well-educated parents. Detailed inspection of the table shows that the expansion in this period was of most benefit to those whose father was in a manual occupation and who had the benefit of parental cultural capital, in the sense of having a parent educated to age 17 or older. The increase in the proportions entering higher education for people with well-educated parents in this sense was 124 per cent in the skilled-manual group, 98 per cent in the semi-skilled manual group, and 175 per cent in the unskilled manual group.[8] By contrast, those with fathers in non-manual jobs and with little cultural capital to draw on benefited on the whole relatively less. The increases were 102 per cent in the professional and managerial group, 80 per cent in the intermediate group, and 66 per cent in the junior non-manual group.

There is evidence, then, that the old system of transmission of advantage based directly on parental occupation, as discussed in Chapter 6, may be in the process of being replaced by one in which parental cultural capital plays a larger independent role. Of course, the two sources of stratification can never be separated, precisely because of selection by merit. Entry to the professions has depended on the successful completion of at least a secondary education, and mostly some kind of higher education, for a much longer period than is covered even by the life-span of the oldest parents in these cohorts. So, when we say that there was stratification based on parental social class in the third quarter of the twentieth century (as reflected in the 1980 sample here), we are inevitably also saying that there was stratification based on parental education. What may be changing then, is, not the fact of education's relevance to stratification, but the way in which it operates and the strength of its influence. Previously it operated indirectly, enabling some groups of parents to lead more affluent lifestyles and to acquire social status because of them. Now, perhaps, education is coming to operate more directly by cultural transmission. The passing-on of culture acquired through education now itself offers significant advantages to young people, more independently than previously of whatever vocational advantage their parents have gained with that culture.

Education has also more diffuse effects, conferring a great range of benefits on its holders. People with degrees are much more likely to have large quantities of 'social capital' than those without – that is, they are more likely to take part in civic networks, to trust their fellow citizens, and through all that to exercise power and influence. For example, in the Scottish Social Attitudes Survey of 2000, 39 per cent of people with degrees were a member of at least one local group (for example, neighbourhood watch schemes), compared with only 14 per cent among those with no better than an Ordinary Grade or a Standard Grade pass. The proportions were 34 per cent and 7 per cent for membership of at least one national group (for example, RSPB or CND), and 81 per cent and 66 per cent for having taken part in some kind of political activity. (Further details are in Table A7.17.)

CONCLUSIONS

Four points may be made in conclusion. One is that quite lengthy periods of initial education have become normal. A century ago, well over 80 per cent of children experienced no more than about five years of full-time education, because many started at age six and most ended by 12. Now everyone goes through at least 11 years (ages five to 16), over two-thirds go through at least 12, and half stay on into higher education to complete at least 15 years. What is more, the educational institutions through which they travel have, compared even to two decades ago, become more flexible, and are able to offer worthwhile courses and certification to a much broader range of students. The long-term consequences of this expansion will take well into the new century to be fully evident. For example, if (following Trow (1973: 7)) we define mass higher education as having been reached when the proportion of young people entering it surpasses 15 per cent, we have had that in Scotland since the late 1970s. If we assume that people graduating in about 1980 have a 40–year working life, it will be about 2020 before even the first full impact of a mass system will have pervaded the workforce. It will obviously take even longer before Scotland feels the effect of participation rates of 40 per cent or higher, because, as we have seen in this chapter, these were first reached in the late 1990s.

One consequence of this therefore has to be speculative, because we are still living through only the first years of the effects of mass higher education. Mass secondary education was achieved in Scotland by the 1930s, and was consolidated after the war, somewhat earlier than in many European and North American societies, but broadly happening in parallel to developments there too. From the 1960s onwards, these better-educated generations then became the source of sharp reductions in deference, increasing challenges to authority, and insistence on choice in both public services and the operation of the market. Changes in production, in distribution, and in technology – some of them detailed elsewhere in this book – were important too, but even they depended for their effects on the capacity of the newly educated populations to take advantage of them. In short, the participation revolution in Europe and North America in the last couple of decades of the twentieth century probably owed a great deal to the earlier expansion of secondary education. What then might we expect from the expansion of higher education? One answer may be summed up by the US political scientist Amy Gutmann, who argued in 1987 that

> learning how to think carefully and critically about political problems, to articulate one's views and defend them before people with whom one

disagrees is a form of moral education to which young adults are more receptive [than school children] and for which universities are well suited. (Gutmann 1987: 173)

She argued that mass higher education has the potential to become the basis on which a more critical citizenry emerges. If she is correct, then the long-term effects could be a renewal of democracy, but not in ways that would necessarily be comfortable to political elites, and requiring much more participation than representative structures have traditionally allowed.

Third, although the proportion of adults who have passed through higher education will radically increase, one such consequence may not be particularly democratic at all. Formal education is becoming increasingly important in gaining access to good jobs, especially at the top end of the class structure and of the distribution of income. It has also become an influential means by which people take part in the social networks which govern society, both in the sense of regulating norms and values, and in the sense of ruling through the state and its associated institutions. As we noted in the conclusion to Chapter 6, the new Scottish Parliament has been able to take advantage of the resulting networks of well-educated professionals, but their sheer cultural self-confidence and articulacy may also be standing in the way of the parliamentarians reaching out beyond them to the wider society. There may well be wide consultation with professionals, but precisely because there are many of them and they dominate the channels of communication and debate, people who are not professionals may find it even more difficult than before to have their voices heard (Paterson 2002b).

That brings us, last, to one of the paradoxes of educational expansion. Conceived of as a movement with liberatory potential, especially by radical activists earlier in the century, it can become the basis of a new structure of social stratification. The paradox was summed up eloquently in 1963 by the daughter of one of these radicals, Jennie Lee. As a minister in the Labour government of the 1960s, she ambivalently helped to entrench the meritocracy about which she had earlier had doubts. In the first volume of her autobiography of growing up in south Fife in the 1930s she wrote:

I know how my grandfather's, even my father's, generation felt about education. They were very romantic about it. They thought of it as a kind of lamp to light the feet of their children, so that we need not stumble and hurt ourselves as they had done, or as armour buckled around us so that we could meet in fair fight all who stood in our way. They never doubted that our fight would be anything other than their fight and with them and of them and for them.

But the interaction of class and education ensured that the ideals could not be sustained: 'it is very hard for the old idealistic socialist when he sees graduates from the working class homes turn into small-town snobs' (Lee 1963: 92).

Education has helped to reduce the impact of older inequalities, those related to gender, religion, perhaps ethnicity, and probably also social class, as measured by occupation. But it has done so by elevating the principles of meritocracy to a position of unchallengeable hegemony: worth is measured by certificates, especially in Scotland with its very long tradition of adherence to at least partly meritocratic principles. The social democratic politicians, such as Lee, of the mid-century who introduced the reforms would, despite their memories, not have demurred (Paterson 2003). This may seem unfair, although faced with the evidence of apparently steadily rising attainment most people would probably conclude that barriers to the opportunity to gain the necessary certificates are steadily diminishing. Meritocracy has very real merits despite the damage it does to those who cannot or will not take advantage of it. The problem for people who would want to challenge its dominance is finding any credible alternative principles that would not take us back to the very widespread restriction on educational, occupational and cultural opportunity which the last two decades seem to have put firmly in the past.

NOTES

1. Higher education consists of courses leading to degrees and diplomas (including courses leading to school teaching or to qualifications from various professional bodies). Further education is a rather amorphous category of mainly vocational courses below that level and above school level, but also of non-vocational courses that could alternatively be followed at school. Full-time and part-time are even more nebulous, and the government statistical bulletins from which the data in Table 7.1 are taken provide no definitions. The category of 'full-time' used to be defined administratively as courses which were funded (by government agencies) as full-time, and for which mandatory student grants were available; 'part-time' therefore covered everything else. That is still broadly the case: a full-time course is one which students are expected to attend as they would a full-time job, for those weeks in the year when it runs (usually between about 30 and about 40). Schuller et al. (1999: 49–52) provide a discussion of the issues of definition.
2. About 15,000 of the figure in 2000 is part-time continuing education students who were included in the figures for the first time in 1995: these are students attending adult education classes, usually not leading to formal certification.
3. This is likely to be an underestimate of completion rates, because full-time courses tend to have higher rates of completion than part-time ones, and also the first year tends to be the time of maximum drop-out. We also assume that other lengths of full-time course in the colleges may be ignored for purposes of this approximation.
4. In 2001, for example, the proportions with degrees were 16 per cent of men and 18 per cent of women, and the proportions with diplomas were 10 per cent of men and 9 per cent of women (Table A7.5).

5. And the survey of leavers in 1994 has some technical problems: see Tinklin and Raffe (1999: 3).
6. Highland and Argyll, Grampian and Tayside, Central and Fife, Lothian, Strathclyde apart from Argyll, and Borders, and Dumfries and Galloway
7. The meaning of occupational mobility has been discussed in Chapter 6: it is essentially the extent to which a person works in a different class of job from their father. We may measure this both for the person's current job and for the job they were in when they first entered the labour market.
8. We must be cautious about the last of these because of the small sample sizes.

CHAPTER 8

Consumption, Lifestyle and Culture

In a relatively brief book of this kind we can only brush the surface of a topic as extensive as consumption, lifestyle and culture in a highly selective way. The data we present must be seen as indicative rather than exhaustive. In general, however, the story we have to tell of how we live in Scotland today and how this has changed in the last 20 years follows a pattern which will by now be familiar to our readers.

People in Scotland today enjoy for longer and in better health a varied lifestyle which would have been literally inconceivable 50 and even 30 years ago. Households have access to, and can in general afford to buy, a wide range of consumer goods, and things which were luxuries then are now owned even by many in the poorer section of the community. The standard and quality of life for a large proportion of Scotland's citizens is high. Changing technology has dramatically altered not only the consumer goods available in the shops but the ways we are able to communicate and the ways in which we store and access knowledge, music and all kinds of entertainment. Many people in Scotland enjoy opportunities for affordable travel both within and furth of Scotland which were not available even 30 years ago. All this takes place in a context in which emphasis has shifted from work to leisure.

Yet as we said when discussing income in Chapter 5, the lifestyle and opportunities open to high income earners and the wealthy are very different from the experience of the majority of Scotland's citizens. The advantages of that majority contrast just as sharply with those on low incomes and with little or no savings. It is of course not necessary, as we shall see, to belong to the high income group to enjoy many of the advantages of living in Scotland in the early twenty-first century but the theme to which we have repeatedly returned in this book also runs through this chapter. Against the general background of well-being for the majority, those without the necessary resources of income and education, especially if they are also young, are unable to enjoy these advantages to the full, and their inability to do so is a form of social exclusion.

PATTERNS OF CONSUMPTION AND SOME OF THEIR CONSEQUENCES

How then do people in Scotland spend their incomes which, as we have seen in Chapter 5, are higher than ever before? Table 8.1 provides details of the pattern of expenditure across 13 categories. First, we shall concentrate on just three – food, housing, motoring and fares – which for the last 20 years have made up half (49 per cent) of the average weekly household expenditure. The proportion has remained the same since 1980, but, as Figure 8.1 shows, the balance between them has changed considerably.

Table 8.1 Average weekly household expenditure, 1980–2000

% in columns	Year		
	1980	1990	2000
Housing (net)	10.5	14.3	14.7
Fuel, light and power	6.3	5.3	4.1
Food	24.4	19.8	18.2
Alcoholic drink	5.4	4.7	4.6
Tobacco	4.1	2.9	2.6
Clothing and footwear	9.5	7.9	6.6
Household goods[1]	8.6	8.5	8.0
Household services	2.4	4.6	4.9
Motoring and fares	13.9	14.8	16.3
Personal goods and services	2.5	3.8	3.4
Leisure goods[1]	4.8	4.4	5.3
Leisure services	7.0	8.4	11.0
Miscellaneous	0.6	0.5	0.3

Sources: Scottish Executive (2001d: Table 3.9), Scottish Office (1992a: Table 10.1), and Scottish Office (1988: Table 10.17).
1. Stationery is classified with household goods in 1990 and 2000 but with leisure goods in 1980. Note that the 1980 figures have been re-classified from the published version, and so categories may not be fully consistent (even in ways other than that noted).

The proportion spent on housing has gone up sharply (by roughly half), and on motoring and fares has risen somewhat, whereas the proportion spent on food has fallen by a quarter. These changes in expenditure since 1980 have to be seen in the context of the one-fifth rise in incomes which makes the rising proportion spent on housing the more remarkable. The fall in the proportion spent on food is also partly explained by this rise in total incomes. The money spent on housing partly reflects rising house prices, but also that the funds are now in many cases going towards house purchase rather than rent, largely as a result of council house sales. For many people these changes also involve potentially rising capital values in the property market which until fairly recently was booming. While the house owners themselves are unlikely to realise this capital, the impact on the next generation may be significant.

Figure 8.1 Average weekly household expenditure on selected items, 1980–2000

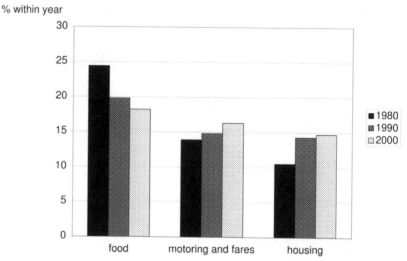

Source: Table 8.1.

As Figure 8.2 shows, the extent of the shift in tenure is striking, with owner occupation rising from around 35 per cent in 1979 to 62 per cent in 1999, as public renting declined correspondingly from 54 per cent to 25 per cent; housing association tenure rose from 2 per cent (in 1984) to 6 per cent, and private rented tenure fell from 11 per cent to 7 per cent. The implications of these changes are far-reaching, involving relationships with local authorities, patterns of local government expenditure, the nature of the housing market, pressures on younger people trying to get on the housing ladder, and even the popularity of DIY activities and garden centres.

Returning to Table 8.1, we see that the 38 per cent rise in the proportion spent on leisure goods and leisure services taken together is also considerable, especially in the context of rising incomes. Alcohol and tobacco on the other hand show falling proportions, reflecting a real fall in tobacco expenditure but a real rise in alcohol expenditure.

Figure 8.2 Changes in housing tenure, 1979–99

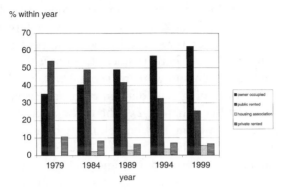

Source: Table A8.1.

The last two items remind us that increasing affluence and expenditure may be a two-edged sword. People in Scotland choose to spend their disposable income in different ways, the majority enjoying more choice than ever before. We shall see that, in this respect, the sharp distinctions are less obviously between the 'haves' and the 'have-nots' in society but are more likely to be class-related. There is, of course, a relationship between affluence and class, but in this area the impact of class is more a matter of making different choices than having the necessary resources. It is a matter of frequent comment that the choices made by the people of Scotland are not always in the best interests of their health. The health of individuals is not simply a matter of individual concern but has an impact on the society in general, affecting as it does health provision, their families and those around them, sometimes even their conduct in the workplace. The balance between the freedom of the individual and the role of government is a complex one, especially in this area.[1] We shall look at smoking, alcohol consumption, other forms of drug use, diet and physical exercise.

Smoking is a major health risk to both the smoker and others around them, and the extent of smoking among children is giving rise to real concern. In 1998 well over a third (37 per cent) of boys and nearly half (46 per cent) of girls had smoked at some time by the age of 15. As early as the age of 12, the corresponding figures are 16 and 22 per cent (Table A8.2). Among adults, in 1980, nearly half of men (45 per cent) were 'current smokers', six in every ten of them smoking more than 20 per day. As one might expect, nearly 20 years later in 1998 these figures had fallen considerably in both respects, with 34 per cent of men smoking, and more than 20 a day being smoked by four in every ten of them (Table A8.3).

This is an area of social life where gender now makes relatively little difference: among women nearly the same proportion smoke. In 1980, 41 per cent smoked, with four in every ten smoking more than 20 per day. In 1998, 32 per cent of women smoked, 3.4 in every ten smoking more than 20 a day. Smoking also varies very little by age. The percentage currently smoking cigarettes in each age band is much the same in 1998 up till the age of 60 or older for both men and women (Table A8.4). Smoking, however, contributes to the continuing class differentials in morbidity to which we have already referred (see Chapter 2). There is a steep class gradient in percentages currently smoking. In households where the chief income earner is in class IV or V the proportion of current smokers is around four times as high among men and five times as high among women as in households where the chief income earner is in class I (Table A8.5).

Alcohol, while it has undoubtedly been a source of real enjoyment and an important element of congenial social interaction in Europe over a very long period, has its own hazards, both direct and indirect. Again there is considerable concern about alcohol consumption among the young. Alcohol consumption measured in mean units per week was virtually stable at around 20 for men (all ages) between 1995 and 1998 but rose from 6.3 to 7.1 for women. These overall figures conceal a rise among the youngest age group, those aged 16–24 (from 20.8 to 23.4 for men and 8.4 to 10.0 for women), this group consuming more than any other age group in 1998 (Table A8.6). Because these figures represent the mean number of units consumed, it is clear that since some people will drink considerably less, others drink considerably more, well over the recommended maxima.[2] Among children, the proportion having had a 'proper alcoholic drink' rises steadily with age as one might expect but reaches two-thirds by age 15 for both boys and girls, and is already four in ten by age 13. Even at the age of ten or below the proportion is around one in ten for boys and one in 20 for girls (Table A8.7).

Turning to illicit forms of drug use we find a dramatic rise in new drug addicts notified to the Home Office between 1980 and 1996 (Table A8.8). There were 58 men and 32 women in this category in 1980 and the figures rise to 1,032 for men (mean age 25) and 431 for women (mean age 24) in 1996. The figures rose very steeply between 1980 and 1986, less dramatically between 1986 and 1991, and then doubled between 1991 and 1996. Addicts notified to the Home Office are an extreme group, a tiny proportion of the population of Scotland, and undoubtedly only a very small fraction of users of drugs of various kinds, but they do seem to reflect an underlying trend. Statistics on drugs are notoriously difficult to collect and interpret. The Scottish Crime Survey collects data on reported drug misuse, which could cover everything from cannabis to heroin. In 1996, the proportion reporting use in the last 12 months was 26 per cent for men aged 16–19, rising to 37 per cent in the 20–4 age group, and then falling steadily to 2 per cent in the 40–59 age group. For women the pattern was not dissimilar, 20 and 21 per cent in the two youngest age groups and 1 per cent at 40–59 (Table A8.9). It is, of course, impossible to say with certainty whether this pattern by age will continue into the future or whether the younger cohorts will continue to report drug misuse as they get older. One authority on drug use in Scotland (Neil McKeganey of Glasgow University, private communication) suggests that because drug use is to some extent about lifestyle, the pattern will vary from drug to drug. Thus, use of heroin, especially among marginalised, dependent groups, is likely to continue as they get older, whereas the use of ecstasy, unless it were to transfer from semi-public consumption among younger people to domestic use, is likely to decline with age. The recreational use of cannabis probably makes up a good deal of the reported current drug use, and there seems no reason to believe that the pattern by age will change in the future. On balance, then, the continuation of existing age patterns seems more likely.

The crude categories in Table 8.1 showing broadly on what we spend our income may conceal crucial variations. Nowhere is this more apparent than in diet, another area of consumption which may have far-reaching consequences. People in Scotland, as we have seen, spend just under one-fifth of their income on food and, like alcohol consumption, smoking and taking drugs, this can have effects on their health. Concerns about obesity, especially among the young, are commonplace. It is becoming increasingly clear that what we eat impinges on more than our taste buds. *Scottish Social Statistics* (Scottish Executive 2001a: 84) states that 'links between health and diet are well documented. Diet is the second most important factor in preventable ill health in Scotland behind only smoking.'

Although somewhat complex in detail, Table 8.2 broadly shows that women eat more healthily than men, that there are clear class differentials with the higher classes eating more healthily than the lower, and, encouragingly, that there were modest improvements between 1995 and 1998.

It is, then, apparent that there is a considerable variation by social class in lifestyle factors affecting health – with greater affluence which does allow consumers more choice, which they may or may not exercise wisely, education and cultural factors all playing their part. Figures for 1998 giving the prevalence of any cardiovascular disorder by social class of chief income earner and sex reflect this clearly (Table A8.10). For men the percentage prevalence in class V (30.4 per cent) is 1.7 times, and for women (28.8 per cent) twice, that for class I where the corresponding figures are 18.2 and 14.0 per cent.

Table 8.2 Aspects of diet, by sex and social class of chief income earner, 1995 and 1998

%	Social class of chief income earner[1]						Total[2]
	I	II	IIInm	IIIm	IV	V	
Male							
Uses skimmed or semi-skimmed milk							
1995	68	68	64	57	53	49	60
1998	74	70	69	60	51	51	64
Eats potatoes, pasta or rice five or more times a week							
1995	68	60	53	50	45	41	53
1998	71	69	61	59	57	63	63
Eats fresh fruit once a day or more often							
1995	57	44	41	35	32	26	39
1998	60	52	44	42	34	34	45
Usually [1998] or generally [1995] adds salt to food at table							
1995	39	46	52	59	59	60	53
1998	36	41	50	57	59	56	49
Female							
Uses skimmed or semi-skimmed milk							
1995	80	73	68	63	57	56	67
1998	80	75	74	66	61	58	70
Eats potatoes, pasta or rice five or more times a week							
1995	77	66	59	55	51	42	59
1998	81	76	70	63	62	56	68
Eats fresh fruit once a day or more							
1995	67	62	54	49	39	39	52
1998	73	70	59	54	43	35	58
Usually [1998] or generally [1995] adds salt to food at table							
1995	33	32	40	46	45	51	41
1998	27	36	39	44	48	49	40
Sample sizes (unweighted)							
Men							
1995	240	886	389	1148	521	196	3524
1998	256	1025	420	1290	607	191	3789
Women							
1995	253	1088	851	1039	677	273	4408
1998	243	1340	1036	1094	816	369	4898

Source: Deepchand et al. (2000: Table 10.24), using Scottish Health Survey 1998.
Percentages weighted.
1. Registrar General's class.
2 The 'total' column includes those for whom social class could not be determined.

Data on class differentials in overall participation in physical activity (Table A8.11) also show a class gradient but a somewhat more complex one, partly because unavoidable physical activity at work is class-related. The Scottish Health Survey sought to measure activity whether during leisure, paid work or housework. Moderate or vigorous activity included being 'very physically active' at work; doing heavy housework or gardening; walking briskly for 15 or more minutes; sport and cycling. Individuals are then classified as High, Medium or Low on physical activity. Thirty minutes or more of such moderate or vigorous activity on at least five days per week leads to a classification of High; 30 minutes or more on one to four days per week as Medium; and all activity below Medium as Low. An individual classified in the High category is certainly involved in a good deal of physical activity, and in the Low category in very little; the Medium category covers a wide range. If, then, we focus on the clear-cut extremes we find that the proportion of men classified as Low rises steadily as we move down the social classes (from 23 per cent in class I to 43 per cent in class V), whereas the proportion classified as High shows a much smaller gradient, the range being 36 per cent to 43 per cent. Those in the higher, non-manual groups who are classified as High are presumably deliberately taking more exercise whether for health or pleasure or both. The heavier physical activity of some manual workers puts them in this category, compensating for a lower proportion choosing this level of activity. Overall, 33 per cent of men in Scotland are in the Low category and 38 per cent in the High. In the case of women, the data patterns are more clear-cut and their levels of physical activity lower. Overall 38 per cent are in the Low category and 27 in the High. As in the case of males, a much higher proportion of class V females (42 per cent) are in the Low category than class I females (29 per cent); the figures for the High category show much less variation – 28 per cent in class I and 26 per cent in class V.

The most salient summary finding is that one-third or more of the people in Scotland may be damaging their health by taking very little physical exercise indeed, and that this is clearly class-related. Of course, as one would expect, young adults exercise more than old. Nevertheless the data show that by age 35, 29 per cent of men and 28 per cent of women are already in the Low category, a figure which then rises steadily (Table A8.12). Concern is frequently expressed about the lack of physical activity among children, and the above data suggest that for many their parents do not offer outstanding role models. The data on children are indeed anything but encouraging, as is shown by Table A8.13, drawn from research at the Child and Adolescent Research Unit at Edinburgh University. In 1998 only half (49 per cent) of boys and well under a third (29 per cent) of girls exercised for six or more hours per week in or out of school. The corresponding figures for exercise in free time for four or more hours per week were 42 and 24 per cent. This latter measure is available since 1990 and, interestingly, there has been a modest proportional rise between 1990 and 1998 by 16 per cent for boys and 24 per cent for girls; this does not support the frequently expressed view that the impact of television and the computer is steadily turning more and more children in Scotland into couch potatoes year on year. Information on a slightly different basis, collected by the same research group in 2000–1, may indicate continuing improvement, but there is clearly no room for complacency. The national guideline of at least one hour of moderate-to-vigorous physical activity on at least five days per week is being met at age 11 by 56 per cent of boys and 41 per cent of girls. By age 15, however, the proportions fall to 39 per cent of boys and 24 per cent of girls (Alexander et al. 2003).

We have looked in considerable detail at how people in Scotland spend their incomes and the way in which this is still patterned by class, often with consequences that show that, although people have more to live on than before, the impact on health is not universally beneficial. It is of course important to maintain a sense of historical perspective. People may not always choose a healthy diet but most have sufficient to eat. We may bemoan the lack of physical exercise but working hours, in principle at least, would allow time for exercise if people chose to take it, and ill-health is less often a barrier. A further implication is that class differentials in this area are, to some extent, though by no means entirely, a matter of education and class cultures rather than brute necessity. Encouraging the population to smoke less, drink in moderation, eat a healthier and more balanced diet, and take more exercise is, then, a realisable goal even if not one which it is easy to achieve. It is one thing to cast a somewhat critical and mordant eye over the *choices* that people make, but as we move through the twenty-first century a large majority are at least able to make them.

OWNERSHIP OF HOUSEHOLD GOODS

One consequence of rising affluence which it would be hard for anyone to criticise, except perhaps sometimes on ecological grounds, is the far wider distribution of household goods, and it is to this that we now turn. It is well known that household goods which were once restricted to relatively wealthy families are now to be found in many households, and our everyday experience of other people's households and what we see on television reinforces this perception. Nevertheless, the figures in Table 8.3, which show the proportion of individuals living in households possessing various household items, may hold a few surprises. On the reasonable assumption that the figure for fridges has risen since 1980, more than 95 per cent of individuals have access to vacuum cleaners, washing machines, refrigerators, freezers, telephones, and colour television. Possession of some of these goods is at or near saturation; for instance some people choose not to possess a television set or a telephone so that these figures are about as high as they can go (but see below). Central heating, microwaves and video recorders, at around 90 per cent, are heading in the same direction. Since 1980 possession of central heating and freezers has roughly doubled, and other items such as the telephone and colour television which were already common have become almost universal. Widespread ownership of consumer goods is, of course, no guarantee of acceptable physical conditions. The Scottish Household Survey shows that while only 3 per cent of households have fewer rooms than it is estimated they require, this rises to as high as 17 per cent in large family households (Scottish Executive 2003c: Table 4.13). The Scottish House Conditions Survey (Scottish Executive 2002f:12) shows that 6 per cent of dwellings in Scotland are affected by some form of structural dampness, and that condensation and mould growth are found in 11 per cent. Nevertheless, most people in Scotland do live pretty comfortably with access to devices which save labour and provide entertainment in the home, and the considerable number of people alive today who were born before, say, the end of the Second World War have seen extraordinary changes.

Table 8.3 Possession of household items, 1980–2000

% of individuals	Year		
Item	1980	1990	2000
Central heating	53.3	78.6	92.7
Vacuum cleaner	95.7	not asked	not asked
Washing machine	89.7	94.2	96.8
Tumble drier	27.0	55.7	61.5
Dishwasher	2.9	12.3	27.7
Microwave	not asked	49.9	87.7
Fridge	91.8	not asked	not asked
Freezer	41.0	80.9	95.6
Phone	75.3	84.5	98.0
Mobile phone	not asked	not asked	63.9
Television	99.1	98.7	99.2
Colour television	81.0	96.0	98.7
Video recorder	not asked	72.4	92.7
Computer	not asked	25.3	45.9
Sample size	3224	5356	1637

Sources: General Household Survey 1980, 1990 and 2000. Weighted in 2000, unweighted in other years (all sample sizes unweighted).
Base is individuals: i.e. percentages show proportion of individuals living in households with item.

Here we return to the sharply contrasting world of the 'haves' and the 'have nots' and this theme runs through the rest of this section of the chapter. The small numbers of people who do not possess these items, ownership of which has come to be taken for granted, will undoubtedly feel a strong sense of relative deprivation. Furthermore, some items are less widely distributed. Possession of tumble driers more than doubled between 1980 and 2000 but only around six in ten individuals are in households which have them; possession of dishwashers has risen from 3 per cent in 1980 and doubled between 1990 and 2000, but the figure still remains less than 30 per cent; and perhaps most dramatically of all, the proportion of individuals in households which possessed computers in 2000 stood at 46 per cent, having nearly doubled since 1990. Life without a tumble drier or dishwasher is perhaps no great hardship, although the former can make life a good deal easier for those with small children, but – and we shall return to this – the computer may have a greater and growing impact.

As can be seen from Table A8.14, which covers some but not all of these items, ownership varies systematically by income. Ownership of a freezer or refrigerator, washing machine, and telephone is so high that even in the poorest category the figure is 88 per cent. It has long been argued that people's sense of deprivation relates to those with whom they compare themselves (Runciman (1964) is the original source). It is accordingly likely that the members of the one in eight households in the poorest category (net income less than £6,000) lacking these items will be only too well aware that in this respect they do not share the lifestyle of many of those on similarly low incomes to themselves, let alone most people living in Scotland.

As one might expect, car ownership is heavily skewed, with 19 out of 20 households in the highest bracket (net income over £20,000) owning a car in 2001, but just one-third in the lowest. In the highest bracket, the lack of a car is often likely to be from choice or some infirmity which makes driving impossible or unwise. In today's society, however, the lack of a car, especially in rural areas, can have a major impact on the ability to get to work easily, to interact with family and friends, to have access to leisure facilities, and even to take ready advantage of supermarkets and other retail outlets.

The importance of the car is underlined by the statistic that in 1999 over two-thirds of people in Scotland (69 per cent) used the car as their normal means of travel to work (either as driver or passenger), a figure which has risen threefold from 21 per cent in 1966. The proportion using buses has declined fourfold from 43 per cent to 11 per cent, and only 13 per cent now walk to work compared to 24 per cent doing so in 1966, thus contributing to the nation's lack of exercise (Table A8.15). These figures vary across Scotland, as one might expect (Scottish Executive 2001c: Table 10). The percentage travelling to work by car is significantly lower in Edinburgh (52 per cent) and Glasgow (55 per cent) and somewhat lower in Dundee (61 per cent), Aberdeen (62 per cent) and Moray (61 per cent). Between one-fifth and one-quarter use the buses in Edinburgh (25 per cent), Glasgow (21 per cent) and Midlothian (20 per cent), and the proportion is approaching that level in Dundee (18 per cent) and Inverclyde (18 per cent). Walking to work is most common in 'remote' small towns, where over one-fifth travel in this way.

Nearly two-thirds of the households with net annual household income below £10,000 do not own a car (Table A8.14), and the effect of this must be seen against a background in which the car has assumed a central place in the lives of more affluent Scottish people. Distances travelled per adult per year have risen steadily between 1985–6 and 1997–9 (Table A8.16) and, although this travel is not necessarily all in Great Britain, that change is a reminder of the car's impact on the nature of leisure. The number of cars licensed has risen by 52 per cent in the past two decades, from 1,398,000 in 1980 to 2,131,000 in 1999, while the available road lengths have increased only by 8 per cent, greatly increasing road congestion (Table A8.17). Under the circumstances, it is a relief to note that casualties have actually declined by 28 per cent.

SOCIAL PARTICIPATION AND LEISURE

We mentioned earlier that differential access to the computer, and especially access to the internet, has a greater importance than is at first glance apparent, and one which we can expect to increase. Table A8.14 shows that 36 per cent of all households own a computer[3] but the 68 per cent doing so in the highest income group is more than four times greater than the 15 per cent in the lowest two categories. The computer is itself a very useful tool and a valuable source of entertainment, as the popularity of computer games testifies. For those with access to the internet and e-mail, its impact on social life is vastly increased, generally for the good, although the problems raised by easy access to all forms of pornography, and the perils of chatrooms, are well known. Crucially, e-mail allows quick, easy and relatively cheap communication across the entire world in what is, in some ways, a revival of the habits of letter writing, and the world wide web is the gateway to a wealth of information formerly only available to those with easy access to major libraries, and with both the expertise and the prior information required to locate the printed information. It also provides opportunities to purchase a wide range of consumer goods and services, often at prices well below those in other retail outlets.

Slightly under a quarter of Scottish households (22.7 per cent) had internet access in 2001, but this figure ranges from 7 per cent in households with net income below £10,000 to nearly half (48 per cent) in those with net income over £20,000. Table A8.18 shows that internet users are younger, more highly educated and richer than non-users. The differentials are striking and the conclusion that there is a digital divide at present is inescapable.[4] Those with a university degree are seven times more likely to use the internet than those without any educational qualifications; those in households with an annual household income of £26,000 per year or more are over four times more likely to use it than those with less than £6,000 per year; men are somewhat more likely to use it than women; and age has a dramatic effect, with only 14 per cent of those aged 55 or over logging in, whereas nearly 60 per cent of those aged 18 to 34 do so.

Gardner and Oswald (2001) relate their discussion of the 'digital divide' interestingly to the widely discussed book by Robert Putnam, *Bowling Alone* (2000). He argues that in the United States there has been a decline in what he refers to as 'social capital', 'connections among individuals – social networks and the norms of reciprocity and trustworthiness that arise from them' (2000: 19) and which he sees as 'closely related to what some have called "civic virtue" '. The overall thrust of Putnam's book is to show that, in America, 'the bonds of our communities have withered, and we are *right* to fear that this transformation has very real costs' (Putnam 2000: 402).

Gardner and Oswald find that, contrary to popular belief, 'internet users are much more likely to take part in social activity and be good citizens. They attend church more, join voluntary organisations more, are more likely to have friends whom they can rely on in times of trouble, read more books, are not less trusting of other people, and watch fewer hours of television' (Gardner and Oswald 2001: 168). Internet users in Britain would therefore be regarded by Putnam as high in social capital. The unequal distribution of internet access then implies that, to some extent at least, there is stratification in the possession of social capital. The importance of access to computers and the internet may be even greater than the immediate benefits to which we have referred earlier. In what follows, we shall discuss various aspects of the possession of social capital in Scotland.

First, we want to place these findings in the context of the argument one of us has developed elsewhere (Paterson 2002a: 5–32). Data from the Scottish and British Social Attitudes Surveys of 2000 presented in that chapter suggest strongly that social capital and social trust remain strong in

Britain despite, for instance, declining turnout in elections. Michael Johnston and Roger Jowell (Johnston and Jowell 2001) also directly address Putnam's argument using over-time data for Britain as a whole, and come to the same conclusion, saying, 'Civil society here remains as strong and active as it was' (2001: 194). In Scotland, the evidence summarised by Paterson (2002a: 21) shows that social capital does underpin political engagement in precisely the way that Putnam suggests: high trust, strong norms and many memberships are associated with a resistance to political cynicism. However, this state of affairs where strong social capital prevails, however desirable in one regard, is associated with support for the existing social and political order, for example with holding more conservative views on redistribution of wealth.

These arguments (supported albeit from a somewhat different angle by Johnston and Jowell) have very important implications for the future governance of Scotland, and also for our running theme of social exclusion. Johnston and Jowell, writing quite generally about Britain as a whole, sound a familiar warning note:

> But to a significant extent too, this enviable degree of participation remains concentrated within familiar subgroups who start off with many advantages and then bolster those advantages in the course of their voluntary 'joining' activities. In time, as their social capital (in common with other forms of capital) generates increasing returns, these advantages will tend to be reinforced. This matters for those who are left out, restricting their access to important sources of support, influence and confidence. And it matters too for society at large, tending to perpetuate old divisions. (Johnston and Jowell 2001: 194)

The first part of this conclusion relating to advantage and social exclusion is also to be found in the analysis of the Scottish Social Attitudes Survey (Paterson 2002a). The initial drive to devolution may indeed have been fuelled by high levels of social capital. Now that Scotland has an established parliament, the coalition between liberal reformism and a more radical view is possibly beginning to unravel. People high in social capital, exactly as Johnston and Jowell suggest, see it as supportive of their particular view of liberal democracy, wishing to embed the parliament in their vision of civil society as it exists within the UK. The more socially excluded see the parliament as a medium of challenging the Union and that view of civil society.

To fill out this picture, let us look directly at social capital and examine the extent to which people in Scotland are involved in various kinds of social and leisure activities. Data in Paterson (2002a: 13) show that nearly a

quarter (22 per cent) of people in Scotland are *members* of local organisations,[5] four out of five of them of one only, the rest of two or more. Just over
a quarter (27 per cent) are members of sports and cultural groups – again
around four out of five only of sports groups, the rest of cultural groups or
both. Giving up one's time to help as a volunteer or as an organiser for a
charity, club or organisation rather than just participating is a significant
contribution to social capital. It must be emphasised at this point that social
capital can be of the kind which increases 'bonding' *within* a social group or
'bridging' *between* social groups. The latter will decrease social exclusion, the
former may increase it, depending on the group involved, and charities,
clubs and other voluntary organisations vary greatly in their aims. That
said, around one in five people in Scotland do give up time, with women,
the more affluent and those in rural areas doing so more than men, the less
affluent and those in urban areas (Scottish Executive 2001a: Chart 10.9 and
pp. 151–2). Volunteers help with church or religious organisations (23 per
cent of them); work with young children (21 per cent); with the elderly or
disabled (12 per cent in each case); or with arts, culture and sport
organisations (13 per cent).

Traditionally, church membership has been an important contributor to
social capital. Active membership of churches fell considerably between
1980 and 2000, especially among Presbyterians where the proportional fall is
35 per cent to 639,000 in 2000. Even among Roman Catholics the fall is 24
per cent to 225,0000. Other Christian denominations have held steady at
around 150,000, while the relatively small numbers of those classified as
non-Trinitarians and as Other Religions have risen from around 25,000 to
42,000 and 59,000 respectively (Table A8.19).

LEISURE ACTIVITIES MORE GENERALLY

It is, of course, not necessary to be a member of a club or organisation to
participate in leisure activities which are important as a potential form of
social interaction and general involvement in the affairs of the society.
According to *Scottish Social Statistics* (Scottish Executive 2001a: 160), 63 per
cent of the population participated in sports during 1997–9. There are 12
sports in each of which more than one in 20 men participated; six sports
have this rate of participation for women. Walking, football, swimming and
golf for men, and walking and swimming for women, all register rates over
15 per cent. The Scottish Household Survey of 1999–2000 (Scottish
Executive 2001b: Table 5.31) shows that 11 per cent used a swimming
pool and 14 per cent visited a sports or leisure centre in the past week (38 per
cent and 35 per cent respectively in the past year), but 27 per cent and 32 per

cent have never done these things. However, more people in Scotland do take a gentler form of exercise and the same table shows that only 12 per cent had never visited their local park, whereas one-third (34 per cent) had done so in the past week and two-thirds (67 per cent) in the past year. Gershuny and Fisher (2000: 642–3), looking at British social trends, come to the conclusion that

> while it remains true that the members of the professional classes are still substantially more likely to take exercise than are members of the working classes, the *rate of growth* in participation among the working classes has generally been much higher than among the professional classes. Therefore, in short, at the end of the century, British society as a whole was converging on higher levels of participation (in at least the non-team sports) than it had 30 years ago. [emphasis in the original].

Since taking part in sport is a fairly high level of exercise, these conclusions are in line with the Scottish data cited earlier in this chapter.

Football, often regarded as a national obsession, attracted 3,236,857 attendances at premier league matches in 1997–8 (Scottish Office 1998: Table 15a5) a figure which has fluctuated up and down from the 3,003,318 in 1992–3 going as low as 2,547,827 in 1994–5, but figures for earlier years show that, while it has always fluctuated, popularity has not fallen away since 1979–80 when the figure was 2,225,600 (Scottish Office 1992a: Table 8.3).

Scottish Social Statistics cites the Scottish Arts Council as finding that 'the three most popular arts activities participated in at least twice in 1998 were, reading books (73 per cent), attending the cinema (57 per cent) and buying a work of fiction or poetry (41 per cent)' (Scottish Executive 2001a: 162). We shall look at reading habits in more detail shortly but figures from *Scottish Screen Data* (Scottish Screen 1998: 40) (obtained from the Cinema Advertising Association) indicate that annual cinema admissions in Scotland in 1998 were 13 million, down a million from the year before, but still higher than the 11 million, 10 million and 12 million in 1994, 1995 and 1996. These figures follow fairly closely the pattern for the UK as a whole, and, if we assume this holds more generally, Table 10b (1998:41) shows rising frequency of attendance at all ages between 1994 and 1998, with the highest frequency in the 15–24 age group. This must, of course, be seen in the longer-term context of massive decline in the number of cinemas and admissions. This is documented for the UK by Gershuny and Fisher (2000: 638–9) and is part of the general phenomenon which they describe well as the process whereby 'home-based provisions replace job-creating service consumption outside the home'.

We have seen that reading (and indeed buying books) is a popular 'arts activity' but it is eclipsed in terms of time spent by watching television (Table A8.20). Even professionals and managers, who, of the six broad socio-economic groups, spend least time watching television, do so for 2.5 hours per weekday evening, and the figure rises steadily as one descends the socio-economic groups reaching 4.5 hours for the unskilled manual. Book reading for pleasure is less unequally distributed, the lowest figure being 3.3 hours per week in the skilled manual group, rising to 3.7 in the unskilled and semi-skilled groups and 4.9 in the intermediate non-manual, a figure which is higher than that for professionals and managers, possibly because work-related reading occupies more of the last group's time even outside office hours. Even professionals and managers then, who spend only 12.5 hours in the evenings Monday to Friday watching TV, do spend two and a half times more hours on that than the most diligent book readers spend reading. A very similar pattern emerges if these data are tabulated by highest educational attainment (Table A8.21). Those with a degree or professional qualification read for pleasure 4.7 hours per week and this falls to 3.9 among those with no or low qualifications; television viewing per weekday evening rises from 2.2 hours among those with a degree or professional qualification to 4.0 hours among those with no or low qualifications. It is an inescapable conclusion that television viewing occupies over twice as many hours as reading even among the most highly educated and highest socio-economic groups. The content of their viewing and reading may, of course, differ greatly between socio-economic groups. The percentage of each of these groups who have used a public library in the past month is patterned very similarly with respect to education level: around a quarter overall have done so, and use in the past month among those with a degree or professional qualification (37.3 per cent) is double that of those with no or low qualifications (18.4 per cent) (Tables A8.22 and A8.23).

It is clear that viewing television and listening to the radio absorb sizeable amounts of the leisure time enjoyed by the people of Scotland and the detail is worth closer examination (Table 8.4).

Television viewing increases steadily with age and the data do not support the view that children view television more than their elders, though it is undeniable that, at 18.5 hours per week, television has changed the pattern of childhood leisure over the past 50 years. Gender differences are small, and differences by 'social grade' are as one would expect, with the DE grade viewing around 40 per cent more than the AB. Radio listening figures show both rather smaller differentials and that radio remains very popular. Such is the amount of time spent viewing television that

Table 8.4 Television viewing and radio listening among people aged 4 and over, by gender, by age and by social class, 1999

| | Hours per person per week | |
	Television	Radio
Sex:		
Male	26.2	19.0
Female	29.5	16.1
Age:		
4–15[1]	18.5	7.8
16–24[1]	19.2	18.9
25–34	27.1	20.6
35–44	26.2	20.3
45–54	30.9	20.0
55–64	35.1	19.2
65+	39.6	16.8
Social grade		
AB: professional, managerial and intermediate	23.5	16.6
C1: skilled non-manual	24.1	16.7
C2: skilled manual	28.0	19.3
DE: semi-skilled and unskilled manual	32.8	17.4
All aged 4 and over	27.9	17.5

Source: Scottish Executive (2001a: Table 10.14), using data supplied by the BBC but relating to all channels.
1. Radio age groups are 4–14 and 15–24.

Scottish Social Statistics is clearly right to suggest that many people spend most evenings viewing, and that the figures seem to show that the radio is often on in the background while people go about their everyday lives, driving, doing housework and other jobs around the home, or even working (Scottish Executive 2001a: 155). These findings must, however, be kept in perspective. Assuming Scotland is not dissimilar to Britain as a whole in this regard, it is worth noting Gershuny and Fisher's observations on change between 1961 and 1995 (2000: 646–7) that 'time devoted to radio and television (as a main activity) has not changed much over the whole of this period' and that 'though television watching is by far the largest single activity within the household in terms of time use, at the end of the television century it shows no signs of progressively taking over all life outside paid work'.

CONCLUSION

The material we have discussed in this chapter is, in one respect, different from the earlier chapters of this book. The ways in which people spend their income and other resources, owning or renting their houses, their enjoyment of consumer goods, consumption of food, tobacco, alcohol and drugs, their leisure activities, and use of computers and the internet, are in a sense the *consequences* of many of the things we have discussed earlier. Most obviously, they require income which derives largely from work and employment. Consumption and lifestyle are nevertheless strongly structured by education and social class in ways which are partly irrespective of affluence. The data in this chapter put flesh on the idea of living in Scotland, the title of this book. Many of the activities we have discussed describe the ways in which the people of Scotland enjoy their lives and contribute to the civic culture of their country. Other data reveal darker and less desirable facts. Running through the chapter is the recurring theme of the highly structured way in which the benefits and goods of Scotland are distributed, partly as a result of resources and partly for cultural reasons. Where income is lower, or we move down the levels of class and education, people have less and less access to the goods and services they seek and value. That said, the majority of Scotland's people enjoy a higher standard of living than ever before and are able to live relatively comfortably in ways which few would have predicted 20 or 30 years ago They may not always spend their resources in the way that health professionals or educationalists might think best, but that is their choice. This picture is, however, severely blighted by the ever more salient gap between the 'haves' and the 'have nots' whose relative disadvantages appear all the more stark against the way that those around them live.

NOTES

1. At the time of writing, a good example is the debate over the control of smoking in public places, not just in Scotland but throughout Europe.
2. Currently 14 units per week for women and 21 for men.
3. To avoid confusion, note that this figure is the proportion of *households*, and the figure cited previously is proportion of *individuals* in households, owning a computer.
4. An interesting paper by Jonathan Gardner and Andrew Oswald (2001) using data from the British Social Attitudes Survey 2000 discusses this question in some detail for Britain as a whole.
5. Tenants' or residents' association; parents' association; school board; political party; community council or local council; neighbourhood council or forum; Neighbourhood Watch Scheme; local conservation or environmental group; or other local community or voluntary group

CHAPTER 9

Conclusions

Before we finish by speculating about the possible consequences of the structural patterns we have traced in this book, let us start by reviewing their main features, revisiting some of the themes which we adumbrated in Chapter 1. In no more than two decades, Scotland has gone through such profound transformations that, in some important respects, it is barely recognisable as the same place. All three of us have lived through this whole period, and yet it comes as a surprise to see just how large the changes have been: the incremental change that one experiences from year to year does not prepare one for the starkness of some of the contrasts revealed by studying the data in detail. We have frequently taught our students that one of the things you learn as a sociologist is that societies generally change more slowly than is often supposed, except at times of revolution, and even then that change is often more apparent than real. This is just plain wrong for Scotland since the 1960s and 1970s, as in other western, post-industrial societies. Scotland is a very different place now from 1980 and, although some of the changes started well before that, this last period has been crucial. There is possibly an analogy with the way that people have come to look on the Second World War as something of a watershed. It is not that the changes of the post-war period did not have their origins in the 1920s and 1930s; it is, rather, that experience of war intensified them and made them more apparent. The difference now is that there has been no war, no revolution, no cataclysmic event to which change could be approximately attributed. No single event has brought the changes into sharp focus.

We do not need to go over the detail of change again here, but it is worth just reiterating in outline what the data have shown. First are changes of a structural nature, driven by some of the various forces that were summarised in Chapter 1 and which have been referred to in explanation in all the chapters. By structure we mean many things. There is demography – declining birth rates and death rates, greater longevity and an ageing population, changing causes of death, shifts in the patterns of disease, and the coming to an end of Scotland's historically very high levels of emigration. There are changes to the family and household – different patterns of marriage, the growth of new kinds of cohabitation, different amounts and timings of child-bearing, consequently different types of household. There have been enormous changes in the industrial and occupational structure, perhaps the topic where consciousness of change has been most widespread but easily also the one with the greatest capacity to astonish: would any politician in the 1974 general elections – the start of the political process that has now led to limited Scottish self-government – have been willing to believe that within a generation only 13 per cent of Scottish workers would be employed in manufacturing industry? Or that this proportion would be comfortably exceeded by the numbers working in finance and business services?

From these occupational changes have come profound alterations in the very nature and significance of social class, changing the life chances of Scotland's citizens, in the market place, in social interaction with others, and perhaps above all in the opportunity for what they experience subjectively as upward mobility. For all the longevity of Scotland's self-belief as a land of open opportunity, never before in its history has it had so many lads and lassies o pairts. That has been driven partly by changes in supply – by the changing roles of women, by the shrinking of the working class. It has also been shaped partly by changes in demand for skilled labour – the growth of professions with their insistence on credentials and on formal development of careers. But the changing nature of social opportunity has also been shaped by changes to the system of education itself, partly by deliberate governmental action – such as in the growth and thorough democratisation of secondary schooling, or the growth and incipient democratisation of higher education – but more often by the pressures of students and their families. It was not the rather laggard Scottish policy makers who brought equal gender opportunities to the attention of Scottish schools, but rather the persistence of thousands of girls in using somewhat broadened curricula to overtake boys' attainment in the late-1970s and then to surpass boys by a large margin 20 years later. That specific change, too, would have been unimaginable to the generation of Miss Jean Brodie, although it would have rather pleased them.

We can be amazed by all this change without having to declare that it is good or bad, and in truth both reactions are appropriate. Good news first. Scotland is now a country where more people are in work. Work, moreover, is by and large less dangerous and less heavy, and earnings are higher for a majority of individuals and families. All this implies not only that most people at least avoid the uncertainty and indignity of involuntary unemployment, but also that they have access to the fulfilment and wide social networks that working outside the home may bring. Most families have modest cushions against hard times, in the form of pensions, insurance, some level of savings and so on, even if overall inequalities of wealth are greater than they were two decades ago. However great the importance of relative deprivation (to which we return in a moment), what matters is that most of Scotland's people have access to sufficient resources to lead a tolerably comfortable and decent life. Once again, it may be women who have benefited to the greater extent – more opportunities, more independent sources of income – although the financial security which the poorest kind of female employment offers is of only a very minimal kind.

Along with these changes have come rising levels of ownership of consumer goods. The most basic have been those pieces of equipment which make house-management no longer the unrelentingly exhausting chore it once was for nearly all women and some men. But there is also much wider access to broadcasting and to computers which in turn, especially coupled with rising levels of education, have brought new possibilities of communication and access to information. Computer literacy is both a means for advanced leisure and easier social interaction, and also a way of acquiring marketable skills. More generally, leisure opportunities are wider and more varied. In short, for most people, Scotland is a more affluent, comfortable and pleasant place to live in than it was just two or three decades ago.

We have started this discussion with the positive conclusions, and even the sociological tendency to focus on social stratification and social inequality shows some beneficial changes. Nevertheless, one would require truly rosy spectacles not to see a much darker side. Amidst this largely benevolent change, Scottish society is seriously divided and stratified. The basis of stratification has changed somewhat, and the size of the disadvantaged segments of society has shrunk, but the nature and experience of the resulting exclusion may, if anything, have worsened. People may be better-off than their parents were, but feel deprived relative to the way their peers live and may realistically aspire to. They may well understand how different their lives are from those of their parents and grandparents but may also feel excluded from what is common to most of their generation. For most people it is their contemporaries who provide their reference groups. Occupational class still matters, though changes in structure have perhaps made it less dramatic and obvious in terms of style of life: thus it probably matters more now than three decades ago whether someone has high levels of formal educational attainment, and it matters rather less (in a direct sense) in what occupation their father earned a living. As we explained at the end of Chapter 7, that change may be liberating for some, perhaps for a majority at a time when education has expanded so massively, but it may leave those with minimal amounts of educational achievement, and with no inherited wealth, even more inescapably at the bottom of every ladder of opportunity. There is also the question of changes over the life cycle. We have seen that individuals' and families' economic circumstances change as their circumstances change – having children, children leaving home, retiring, becoming old. In addition, professional and managerial workers have higher and more secure earnings than manual workers over their lifetimes. Consequently, adding up lifetime earnings would give us a different picture of deprivation from that which we get by simply taking a snapshot at one particular point in time. Similarly, the 'poor' may dip in and out of work, not out of choice, but because the jobs they end up doing are precisely those expendable and badly-paid ones which are swept away by technological change or exported overseas. The changing nature of work and the decline of a collective work ethos precisely in the jobs and sections of industry in which the worst-off are to be found increases the sense of deprivation, and it is exacerbated further by the virtual disappearance of the occupational communities which once provided emotional and material support.

Even beyond that point about the changing nature of stratification, there are distinctive groups of Scottish citizens who live in and under conditions which appear even more scandalous in the light of the improved conditions of many. Some of these groups are now much more important numerically than they were 20 years ago – the long-term unemployed, single parents and old people managing on no more than the state pension being particularly notable examples. Gender stratification may have diminished significantly for those who enter the professional labour market (although, even there, it has by no means vanished). But outside that it has barely diminished, even in the workplace despite legislation. Among people from Asian and Chinese backgrounds there is, alongside a significant amount of entrepreneurial and meritocratic success, also a group of workers in low-skilled, poorly-paid and probably insecure employment. The deprivations and inequalities of these groups are the more striking, and indeed shocking, against the possibilities of what might be. The very nature of some of the benefits enjoyed by the majority in itself accentuates the inequalities. Thus, for instance, the rise in computer access excludes those without it in an unprecedented way.

The consequences of all these somewhat contradictory changes cannot be foreseen clearly, but as we draw this book to a close we wish to allow ourselves to speculate about what they might be in the light of Scotland's still new political autonomy. It seems to us that questions are raised, the resolution of which cannot with any certainty be foreseen, questions about the way in which the country might respond both to the astonishing changes (many for the better) we have discussed, and to the persistence of invidious social stratification.

One version of Scotland's political story in the past three decades goes like this (for a fuller account, see McCrone (2001: 104–26) and Paterson (2002c)). A country of strong community ties, built around the inherited social institutions of its civil society, suddenly came up against a Conservative government that distrusted them in the light of its commitment to individual rather than collective autonomy. The resulting crisis was exacerbated by the background changes we have been describing, especially by the decay of the old economic base of old kinds of Scottish community, but also by the erosion of the authority of the rather socially conservative intellectual class which ran these same social institutions. The challenge to them was intensified because the old outlets through emigration had been blocked off with the collapse of the British Empire to which educated and ambitious Scots had contributed enormously. The Thatcher government presided over the critical years of the changes we have seen here, not only the changes in social structure but in particular the real and substantial growth of individual opportunity. By the 1990s there was, then, a tension between a newly educated, newly individualised populace articulating the inherited values of community, and the intransigence of a sclerotic UK state. According to this view, the tension was, at least to a considerable extent, resolved in the referendum on self-government in 1997 and, from 1999, the new Scottish governing system.

But the contradictions could not be resolved that easily, because in reality they were structurally indigenous to Scotland, not between that country and the state. They were tensions between community and individual choice. The Scottish National Party attracted support from upwardly mobile, aspiring young workers in the 1970s (McCrone 2001: 118–21), and – despite the rhetoric of much of the self-government movement – there were tensions between a persistent social democratic belief that public, political action could help to free individuals from social constraints and the distrust of old social democracy which the newly freed citizens then evinced. The rhetoric of community values pervaded the long campaign for self-government (Paterson 1998: 1–11). Not only did this come from the sense that government itself had never been distrusted in Scotland in the way that it seemed to be by Thatcher and her allies: belief in public action long pre-dated social democracy, and had origins in presbyterian notions of a well-governed commonwealth that go back for at least four centuries. The rhetoric also was inseparable from the very idea of a national community.

Because belonging requires somewhere to belong to, that required the reinvention of Scottish culture. This resurgence was a much more insistent and immediately apparent theme of intellectual discourse in the 1980s and 1990s than the silent background changes in structure that we may see only retrospectively. The ideas of a civic culture pervaded the deliberations of the Constitutional Convention, and spread from there through the Consultative Steering Group into the working practices of the new parliament. A government of and for the community of the realm has been trying to base its whole practice on the networks of social capital of the kind which we described briefly towards the end of Chapter 8.

Yet the rhetoric that was mobilised to defeat the Tories, and that was mobilised probably for the last time in the 1997 referendum, cannot coherently persist now that the tensions can be seen to have been domesticated. The ideological consequences of the structural changes we have delineated in this book have, at best, opened up new political options: in Scotland today there are more significant political parties, and more new ideas on policy, than at any time since at least the 1920s. At worst, however, they have induced in Scotland's people the same alienation from the political system as is experienced by all European societies, and for much the same reason: a more individualised, better educated, and more affluent population is no longer satisfied with deferentially accepting what politicians tell it, and no longer sees politics as a particularly efficacious way of bringing about desirable change (Curtice 2002). In particular, moreover, the change that might be envisaged is, for this relatively affluent majority, no longer as profound as seemed possible only a couple of decades ago, when the onslaught from Thatcher's government seemed to mark the beginning of a revival of Scottish utopian thought and action. This may not quite be what J. K. Galbraith famously characterised as a culture of contentment, insofar as people in Scotland show no signs of shifting their allegiance from the provision of major public services by mainly public means paid for mainly by taxation (Paterson 2002d). But it does not seem to be the ideological basis for the kinds of radical political action that, as we noted at the end of Chapter 5, would be required truly to bring the persisting poverty and social exclusion to an end.

There is a similar tension in all European societies at the moment, but the strength of the lasting attachment to community in Scotland makes its resolution here very difficult to bring about. The country has never shown itself to be particularly friendly to flaunting individualism, and it is difficult to see any circumstances in which a government of the radical right could capture power in the Scottish Parliament. There will be no programme of radical privatisation or deregulation, no shift to vouchers as the basis of providing public services, not much taste for these services to be differentiated in any fundamental ways. To that extent, Scotland remains attached to some kind of egalitarian collectivism. However, as we have seen in this book, the old social basis of collectivism, which supported what we may think of as 'traditional Labour', is dead, and for that reason the attachment to collectivism is not at the moment strong enough to underpin a social movement supporting truly radical politics. This is not to deny that the Scottish Executive has made, and continues to make, modest changes which attack some injustices and ameliorate some of the worst deprivations. But any new social ethic that might eventually generate and assent to a political programme that could eradicate poverty will have to be based on the freely chosen values of the newly individualised majority, never again on the inherited solidarity of an oppressed class. These values themselves will not come from politicians, nor from any of the social institutions – such as churches or schools – that used to instil them in the past. They can only come from citizens themselves. And, although social science can analyse the problem and offer explanations, predicting how a new social ethic might come to prevail in Scotland is something of which it is simply incapable, however willing its practitioners might be to help bring it about.

Supplementary Tables

SUPPLEMENTARY TABLES FOR CHAPTER 2

Table A2.1 Death rates, by sex and selected ages, 1946–2001

Males – rates per 1,000 population

Year	45–54	55–64	Age 65–74	75–84	85 +
1946–50	10.6	25.0	54.5	127.7	277.5
1951–55	9.6	25.6	57.0	130.4	278.1
1956–60	9.2	25.3	58.9	127.7	268.6
1961–65	9.3	25.9	59.8	128.7	266.8
1966–70	8.8	24.4	57.7	122.3	256.3
1971–75	8.9	23.8	57.3	122.7	246.4
1976–80	8.6	22.7	54.2	119.0	243.5
1981–85	7.6	21.2	51.8	113.4	229.7
1986–90	6.6	19.3	47.8	107.1	224.6
1991–95	5.5	16.4	42.6	95.7	210.6
1996–2000	5.5	15.2	39.4	91.1	203.8
2001	5.3	14.1	34.7	81.7	191.3

Females – rates per 1,000 population

Year	45–54	55–64	Age 65–74	75–84	85 +
1946–50	6.6	15.6	40.6	103.7	243.4
1951–55	6.0	14.4	39.5	104.6	240.6
1956–60	5.4	13.5	37.0	99.3	239.8
1961–65	5.4	13.1	35.1	93.8	217.4
1966–70	5.4	12.4	32.4	85.8	212.4
1971–75	5.3	12.6	30.3	80.1	198.5
1976–80	5.2	12.5	29.6	75.8	190.1
1981–85	4.5	12.0	29.5	71.5	183.2
1986–90	3.9	11.3	27.9	68.5	174.5
1991–95	5.5	16.4	42.6	95.7	210.6
1996–2000	3.4	8.8	24.0	61.5	174.6
2001	3.2	8.3	21.3	57.5	162.4

Source: Registrar General for Scotland (2002a: Table 5.1).

Table A2.2 Perinatal and infant mortality, by sex, 1946–2001

Year	Perinatal death rate per 1,000 live and still births		Infant death rate per 1,000 live births	
	male	female	male	female
1946–50	51.5	44.9	53.2	41.1
1951–55	45.1	39.7	36.8	28.8
1956–60	40.9	36.6	31.5	24.1
1961–65	35.4	31.6	28.3	21.6
1966–70	27.8	25.3	23.8	18.4
1971–75	24.3	21.6	21.0	16.5
1976–80	16.9	14.6	15.4	11.9
1981–85	11.9	9.9	11.7	9.2
1986–90	9.7	8.4	9.5	7.1
1991–95	9.0	7.1	7.5	5.6
1996–2000	7.6	6.3	6.2	4.9
2001	8.0	6.7	5.8	5.2

Source: Registrar General for Scotland (2002a: Table 4.2).

Perinatal death is stillbirth or death in the first week of life. For this table, stillbirth is defined to be losses to gestation periods of 28 weeks or longer, in order to maintain continuity with the period before 1992 when the legal definition was changed to 24 weeks gestation. Infant deaths are all deaths in the first year of life (and hence include some of the perinatal deaths).

Table A2.3 Death rates from selected causes, by sex, 1950–2001

Males – rates per 100,000 population

Year	Cancer			Ischaemic heart disease	Cerebrovascular disease
	All sites	Trachea, bronchus and lung	Prostate		
1950–52	206	48	13	276	155
1960–62	241	86	16	360	166
1970–72	272	112	14	407	158
1980–82	291	119	19	408	139
1990–92	310	110	27	363	118
2001	319	94	32	257	100

Females – rates per 100,000 population

Year	Cancer			Ischaemic heart disease	Cerebrovascular disease
	All sites	Trachea, bronchus and lung	Breast		
1950–52	185	10	31	203	213
1960–62	195	13	35	262	230
1970–72	218	24	40	289	226
1980–82	247	41	45	304	210
1990–92	278	57	48	297	191
2001	282	62	43	215	159

Source: Registrar General for Scotland (2002b: Table 4.1).

Table A2.4 Morbidity: top ten GP consultation rates per 1,000 population, 2000

Condition/illness	
Depression	152
Hypertension	143
Upper respiratory tract infection (excl. sore throat)	124
Back problems	115
Lower respiratory tract infection	94
Anxiety	86
Sore throat	63
Miscellaneous	62
Abdominal pain	58
Itch/rash	56

Source: Common Services Agency (2001).

Table A2.5 Health and religion, 2001

% in columns	All	Religion				
		None	Church of Scotland	Roman Catholic	Other Christian	Other religion
General health						
good	55.3	59.5	54.0	51.5	56.3	56.2
fairly good	30.9	28.0	32.1	31.1	31.4	32.6
not good	13.8	12.5	13.8	17.4	12.3	11.2
Disability or long-term illness						
disability only	6.6	4.8	7.4	7.2	6.4	5.3
long-term illness only	8.9	6.5	9.3	11.6	9.1	8.2
both	4.2	3.2	4.6	5.1	3.8	2.4
neither	80.2	85.2	78.6	76.0	80.6	83.8
Sample size	14643	3771	7334	2067	1162	309

Source: Scottish Household Survey 2001, weighted (sample sizes unweighted).

Table A2.6 Health and broad ethnic group, 2001

% in columns	All	White	Non-white
General health			
good	55.3	55.2	64.4
fairly good	30.9	30.9	29.9
not good	13.8	13.9	5.7
Disability or long-term illness			
disability only	6.6	6.6	2.1
long-term illness only	8.9	9.0	3.6
both	4.2	4.2	1.0
neither	80.2	80.1	92.8
Sample size	14643	14476	160

Source: Scottish Household Survey 2001, weighted (sample sizes unweighted).

Table A2.7 Birth place, by area, 1999

% in rows Area of birth	Same area of Scotland	Elsewhere in Scotland	England	Rest of UK	Rest of EU[1]	Rest of world	Sample size
Area of residence							
Lothian	55.9	26.3	12.7	1.4	1.2	2.5	638
Central and Fife	59.7	29.7	7.2	0.7	2.0	0.7	327
South West	40.5	33.6	21.4	0.0	3.8	0.8	120
North East	66.8	18.1	10.8	0.6	1.3	2.5	419
Tayside	66.7	23.2	5.8	1.9	1.0	1.4	214
Highlands and Islands	46.6	35.6	16.9	0.8	0.0	0.0	136
Strathclyde outside Glasgow	46.3	43.2	7.2	1.2	0.8	1.2	735
Glasgow	59.3	22.0	8.8	1.4	3.0	5.5	335
Total	55.2	30.3	9.9	1.1	1.5	2.1	2924

Source: British Household Panel Survey, waves 1 and 9.
1. EU countries as defined in 1999.
Percentages weighted, sample sizes unweighted.
Example of what the first two columns of this table mean: of all people living in Lothian, 55.9% were born in Lothian and 26.3% elsewhere in Scotland.

SUPPLEMENTARY TABLES FOR CHAPTER 3

Table A3.1 Family size and socio-economic group, among school leavers, 1981–99

Father's broad socio-economic group	Year of survey		
	1981	1991	1999
Professional and managerial	3.0 (1165)	2.5 (673)	2.6 (1498)
Intermediate non-manual	3.0 (330)	2.6 (245)	2.6 (679)
Junior non-manual	3.0 (313)	2.5 (166)	2.6 (429)
Skilled manual	3.6 (2002)	3.0 (1005)	2.8 (2400)
Semi-skilled manual	3.7 (652)	3.1 (254)	2.8 (565)
Unskilled manual	4.1 (309)	3.0 (119)	2.9 (203)
All	3.5 (5548)	2.9 (2952)	2.8 (7249)

Source: Scottish School Leavers Survey 1981 and 1991 (leavers in sessions 1979–80 and 1989–90), and survey in 1999 of pupils who were in fourth year of secondary school in session 1995–6. Thus respondents were aged approximately 16–18. Being conditional on families having at least one member (at school), the data here over-estimate family size, but that over-estimation should perhaps remain roughly constant over time. The 1999 survey is, strictly speaking, not comparable to the other two, since (roughly) it surveyed a single year cohort, whereas the other two surveyed single leaver cohorts. However, since the latter spans only about three year cohorts, the discrepancies are small.

The numbers shown are 1 plus the number of reported siblings. Those with no father's occupation recorded, or with father in armed forces, are excluded from body of table but are included in the row labelled 'all'.

Data are weighted. Unweighted sample sizes in brackets

Table A3.2 Migration of individuals, by household type in which living, 1999

% individuals in rows Household type	Scotland, same area[1]	Place of birth Scotland, different area[1]	England	Rest of UK	Rest of EU[2]	Rest of world	Sample size
Couple,[3] dep. child(ren)	51.9	32.5	10.8	1.4	0.6	2.8	810
Couple,[3] no dep. child(ren)	57.6	29.0	9.6	1.2	1.5	1.2	1138
Lone parent, dep. child(ren)	65.2	28.0	5.6	0.6	0.0	0.6	184
Lone parent, no dep. child(ren)	58.3	34.4	5.2	0.0	1.0	1.0	91
Single person	57.5	28.1	9.2	0.6	2.3	2.3	546
Unrelated adults	14.3	44.8	21.0	2.9	8.6	8.6	95

Source: British Household Panel Survey, waves 1 and 9, weighted (sample sizes unweighted).

1. Same or different defined in relation to place of current residence. Areas defined as in Table A2.7.

2. EU countries as defined in 1999.

3. Married or cohabiting.

Table A3.3 Mean age at marriage, by sex and marital status, 1941–2001

Year	Men all	bachelors	widowers	divorced	Women all	spinsters	widows	divorced
1941–50	29.0	27.6	48.3	37.6	26.0	25.2	40.0	33.7
1951–60	27.9	26.4	52.2	38.5	25.1	24.0	45.9	35.2
1961–70	26.5	24.8	55.4	37.7	24.1	22.8	49.2	34.8
1971–80	26.8	24.3	56.9	36.6	24.7	22.5	51.0	34.0
1981–90	28.9	25.6	57.5	38.3	26.6	23.8	51.7	35.7
1991–2000	32.7	28.8	58.4	41.1	30.4	27.0	52.6	38.4
2001	34.8	30.7	57.2	43.1	32.3	28.8	51.4	40.3

Source: Registrar General for Scotland (2002a: Table 7.3).

Table A3.4 Marital status of people aged 16 and over, 1981–2001

% in columns	Year 1981	1991	2001
Single (never married)	25	27	31
Married (first marriage)	63	53	44
Re-married		5	6
Separated (but still legally married)[1]	na	na	4
Divorced	3	5	7
Widowed	9	10	9

Sources: Census 2001 (Table 2); Registrar General for Scotland (1983a: Table 7).

1. 'Separated' not available as a category in 1991 or 1981.

Table A3.5 Live births, by marital status of parents and type of registration, 1981–2001

% in columns	1981	Year 1991	2001
To married parents	87.8	70.9	56.7
To unmarried parents	12.2		
joint registration		21.8	36.6
(same address)			(27.4)
(different addresses)			(9.2)
sole registration		7.4	6.7

Sources: Registrar General for Scotland (1981: Table S1.1); Registrar General for Scotland (2002a: Table 3.2).

Table A3.6 Mixed-religion households, 2001

% households in rows Religion of highest- income householder	Religion of partner of highest income householder					Sample size
	None	Church of Scotland	Roman Catholic	Other Christian	Other religion	
None	78.6	12.1	5.7	3.0	0.6	2332
Church of Scotland	3.8	89.0	4.8	2.2	0.3	4294
Roman Catholic	7.7	17.9	70.0	3.9	0.5	1200
Other Christian	6.1	14.6	5.2	73.6	0.5	691
Other religion	6.3	6.8	1.0	2.1	83.8	195
Total	24.7	50.5	14.4	8.0	2.3	8712

Source: Scottish Household Survey 2001, weighted (sample sizes unweighted).

Restricted to households where highest-income householder is married or cohabiting.

Table A3.7 Mixed-ethnicity households, 2001

% households in rows Ethnicity of highest income householder	Ethnicity of partner of highest income householder		Sample size
	White	Non-white	
White	99.5	0.5	8564
Non-white	33.6	66.4	110
Total	98.6	1.4	8674

Source: Scottish Household Survey 2001, weighted (sample sizes unweighted).

Restricted to households where highest-income householder is married or cohabiting.

Table A3.8 Divorces, by duration of marriage, 1981–2001

% in columns	Year				
Duration of marriage (years)	1981–85	1986–90	1991–95	1996–2000	2001
0–4	17.6	17.6	16.4	14.0	10.9
5–9	29.9	29.2	28.6	26.7	25.6
10–14	19.4	19.4	19.8	19.5	20.3
15–19	12.9	13.8	13.7	14.3	14.7
20–24	9.3	9.8	10.8	11.7	12.5
25–29	5.6	5.3	5.9	7.8	8.6
30+	5.3	5.0	5.0	6.0	7.4
Median (years)	10	10	11	12	13

Source: Registrar General for Scotland (2002a: Table 8.2).

Table A3.9 Divorces, by ground, 1981–2001

	Year		
	1981	1991	2001
Ground for divorce:			
adultery	1703	1198	473
behaviour	4133	3688	1639
desertion	230	82	24
non-cohabitation:			
2 years and consent	2438	5508	5942
5 years	1369	1919	2552
other grounds	2	0	1
Nullity of marriage	6	4	0
Total	9881	12399	10631

Source: Registrar General for Scotland (2002a: Table 8.1).

SUPPLEMENTARY TABLES FOR CHAPTER 4

Table A4.1 Reasons for part-time work, by sex, 2001

% in columns	male	female
Reason		
Financially secure	22.6	4.8
Earn enough part-time	28.5	4.3
Spend time with family	5.2	40.7
Domestic commitments prevent full-time	9.2	32.1
Insufficient child-care facilities	0.0	2.9
Other	34.4	15.2
Sample size	60	837

Restricted to those in part-time work.

Source: Labour Force Survey March–May 2001, weighted (sample sizes unweighted).

Table A4.2 Temporary work, among people in employment aged 16–74, by sex, 1984–2001

% temporary[1] contract	Year		
	1984	1991	2001
Male	6.3 (3650)	4.4 (3243)	6.9 (2427)
Female	7.9 (2583)	7.3 (2776)	8.0 (2567)

Source: Labour Force Survey 1984, 1991, March–May 2001, weighted (sample sizes unweighted in brackets).

1. Seasonal, temporary, casual, contract, agency, other non-permanent.

Table A4.3 Reasons for temporary work, among people in temporary employment aged 16–74, by sex, 1984–2001

% in columns Reason	Year					
	1984		1991		2001	
	male	female	male	female	male	female
Job included training	8.2	5.2	5.9	4.8	7.1	5.3
Could not find permanent job	57.6	44.8	38.1	31.7	43.7	30.7
Did not want permanent job	8.9	21.3	21.5	31.3	17.1	29.2
Other or no answer	25.2	28.8	34.5	32.2	32.0	34.8
Sample size	224	200	138	197	164	203

Source: Labour Force Survey 1984, 1991, March–May 2001, weighted (sample sizes unweighted).

Table A4.4 Sector of work of people in employment aged 16–74, 1979, 1992 and 2001

% in columns Sector	Year		
	1979	1992	2001
Private	57.5	63.5	67.9
Public	42.5	36.5	32.1
public company		7.6	2.0
nationalised industry			0.7
central gvmt., armed forces		4.2	3.3
university etc.			2.2
local gvmt.		16.3	13.7
health board etc.		6.0	6.8
voluntary org. etc.		1.2	2.2
other		1.3	1.2
Sample size	729	957	5569

Sources: Scottish Election Survey 1979 and 1992; Labour Force Survey March–May 2001, weighted (sample sizes unweighted).

Table A4.5 Gross Value Added[1] index, by industry sector, 1975–99

Index, 1975 = 100 Year	Total	Industry sector							
		Agric. & fish. etc.	Mining etc.	Manuf.	Electy etc.	Constr.	Distbn, hotels, etc.	Trnsprt etc.	Fincial & public services
1980	105.0	98.8	134.6	92.7	111.8	90.4	108.5	109.6	118.5
1985	113.8	112.8	161.6	96.4	125.1	84.1	122.0	119.5	133.8
1990	127.2	129.2	163.5	103.9	134.3	98.6	147.1	129.8	150.3
1995	139.3	147.3	157.2	115.2	155.0	110.7	163.1	137.2	162.3
1999	153.1	145.5	179.4	131.2	186.5	112.6	191.7	157.6	190.4

Source: calculated from Scottish Executive (2001d: Table 1.3).

1. Estimates of GDP at constant prices, termed GVA under the European System of Accounts.

Note that, compared to earlier tables, fishing is grouped with agriculture, hotels etc. with retail etc., and all the service sectors with each other.

Table A4.6 Analysis of exports by industry sector, 1996 (producer prices)

£ million	Scottish exports		Domestic content	
	Total exports	Industry as % of total	Exports less associated imports	Industry as % of total
Agriculture, forestry & fishing	1871	4.4	1241	4.7
Mining & quarrying	2131	5.0	1308	5.0
Manufacture of spirits & wines	2390	5.6	1881	7.2
Manufacture of other drinks, food & tobacco	2209	5.1	1266	4.8
Manufacture of textiles, footwear, leather and clothing	1417	3.3	931	3.6
Manufacture of coke, refined petroleum products & nuclear fuel	1441	3.3	1099	4.2
Manufacture of chemicals and man-made fibres	2045	4.8	1146	4.4
Manufacture of metals and metal products	2239	5.2	1466	5.6
Manufacture of machinery & transport equipment	3032	7.0	1650	6.3
Manufacture of office machinery and computers	5860	13.6	2121	8.1
Manufacture of other electrical and optical equipment	3783	8.8	1952	7.5
Other manufacturing	3059	7.1	1836	7.0
Electricity, gas & water supply	200	0.5	147	0.6
Construction	577	1.3	380	1.5
Distribution & catering	3061	7.1	2200	8.4
Transport & communication	2790	6.5	2006	7.7
Financial & business services	2933	6.8	1977	7.6
Public admin., health, education & social services	1777	4.1	1399	5.3
Other services	199	0.5	169	0.6
Total	43015	–	26176	–

Source: Scottish Executive (2001d: Table 1.6).

'Exports' are to rest of the UK and to the rest of the world.

Table A4.7 Manufacturing sector, ownership by industry group, 1998

		Food, drink, tobacco	Textiles, footwear, leather clothing	Petroleum prods, nuclear fuel, chemical & mineral products	Metals, metal goods, mechanical engineering & transport equip.	Electrical/ instrument engineering	Total other manufacturing	Total
Total employment								
UK	%	95	79	70	80	50	89	78
Overseas	%	5	21	30	20	50	11	22
Gross output								
UK	%	89	76	82	68	20	85	59
Overseas	%	11	24	18	32	80	15	41
Gross value added								
UK	%	87	71	68	69	28	89	65
Overseas	%	13	29	32	31	72	11	35
Net capital expenditure								
UK	%	87	66	64	77	23	84	59
Overseas	%	13	34	36	23	77	16	41
Gross value added per head								
UK	£	32700	27100	51100	34600	33300	37600	35400
Overseas	£	90700	41800	54700	62300	82500	39500	67300
Gross value added/gross output								
UK		0.27	0.45	0.18	0.41	0.34	0.46	0.33
Overseas		0.33	0.58	0.38	0.40	0.21	0.33	0.27

Source: Scottish Executive (2001d: Table 2.10).

Table A4.8 Median hours[1] worked among people in employment and aged 16–74, by age and sex, 2001

Age (years)	Male		Female	
	median	sample size	median	sample size
16–29	40	634	36	641
30–44	45	1109	35	1123
45–59	43	910	35	827
60–74	40	164	22	107
All	42	2817	35	2698

Source: Labour Force Survey March–May 2001, weighted.

1. Total usual hours in main job.

Table A4.9 Hours worked among people in employment and aged 16–74, by age and sex, 2001

Age (years)	Number of hours worked per week[1]							
	1–2	3–5	6–15	16–30	31–37	38–48	49–59	60 +
Male								
16–29	0.2	0.8	7.1	8.9	15.0	54.5	7.7	5.9
30–44	0.0	0.1	0.8	3.2	15.7	54.6	14.1	11.4
45–59	0.1	0.2	1.3	4.8	17.2	50.5	14.3	11.7
60–74	0.4	1.1	7.1	14.7	14.1	42.4	10.2	10.0
All	0.1	0.4	2.9	5.8	15.9	52.6	12.3	10.1
Female								
16–29	0.2	1.5	13.3	19.8	24.4	36.6	2.6	1.5
30–44	0.2	0.7	8.1	33.8	24.5	27.8	2.9	1.9
45–59	0.2	0.7	8.9	32.3	27.4	24.8	3.1	2.5
60–74	0.8	3.1	22.6	37.5	15.9	14.3	2.5	3.3
All	0.2	1.0	10.3	29.8	25.0	28.7	2.9	2.0

Source: Census 2001 (Table S29).

1. Total usual hours per week in main job.

Table A4.10 Median hours[1] worked among people in employment and aged 16–74, by economic activity, 2001

	Male		Female	
	median	sample size	median	sample size
Employed, part-time	16	173	20	1107
Employed, full-time	43	2236	38	1453
Self-employed, part-time	20	32	15	55
Self-employed, full-time	50	355	40	67

Source: Labour Force Survey March–May 2001, weighted.

1. Total usual hours in main job.

Table A4.11 Median hours[1] worked among people in employment and aged 16–74, by age and industry section, 2001

Section	Male		Female	
	median	sample size	median	sample size
Agriculture, hunting and forestry	50	81	*	*
Fishing	*	*	*	*
Mining, quarrying	52	78	*	*
Manufacturing	42	547	38	250
Electricity, gas and water supply	*	*	*	*
Construction	44	374	*	*
Wholesale, retail and motor trade	43	340	25	443
Hotels and restaurants	42	97	28	186
Transport, storage and communication	44	269	36	93
Financial intermediation	40	89	35	138
Real estate, renting and business activity	42	265	35	196
Public administration and defence	40	200	36	214
Education	38	136	35	320
Health and social work	40	128	33	612
Other community, social and personal	40	141	32	149
Private households with employees	*	*	*	*

Source: Labour Force Survey March–May 2001, weighted (sample sizes unweighted).

1. Total usual weekly hours in main job.

* Sample size less than 50.

Table A4.12 Accidents at work, among people in employment aged 16–74, by sex, by age and by class, 2001

	Whether had work-related accident in previous 12 months			Sample size
	None	Accident causing		
		1–2 days off work	More than 2 days off work	
Sex:				
male	95.5	2.0	2.5	2719
female	97.9	1.1	1.0	2621
Age group:				
16–29	95.7	1.9	2.4	1236
30–44	96.8	1.6	1.6	2168
45–59	97.2	1.4	1.4	1646
60+	97.2	1.0	1.8	290
NS-SEC class:				
Higher manag. & prof.	99.5	0.5	0.0	593
Lower manag. & prof.	98.2	1.0	0.8	1387
Intermediate	98.1	0.8	1.1	705
Small employers and self-empl.	96.0	1.8	2.2	394
Lower supervisory and technical	93.0	2.8	4.1	606
Semi-routine	96.1	1.1	2.8	777
Routine	93.5	3.6	2.8	639
Never worked, unemployed	96.9	2.0	1.1	239
All	96.6	1.6	1.8	5340

Source: Labour Force Survey December 2001–February 2002, weighted (sample sizes unweighted).

Table A4.13 Injuries and deaths at work, people in employment, 1997–2001

	Year	
	1997–98	2000–1
Fatal:		
employees	28	23
self-employed	9	4
Major:		
employees	2337	2237
self-employed	32	71
Three-day:		
employees	10676	8913
self-employed	39	66

Source: Health and Safety Executive (2002: Table 1).

Table A4.14 Trade union membership, among people in employment aged 16–74, by industry section, 1991 and 2001

Section	Year					
	1991		2001			
	% in union or staff association	Sample size	% in union or staff association	% with unions present at work	% with union recognition at work	Sample size[1]
Agriculture, hunting, forestry	10.8	149	14.2	7.4	13.6	86
Fishing	7.9	27	9.6	0.0	0.0	18
Mining, quarrying	30.4	110	10.5	37.8	7.1	87
Manufacturing	41.8	1143	28.7	36.5	35.7	747
Electricity, gas, water supply	88.8	77	62.8	62.8	73.8	51
Construction	27.1	479	19.6	28.3	32.9	365
Wholesale, retail, motor trade	15.8	856	13.0	23.7	22.0	725
Hotels and restaurants	11.4	344	7.1	9.0	8.5	276
Transport, storage, communication	59.0	438	41.0	33.7	52.7	363
Financial intermediation	55.1	201	33.0	57.3	53.1	242
Real estate, renting, business activity	17.1	355	15.5	19.6	15.2	455
Public admin., defence	63.2	518	61.9	78.5	80.8	441
Education	67.1	407	66.5	79.5	78.4	439
Health, social work	59.9	592	48.7	52.9	59.2	678
Other community, social, personal	32.8	311	25.3	22.7	33.7	279
Private households with employees	1.9	43	22.7	0.0	26.4	9
All	39.2	6083	32.5	35.9	43.6	5261

Source: Labour Force Survey 1991 and September–November 2001, weighted (sample sizes unweighted).

1. Sample size for individual union membership. For union presence in 2001, sample sizes are about half those shown, and for union recognition they are about three-quarters of those shown; the balance is accounted for by respondents' giving no reply to these questions.

Table A4.15 Economic activity, by broad ethnic group and sex, among people aged 16–74, 2001

% in columns	White	Indian	Pakistani and other South Asian	Chinese	Other
All					
Employed, part-time	11.2	7.7	8.6	7.0	7.9
Employed, full-time	40.5	32.1	18.8	26.2	30.2
Self-employed, part-time	1.4	2.0	1.9	1.4	1.5
Self-employed, full-time	5.1	10.6	11.2	10.3	3.9
Unemployed[1]	4.0	3.8	5.1	3.2	5.4
Retired	14.1	5.3	4.0	6.4	3.4
Student	7.0	19.5	19.3	30.9	28.2
Full-time looking after home	5.4	8.6	15.2	8.0	8.5
Long-term sick or disabled	7.5	4.2	5.9	2.1	3.6
Other	3.8	6.2	9.9	4.5	7.5
Male					
Employed, part-time	2.9	4.7	8.7	4.1	4.2
Employed, full-time	51.2	39.4	24.8	31.9	36.8
Self-employed, part-time	1.2	1.7	1.9	1.1	1.3
Self-employed, full-time	8.5	15.1	18.7	14.9	5.7
Unemployed[1]	5.3	3.7	6.4	3.6	6.5
Retired	11.6	5.0	3.9	6.0	2.9
Student	6.6	20.8	20.1	32.0	30.0
Full-time looking after home	0.9	0.8	1.6	0.9	1.1
Long-term sick or disabled	8.2	4.1	6.0	2.1	4.1
Other	3.4	4.8	7.8	3.5	7.5
Female					
Employed, part-time	19.0	11.1	8.5	9.9	11.5
Employed, full-time	30.5	23.7	12.2	20.5	23.8
Self-employed, part-time	1.5	2.4	1.9	1.7	1.7
Self-employed, full-time	2.0	5.5	3.2	5.8	2.1
Unemployed[1]	2.6	4.0	3.6	2.8	4.3
Retired	16.4	5.7	4.0	6.8	4.0
Student	7.4	18.0	18.4	29.8	26.5
Full-time looking after home	9.6	17.5	29.9	15.1	15.6
Long-term sick or disabled	6.8	4.4	5.8	2.1	3.0
Other	4.2	7.7	12.3	5.4	7.5

Source: Census 2001 (Table S208).

1. ILO definition

Table A4.16 Industry section, of people in employment aged 16–74, by broad ethnic group, 2001

% in columns Section	White	Indian	Pakistani and other South Asian	Chinese	Other
Agriculture, hunting and forestry	2.2	0.5	0.5	0.7	0.8
Fishing	0.3	0.0	0.1	0.1	0.1
Mining, quarrying	1.2	0.9	0.4	0.5	2.1
Manufacturing	13.3	6.1	5.5	5.2	8.7
Electricity, gas and water supply	1.0	0.8	0.7	0.3	0.5
Construction	7.6	1.5	1.8	1.7	2.6
Wholesale, retail and motor trade	14.3	22.4	38.4	8.2	11.7
Hotels and restaurants	5.5	11.0	14.2	51.0	12.3
Transport, storage and communication	6.7	5.5	6.3	1.8	4.5
Financial intermediation	4.7	4.6	3.6	3.0	3.8
Real estate, renting and business activity	11.2	13.8	8.8	8.3	13.6
Public administration and defence	7.0	4.0	3.5	1.9	5.2
Education	7.3	6.6	4.2	6.6	9.7
Health and social work	12.4	18.8	8.7	7.7	18.1
Other	5.3	3.5	3.3	2.9	6.2

Source: Census 2001 (Table S211).

Table A4.17 Occupation[1] of people in employment aged 16–74, by broad ethnic group, 2001

% in columns Occupation group	White	Indian	Pakistani and other South Asian	Chinese	Other
Managers and senior officials	12.1	20.0	25.8	14.0	11.6
Professional occupations	10.7	30.2	12.1	14.9	20.3
Associate professional and technical	14.0	9.1	8.5	7.3	16.7
Administrative and secretarial	12.8	7.7	7.1	5.8	8.6
Skilled trades	12.2	5.9	8.0	28.1	7.5
Personal service	7.2	3.2	3.2	2.5	7.7
Sales and customer service	8.6	12.3	21.6	9.2	9.5
Process, plant and machine operatives	9.7	3.5	4.1	1.7	4.3
Elementary occupations	12.7	8.2	9.4	16.5	13.7

Source: Census 2001 (Table S209).

1. Standard Occupational Classification 2000.

Table A4.18 Occupation[1] of people in employment aged 16–74, by broad religious group, 2001

| % in columns | Religious group | | | | |
Occupation group	None	Church of Scotland	Roman Catholic	Other Christian	Other religion
Managers and senior officials	13.5	14.3	12.4	15.8	18.2
Professional occupations	11.6	9.5	11.0	17.0	18.2
Associate professional and technical	12.7	10.9	12.2	15.8	13.6
Administrative and secretarial	15.1	16.5	19.2	14.8	17.5
Skilled trades	12.0	11.4	12.1	6.4	4.5
Personal service[2]	18.3	20.0	17.7	20.9	18.8
Sales and customer service	8.2	9.3	8.5	4.3	4.5
Process, plant and machine operatives	8.7	8.0	7.0	5.1	4.5
Sample size	2006	2954	858	495	128

Source: Scottish Household Survey 2001, weighted (sample sizes unweighted).

1. Standard Occupational Classification 2000.

2. The Scottish Household Survey variable used here (RSOC) seems to have conflated 'personal service' and 'elementary occupations' (compare, for example, Table A4.17). This will not affect the patterns shown here for professional employment, which are the only aspects of this table commented on in the text.

Table A4.19 Industry section, of people in employment aged 16–74, by broad religious group, 2001

| % in columns | Religious group | | | | |
Section	None	Church of Scotland	Roman Catholic	Other Christian	Other religion
Agriculture, hunting and forestry	2.1	2.7	0.7	2.1	0.0
Fishing	0.5	0.3	0.1	1.0	0.0
Mining, quarrying	0.9	0.3	0.2	1.2	0.7
Manufacturing	14.6	14.9	15.1	12.6	8.6
Electricity, gas and water supply	1.3	1.3	1.1	0.2	0.0
Construction	6.2	6.3	8.8	3.9	3.9
Wholesale, retail and motor trade	13.4	11.5	10.8	11.5	12.5
Hotels and restaurants	6.0	3.7	5.5	6.0	9.9
Transport, storage and communication	6.5	7.1	6.5	3.3	5.9
Financial intermediation	4.2	4.0	4.1	2.3	3.3
Real estate, renting and business activity	13.0	12.4	11.8	15.4	11.2
Public administration and defence	6.2	8.1	8.8	8.4	7.9
Education	7.1	8.5	8.7	9.9	9.2
Health and social work	11.8	14.1	12.6	17.1	20.4
Other community, social and personal	5.9	4.1	4.8	4.9	6.6
Private households with employees	0.2	0.3	0.3	0.2	0.0
Sample size	2006	2957	859	497	127

Source: Scottish Household Survey 2001, weighted (sample sizes unweighted).

SUPPLEMENTARY TABLES FOR CHAPTER 5

Table A5.1 Household income by source, 1988–97

Year	1980	1985	1990	1997
Average weekly gross income per household (£), current prices, separate assessment of married couples			283.77	367.40
Average weekly gross income per household (£), current prices, joint assessment of married couples	134.85	206.79	294.15	
Average weekly gross income per household (£), indexed to 1980 level at constant prices[1]	100	108	116	124
Source (%):				
wages and salaries	75.6	69.9	64.4	66.0
social security benefits	12.7	14.0	13.5	16.1
self-employment	11.7	16.1	22.1	7.8
other income				10.1

Sources: Scottish Office (1998: Table 7b1); Scottish Office (1993: Table 10.13); Scottish Office (1992a: Table 10.11); Scottish Office (1988: Table 10.13).

1. Using Economic History web site (www.eh.net), splicing together the two series at 1990.

Because of the Inland Revenue's shift to independent taxation of husbands and wives in 1990–1, there is discontinuity in that year (Scottish Office 1993: 127). The 1993 source recalculates the 1988–90 figures as if they had been for individuals separately, and that is the source of the 1990 figure in the first row. The percentage distribution in that year is from the separate-assessment series. The third row splices these together.

Table A5.2 Distribution of average weekly household income, 1988 and 1997

	Year	
	1988	1997
Average	248.31	367.40
Cumulative distribution (%)		
under £75	20.5	8.3
under £125	35.8	21.6
under £200	50.8	36.0
under £275	64.1	49.3
under £350	75.1	57.6
under £425	82.7	70.2
under £600	93.5	83.4

Sources: Scottish Office (1993: Table 10.13); Scottish Office (1998: Table 7B2).

Table A5.3 Percentage of individuals below median[1] and 60% median equivalised[2] income, by family type, 1998–9

%	Below median	Below 60% median
Pensioner couple	64	(22)
Single pensioner	64	(31)
Couple with children	47	19
Couple without children	30	11
Single with children	90	55
Single without children	(49)	25
All family types	50	22

Source: Scottish Executive (2001d: Table 3.2). Figures in brackets are particularly uncertain because of sampling error.

1. Median is for all of Britain.

2. Household income is equivalised to take account of the number of individuals living in the household. After housing costs.

Table A5.4 Percentage of dependent children below median[1] and 60% median equivalised[2] income, by economic status of family, 1998–9

%	Below median	Below 60% median
One or more full-time workers:		
self-employed	49	27
employees, 1–2 children	38	7
employees, 3+ children	56	27
Others:		
lone parents	96	64
couples	94	69
All economic types	59	30

Source: Scottish Executive (2001d: Table 3.3).

1. Median is for all of Britain.

2. Household income is equivalised to take account of the number of individuals living in the household. After housing costs.

Table A5.5 Average gross weekly earnings of full-time employees, by broad social class and sex, 1980–2000

£ (current prices) Year (April):	Occupational class[1]					
	Manual			Non-manual		
	male	female	female as % of male	male	female	female as % of male
1980	112.2	66.3	59.1	139.8	78.2	55.9
1985	164.2	99.4	60.5	224.0	125.6	56.1
1990	231.7	141.2	60.9	327.4	200.6	61.3
1995	284.5	186.0	65.4	413.2	272.7	66.0
2000	335.4	217.3	64.8	496.4	335.3	67.5

Sources: Scottish Office (1992a: Table 10.2); Scottish Office (1997a: Table 9C1); Scottish Executive (2001d: Table 4.7). All use New Earnings Survey.

1. Based on occupational group.

Table A5.6 Net annual household income, by socio-economic group of highest income householder, 2001

% of households in rows	Income band[1] (£)					Sample size
Socio-economic group of highest income householder	0–6000	6000–10000	10000–15000	15000–20000	20000 +	
Employers and managers, large establishments	1.8	1.9	5.7	11.7	78.8	918
Employers and managers, small establishments	2.4	5.2	13.0	19.4	60.1	683
Professionals, self-employed	1.7	1.7	7.0	7.8	81.7	116
Professionals, employees	1.3	1.3	5.8	13.3	78.3	507
Intermediate non-manual	1.5	5.0	15.1	20.9	57.5	1486
Junior non-manual	6.1	15.8	29.9	18.2	30.0	1035
Personal service	10.1	28.2	29.9	16.1	15.8	307
Foremen and supervisors	2.0	5.6	13.9	21.0	57.5	611
Skilled manual	3.1	7.9	20.6	28.7	39.7	1124
Semi-skilled manual	6.0	18.4	27.7	22.7	25.2	851
Unskilled manual	12.2	26.7	28.8	18.9	13.4	343
Other self-employed	6.5	9.2	21.1	24.5	38.7	482
All	3.9	9.4	18.3	19.9	48.4	8463

Source: Scottish Household Survey 2001, weighted (sample sizes unweighted).

1. Net income after taxation and other deductions from employment, benefits and other sources, brought into the household by the highest income earner, their spouse, and any contribution from other household members.

Table A5.7 Net annual household income, by religious group, 2001

% of households in rows	Income band[1] (£)					Sample size
Religious group of highest income householder	0–6000	6000–10000	10000–15000	15000–20000	20000 +	
None	9.6	18.5	19.9	16.8	35.1	3959
Church of Scotland	11.9	24.2	21.7	14.2	27.9	7370
Roman Catholic	11.0	22.0	21.8	16.0	29.3	2140
Other Christian	10.8	21.4	19.2	13.2	35.5	1174
Other religion	11.1	21.0	21.3	15.9	30.8	318
All	11.1	22.1	21.0	15.1	30.7	14961

Source: Scottish Household Survey 2001, weighted (sample sizes unweighted).

1. Net income after taxation and other deductions from employment, benefits and other sources, brought into the household by the highest income earner, their spouse, and any contribution from other household members.

Table A5.8 Net annual household income, by broad region, 2001

% of households in rows	Income band[1] (£)					Sample size
Region	0–6000	6000–10000	10000–15000	15000–20000	20000+	
West	11.2	24.1	22.1	14.8	27.7	6561
Central and Tayside	11.6	22.7	20.5	15.3	29.9	2027
East	10.8	19.4	20.2	15.2	34.3	3359
North and Islands	10.6	19.6	19.4	15.8	34.6	3014
All	11.1	22.1	21.0	15.1	30.7	14961

Source: Scottish Household Survey 2001, weighted (sample sizes unweighted).

1. Net income after taxation and other deductions from employment, benefits and other sources, brought into the household by the highest income earner, their spouse, and any contribution from other household members.

Table A5.9 Net annual household income, by broad ethnic group, 2001

% of households in rows	Income band[1] (£)					Sample size
Ethnic group of highest income householder[2]	0–6000	6000–10000	10000–15000	15000–20000	20000+	
White	11.0	22.2	21.1	15.1	30.7	14793
Non-white	17.6	15.3	18.8	17.6	30.6	163
All	11.1	22.1	21.0	15.1	30.7	14956

Source: Scottish Household Survey 2001, weighted (sample sizes unweighted).

1. Net income after taxation and other deductions from employment, benefits and other sources, brought into the household by the highest income earner, their spouse, and any contribution from other household members.

Table A5.10 Ownership of land, 1970 and 1995

% of land[1]	Number of owners	
	1970	1995
10	17	18
20	55	58
30	125	136
40	253	283
50	515	608
57.8	985	1411
60	1136	

1 All kinds: for example, urban as well as rural, publicly as well as privately owned.

Source: Wightman (1996: 158).

Table A5.11 Estate numbers and gross values, UK, 2000

Net estate value (£k, lower limit)	Number	Amount (£k)
0	4134	30288
10	1957	53526
25	2019	95892
40	1129	62464
50	1128	72492
60	1935	154538
80	1654	171385
100	2770	371010
150	1245	233825
200	891	233140
300	657	265781
500	360	252297
1000	113	156596
2000	41	158159
Total	20035	2311392

Source: Inland Revenue web site (Table T13.1).

Table A5.12 Concentration of wealth among adult population, UK, 1986–2000

	Percentage of wealth owned by					
	top 1%	2%	5%	10%	25%	50%
1986	18	24	36	50	73	90
1991	17	24	35	47	71	92
1996	20	27	40	52	74	93
1997	22	30	43	54	75	93
2000	22	29	42	54	74	94

Source: Inland Revenue web site (Table T13.5).

Table A5.13 Amount of savings and investments by net annual household income, 2001

% in columns Amount of savings or investments (£)	Net household income (£)					All
	0–6000	6000–10000	10000–15000	15000–20000	20000+	
<1000	30	30	26	26	14	22
1000–5000	26	29	27	26	25	26
5000–10000	13	15	15	15	17	16
10000–16000	11	10	10	11	12	11
16000–30000	8	6	8	8	10	9
30000–75000	7	8	9	9	11	9
£75000+	4	3	5	6	10	7
Sample size	799	1675	2186	1921	5182	11763

Source: Scottish Executive (2003c: Table 6.36), weighted (sample size unweighted).

Restricted to households with any savings or investments.

Supplementary tables for Chapter 6

Table A6.1 Socio-economic classification of economically active population aged 16–74, 1991 and 2001

% in columns	Year	
Socio-economic classification	1991	2001
Large employers and higher managerial	2	4
Higher professional	5	7
Lower managerial and professional	20	25
Intermediate	17	13
Small employers and self-employed	8	8
Lower supervisory and technical	10	10
Semi-routine	17	16
Routine	19	12
Full-time student	1	4

Source: Census 2001 (Table 16); the balance of the percentages is people who could not be classified.

Table A6.2 Industry section by broad socio-economic group, people in employment aged 16–74, 1981–2000

% in rows Industry section[1]	Prof., m'grl	Inter. non-man.	Junior non-man.	Skilled man.	Semi-skilled man.	Un-skilled man.	Unclass. or armed forces	Sample size
1981								
Agriculture, hunting, forestry and fishing	34.7	0.5	1.8	6.9	6.9	49.1	–	366
Mining, quarrying	11.3	2.1	7.7	42.3	30.8	5.3	0.4	230
Manufacturing	9.7	3.8	13.3	40.6	25.9	6.5	0.3	2174
Electricity, gas, water supply	12.0	3.1	28.9	37.1	11.8	5.7	1.5	126
Construction	13.3	2.4	7.1	57.5	9.5	10.2	–	740
Wholesale, retail, motor trade	19.7	3.3	47.5	20.5	5.7	3.2	0.1	1160
Hotels, restaurants	14.2	0.3	8.0	6.6	58.8	12.1	–	310
Transport, storage, communication	8.7	3.6	18.3	47.8	16.7	4.9	–	589
Financial intermediation	14.0	2.9	77.0	2.2	0.4	3.6	–	228
Real estate, renting, business activity	26.8	8.1	40.8	12.9	6.9	4.1	0.3	292
Public admin., defence	12.2	12.9	35.9	9.8	12.2	7.2	9.7	769
Education	10.6	46.4	6.9	2.1	14.6	19.5	–	568
Health, social work	10.1	41.8	10.1	5.5	28.5	4.1	–	768
Other community, social, personal	15.5	4.8	18.7	12.6	28.6	19.0	0.8	252

cont'd over

Table A6.2 cont'd

% in rows Industry section[1]	Broad socio-economic group							Sample size
	Prof., m'grl	Inter. non-man.	Junior non-man.	Skilled man.	Semi-skilled man.	Un-skilled man.	Unclass. or armed forces	
1991								
Agriculture, hunting, forestry and fishing	37.4	1.7	3.0	14.0	8.5	34.9	0.5	180
Mining, quarrying	33.6	11.4	14.9	23.8	11.5	4.9	–	110
Manufacturing	14.6	7.1	9.7	41.3	23.5	3.7	–	1152
Electricity, gas, water supply	19.7	8.2	13.2	44.4	12.1	2.5	–	79
Construction	18.6	3.3	7.1	55.0	7.7	8.1	0.2	487
Wholesale, retail, motor trade	19.5	8.4	41.9	21.5	6.3	2.3	–	864
Hotels, restaurants	15.0	2.3	8.8	5.9	50.0	18.0	–	344
Transport, storage, communication	15.1	6.3	9.6	46.5	17.5	5.0	–	403
Financial intermediation	25.7	21.4	49.1	2.3	–	1.5	–	202
Real estate, renting, business activity	34.0	20.0	29.4	8.7	5.6	1.8	0.5	358
Public admin., defence	14.5	25.5	32.9	8.9	8.6	4.8	4.8	521
Education	30.4	38.7	8.3	2.4	11.3	8.5	0.6	409
Health, social work	13.4	45.4	6.8	5.0	14.9	14.4	0.2	594
Other community, social, personal	12.1	8.3	11.7	17.1	29.4	21.4	–	315
2001								
Agriculture, hunting, forestry and fishing	34.7	1.4	2.4	17.3	7.4	34.4	2.4	138
Mining, quarrying	41.7	12.1	9.7	25.7	7.8	2.9	–	102
Manufacturing	22.0	8.1	9.7	34.6	22.0	3.2	0.4	807
Electricity, gas, water supply	28.6	11.0	14.1	39.0	3.5	3.7	–	56
Construction	23.2	3.6	5.7	51.8	7.1	8.1	0.4	451
Wholesale, retail, motor trade	22.3	9.0	44.0	15.4	5.9	3.0	0.4	810
Hotels, restaurants	19.4	1.5	8.0	6.6	52.5	11.6	0.3	328
Transport, storage, communication	16.3	5.3	16.9	43.0	14.2	3.7	0.7	396
Financial intermediation	27.9	22.1	42.8	4.0	1.9	1.4	–	229
Real estate, renting, business activity	40.1	18.0	20.1	9.5	5.9	5.7	0.8	438
Public admin., defence	17.8	22.7	37.3	4.8	7.7	3.3	6.3	420
Education	26.9	37.5	7.0	3.4	18.8	6.4	–	473
Health, social work	18.1	38.2	8.4	6.0	22.5	6.7	–	716
Other community, social, personal	21.1	15.1	16.2	13.1	23.2	11.1	0.2	337

Sources: Labour Force Survey 1981, 1991, March–May 2000, weighted (sample sizes unweighted).

1. Fishing combined with agriculture etc. to get reasonable sample sizes. Employees in private households, diplomats, and inadequately classified industry section are omitted.

Table A6.3 Socio-economic classification of economically active population aged 16–74, by sex, 1991 and 2001

% in columns	Male		Female	
Socio-economic classification	1991	2001	1991	2001
Large employers and higher managerial	3	5	1	2
Higher professional	7	9	2	4
Lower managerial and professional	19	22	21	28
Intermediate	9	7	27	20
Small employers and self-employed	11	11	4	5
Lower supervisory and technical	16	15	3	5
Semi-routine	13	12	21	20
Routine	20	15	18	9
Full-time student	1	3	1	5

Source: Census 2001 (Table 16); the balance of the percentages is people who could not be classified.

Table A6.4 Socio-economic classification of people aged 16–74, by age group, 2001

% in columns	Age group (years)			
Socio-economic classification	16–29	30–44	45–59	60 +
Higher managerial and professional	7.5	11.4	9.8	8.2
Lower managerial and professional	20.0	27.6	26.3	19.8
Intermediate	17.7	13.1	11.7	10.4
Small employers and self-employed	3.0	8.0	10.7	14.8
Lower supervisory and technical	11.5	10.6	10.3	9.5
Semi-routine	22.5	16.3	17.0	18.2
Routine	17.6	13.0	14.2	19.0

Source: Census 2001 (Table S42).

Excludes those who had never worked, were long-term unemployed, or could not be classified for other reasons such as retirement.

Table A6.5 Socio-economic classification of people aged 16–74, by broad ethnic group, 2001

% in columns	Ethnic group				
Socio-economic classification	White	Indian	Pakistani and other South Asian	Chinese	Other
Higher managerial and professional	9.2	25.4	8.1	12.9	16.6
Lower managerial and professional	23.7	16.1	11.5	12.1	22.5
Intermediate	12.8	7.7	6.9	5.8	10.2
Small employers and self-employed	7.6	16.0	19.3	20.8	6.6
Lower supervisory and technical	10.1	3.6	4.0	6.1	5.9
Semi-routine	17.0	11.9	15.9	23.2	14.0
Routine	14.2	5.3	5.4	7.1	9.4
Never worked, long-term unemployed	5.4	14.0	28.9	12.0	14.9

Source: Census 2001 (Table S213).

Excludes those who could not be classified.

Table A6.6 Socio-economic group of economically active population aged 16–74, by broad religious group, 2001

% in columns Socio-economic group	Religious group				
	None	Church of Scotland	Roman Catholic	Other Christian	Other religion
Employers and managers, large establishments	7.8	7.7	8.6	9.2	8.9
Employers and managers, small establishments	6.4	6.4	4.5	7.4	7.1
Professionals, self-employed	1.3	0.7	0.9	1.7	3.0
Professionals, employees	4.9	3.4	3.7	9.4	7.7
Intermediate non-manual	18.7	17.8	18.8	20.8	21.4
Junior non-manual	17.7	19.4	21.4	17.5	17.3
Personal service	5.2	4.8	4.9	5.0	6.5
Foreman and supervisors	4.3	4.3	4.0	1.7	1.2
Skilled manual	8.3	9.9	8.9	4.2	5.4
Semi-skilled manual	9.3	9.8	8.5	6.8	6.0
Unskilled manual	4.0	3.9	4.6	1.8	1.2
Other self employed	4.1	3.2	3.8	6.8	3.6
Other or inadequately classified	8.2	8.7	7.5	7.6	10.7
Sample size	2171	3159	933	529	142

Source: Scottish Household Survey 2001, weighted (sample sizes unweighted).

Table A6.7 Socio-economic group of economically active population aged 16–74, by place of birth, 1999

% in columns Socio-economic group	Place of birth		
	Outwith Scotland	In a different region[1] of Scotland	In the same region[1] of Scotland
Employers and managers, large establishments	10.2	10.9	7.8
Employers and managers, small establishments	8.3	7.5	6.9
Professionals, self-employed	1.6	2.7	0.7
Professionals, employees	10.6	6.1	2.1
Intermediate non-manual	19.7	23.5	16.7
Junior non-manual	14.6	17.2	18.4
Personal service	4.3	2.9	6.5
Foreman and supervisors	3.5	3.1	4.9
Skilled manual	5.1	8.0	11.0
Semi-skilled manual	5.9	6.3	10.5
Unskilled manual	2.0	3.4	3.9
Other self-employed	7.5	4.2	5.2
Farmers (employers, managers and self-employed)	1.2	1.3	0.5
Agricultural workers	1.6	0.4	1.4
Inadequately classified	3.9	2.5	3.4
Sample size	257	447	899

Source: British Household Panel Survey, waves 1 and 9, weighted (sample sizes unweighted).

1. For definition of these regions, see Table A2.7.

Table A6.8 Social mobility at first job, by birth cohort and sex, among people aged 23–62 in 1999

% in columns within sex Mobility at first job	Birth cohort 1937–46	1947–56	1957–66	1967–76
Male				
Downwards	38.7	36.0	45.0	49.5
Immobile	23.4	20.2	22.3	20.2
Upwards	38.0	43.8	32.7	30.3
Sample size	127	172	224	177
Female				
Downwards	21.4	25.8	30.0	36.6
Immobile	16.8	12.4	17.0	12.8
Upwards	61.8	61.8	52.9	50.6
Sample size	124	190	262	193

Source: see notes to Table 6.3.

Uses 11-class version of Goldthorpe scheme, not the condensed versions in Tables 6.3 to 6.5.

Table A6.9 Perceived absence of class conflict, by socio-economic group, 1979 and 1999

Broad socio-economic group[1]	Year 1979	1999	Sample sizes 1979	1999
Professional and managerial	34.4	45.0	90	292
Intermediate non-manual	28.1	42.3	89	189
Junior non-manual	22.7	38.7	88	237
Skilled manual	20.1	39.8	139	274
Semi-skilled manual	24.2	32.8	95	239
Unskilled manual	34.4	36.7	32	113
All	24.0	39.0	533	1344

Sources: Scottish Election Survey 1979 and Scottish Social Attitudes Survey 1999, weighted (sample sizes unweighted).

Table shows percentage perceiving that classes 'can get along' in 1999 (balance being 'a lot of conflict', 'just a little conflict' or no answer) and that there is 'no conflict' between people on high and low incomes in 1979 (balance being 'not very serious conflict', 'fairly serious conflict', 'very serious conflict' or no answer).

1. Omitting armed forces and inadequately classified.

Table A6.10 Party identification, by self-assigned class, 1979 and 1999

% in rows	Party				Sample sizes
Self-assigned class	Con.	Lab.	Lib. etc	SNP	
Working class					
1979	21.0	46.3	9.4	11.6	458
1999	10.8	46.0	10.5	22.5	1026
Middle class					
1979	59.9	13.8	10.5	5.3	152
1999	29.8	30.3	16.6	14.6	389

Sources: Scottish Election Survey 1979 and Scottish Social Attitudes Survey 1999, weighted (sample sizes unweighted).

Balance of percentages are people identifying with other parties, or with none, and people not choosing any class.

SUPPLEMENTARY TABLES FOR CHAPTER 7

Table A7.1 Staying-on rates[1] in school, by sex, 1979–80 to 1998–9

Year	Male	Female	All
1979–80	42.6	47.9	45.1
1984–85	42.0	50.5	46.2
1989–90	51.2	61.8	56.2
1994–95	61.1	70.3	65.6
1998–99	62.3	71.6	67.0

Sources: 1979–80: Scottish School Leavers Survey 1981 (weighted; unweighted sample sizes 11,038 male and 12,090 female); 1984–85 to 1994–95: Scottish Office (1996b: Tables 2 and 3); 1998–99: Scottish Executive (2001e: Table 1).

1. The percentage of leavers who left in Spring of school fifth year or later.

Table A7.2 Participation rates in education, among people aged 22 or older, 2000–1

% of all in age group	Age group (years)					
	22–24	25–29	30–39	40–49	50+	All 22+
Further education: full-time	1	1	1	0	0	0
Further education: part-time	6	6	6	5	2	4
Higher education: full-time	15	5	2	1	0	2
Higher education: part-time	3	4	4	3	1	2
All education	26	15	12	9	3	8

Source: Scottish Executive (2003d: Table 1).

Some column totals do not equal the figure for 'all education' because of rounding.

Table A7.3 Numbers of students in higher education, by sector, level and mode, 1990–1 to 2000–1

	Sector[1]	Year	
		1990–91	2000–1
Full-time:			
postgraduate	HEI	10768	18001
	FEC	99	69
first degree	HEI	70641	104429
	FEC	59	1025
other HE	HEI	6004	11824
	FEC	9273	30268
Part-time:			
postgraduate	HEI	6731	29332
	FEC	113	419
first degree	HEI	3512	9300
	FEC	489	1299
other HE	HEI	7108	17078
	FEC	23131	39869
Total		137928	262913

Sources: for 1990–91, Scottish Office (1992b: Tables 2 and 3); for 2000–1, Scottish Executive (2002e: Table 1a).

The series has a discontinuity in 1994–5 when the Higher Education Statistics Agency took over the compilation of the statistics on participation in the older universities from the Universities Statistical Record. The largest numerical change seems to have been the inclusion of continuing education students among part-time postgraduate students for the first time, leading to a rise of 78% in their recorded number between 1993–4 and 1994–5 to 17,701: see Scottish Office (1997c: Table 5).

1. Sector: HEI is higher education institution (including both the universities and the central institutions and colleges in 1990–1); FEC is further education.

Table A7.4 Highest attainment of school leavers, by sex, 1981–99

% in rows Year	Highest attainment in public examinations		
	No awards[1]	3 + Higher Grade passes	5 + Higher grade passes
Male			
1980–81	32.3	18.6	9.6
1985–86	26.2	19.1	10.4
1990–91	11.7	23.9	13.2
1995–96	8.1	26.0	15.2
1998–99	4.9	27.2	15.6
Female			
1980–81	27.8	20.8	9.5
1985–86	21.2	22.2	10.8
1990–91	8.9	29.2	15.1
1995–96	6.4	33.3	19.5
1998–99	3.6	36.2	21.0
All			
1980–81	30.1	19.7	9.5
1985–86	23.8	20.6	10.6
1990–91	10.3	26.5	14.1
1995–96	7.2	29.6	17.3
1998–99	4.2	31.7	18.3

Source: for 1980–81, Scottish Office (1992c: Tables 1 and 4.1); for 1985–86 and 1990–91, Scottish Office (1995b: Tables 6 and 7); for 1995–96, Scottish Office (1999: Tables 15 and 16); for 1998–99, Scottish Executive (2001f: Tables 4 and 5). Since 1999, the information has been published in a different format, and so is not directly comparable.

1. For 1980–81 to 1995–96, no awards in Higher Grade, Standard Grade or Ordinary Grade; for 1988–89, no award in these or in National Certificate modules. In that last year, the proportions gaining at most NC modules were 1.9% of males, 1.4% of females, and 1.6% overall.

Table A7.5 Highest educational attainment, among people aged 16–59, by sex, 1981–2001

| % in columns | | Year | |
Highest educational attainment	1981	1991	2001
Male			
First degree, higher degree, professional qualification	7.8	9.7	16.2
HND, HNC, etc	2.1	5.0	10.0
Higher Grade, A level, etc	8.6	26.9	22.0
O Grade, Standard Grade, etc	39.3	16.1	28.5
Scotvec modules, CSE, etc	3.8	6.2	9.9
None of these or no answer	38.3	36.0	13.3
Sample size	6223	3918	3587
Female			
First degree, higher degree, professional qualification	10.0	11.4	18.3
HND, HNC, etc	0.4	2.7	9.2
Higher Grade, A level, etc	9.4	20.3	18.5
O Grade, Standard Grade, etc	18.0	19.0	23.4
Scotvec modules, CSE, etc	6.4	5.2	10.3
None of these or no answer	55.9	41.4	20.3
Sample size	6336	4270	3835

Sources: Labour Force Survey 1981, 1991, March–May 2001, weighted (sample sizes unweighted).

Table A7.6 Highest educational attainment of school leavers, by broad socio-economic group of father, 1980, 1990 and 1993

% Father's broad socio-economic group	Criterion[1]	Year of leaving school		
		1980	1990	1993
Professional and managerial	No awards	9.2	6.5	0.4
	5 or more O/S passes	66.2	71.5	84.1
	3 or more H passes	41.3	52.4	56.6
	5 or more H passes	22.2	33.8	37.1
	Sample size	4554	791	634
Intermediate non-manual	No awards	9.8	8.2	1.6
	5 or more O/S passes	67.3	69.8	78.9
	3 or more H passes	42.9	47.7	59.7
	5 or more H passes	24.0	31.4	38.7
	Sample size	1436	282	269
Junior non-manual	No awards	15.4	8.0	1.7
	5 or more O/S passes	50.3	62.6	62.4
	3 or more H passes	26.2	31.7	32.0
	5 or more H passes	12.7	13.9	19.4
	Sample size	1315	189	237
Skilled manual	No awards	34.3	14.4	2.4
	5 or more O/S passes	26.8	41.5	52.1
	3 or more H passes	10.4	20.2	25.5
	5 or more H passes	4.3	8.8	13.4
	Sample size	8601	1181	1064
Semi-skilled manual	No awards	40.8	20.4	3.1
	5 or more O/S passes	22.5	36.8	45.1
	3 or more H passes	9.4	16.3	19.0
	5 or more H passes	3.6	5.0	9.6
	Sample size	2681	303	262
Unskilled manual	No awards	48.8	25.0	3.4
	5 or more O/S passes	16.8	25.0	37.9
	3 or more H passes	5.5	11.6	19.1
	5 or more H passes	2.4	5.1	8.3
	Sample size	1231	145	92

Source: Scottish School Leavers Survey, weighted (sample sizes unweighted). Omits cases where socio-economic group is armed forces, or inadequate information for socio-economic group.

1 No award means no awards in the Scottish Certificate of Education. O/S means Ordinary or Standard Grade. H means Higher Grade.

Table A7.7 Direct entry to higher education by school leavers, by broad socio-economic group of father, 1980, 1990 and 1993

% entering by autumn of year after left school Father's broad socio-economic group	Year of leaving school		
	1980	1990	1993
Professional and managerial	29.7	42.2	56.4
Sample size	4555	792	668
Intermediate non-manual	31.7	35.1	54.1
Sample size	1436	283	277
Junior non-manual	19.3	19.7	33.6
Sample size	1315	192	248
Skilled manual	7.5	13.0	26.9
Sample size	8602	1195	1108
Semi-skilled manual	5.8	8.6	21.2
Sample size	2682	307	277
Unskilled manual	3.9	7.0	14.5
Sample size	1231	146	98

Source: Scottish School Leavers Surveys weighted (sample sizes unweighted). Omits cases where socio-economic group is armed forces, or inadequate information for socio-economic group.

Table A7.8 Highest educational attainment, by broad religious group and birth cohort, among people aged 25–65 in 2001

% Religious group	Criterion[1]	Birth cohort				
		1936	1937–46	1947–56	1957–66	1967–76
No religion	H Grade or HE qual.	39.6	42.6	59.7	53.6	62.5
	HE qual.	24.2	29.1	39.4	33.7	39.0
	Sample size	75	395	643	917	901
Church of Scotland	H Grade or HE qual.	28.9	32.7	50.8	57.5	63.8
	HE qual.	13.9	18.5	28.7	31.3	37.9
	Sample size	235	1278	1038	1161	731
Roman Catholic	H Grade or HE qual.	15.6	25.2	45.2	50.7	62.5
	HE qual.	7.9	15.6	27.0	31.3	42.7
	Sample size	66	313	307	475	316
Other Christian	H Grade or HE qual.	37.4	52.4	62.8	72.6	74.4
	HE qual.	25.7	35.4	43.7	50.7	52.7
	Sample size	26	183	198	205	123
Other religion	H Grade or HE qual.	12.0	51.6	60.2	63.5	75.8
	HE qual.	3.6	34.5	46.8	54.2	41.2
	Sample size	6	42	61	56	53

Source: Scottish Household Survey 2001, weighted (sample sizes unweighted in brackets).

1. H grade is Higher Grade. HE is higher education (diploma, first degree, postgraduate degree or professional qualification).

Table A7.9 Highest educational attainment and direct entry to higher education among school leavers, by broad region, 1980, 1990 and 1993

% Region[1]	Criterion[2]	Year of leaving school		
		1980	1990	1993
Highlands, Islands and Argyll	No awards	26.4	10.2	1.7
	3 or more H passes	18.1	26.9	32.3
	Entered higher education	11.0	15.9	33.0
	Sample size	1370	288	276
Grampian and Tayside	No awards	27.1	15.7	3.1
	3 or more H passes	17.0	27.2	30.5
	Entered higher education	10.5	23.6	28.5
	Sample size	3341	680	619
Central and Fife	No awards	31.6	16.0	3.5
	3 or more H passes	17.5	25.7	30.2
	Entered higher education	10.9	17.8	30.6
	Sample size	3042	432	489
Lothian	No awards	35.0	11.7	2.8
	3 or more H passes	15.5	28.4	32.8
	Entered higher education	10.6	19.6	29.0
	Sample size	3387	455	480
Borders, Dumfries and Galloway	No awards	27.7	16.6	2.2
	3 or more H passes	17.6	24.6	33.6
	Entered higher education	9.8	19.0	37.0
	Sample size	966	171	180
Strathclyde apart from Argyll and Bute	No awards	34.1	17.3	3.5
	3 or more H passes	16.0	25.3	32.1
	Entered higher education	12.8	16.7	34.7
	Sample size	10103	1523	1249

Source: Scottish School Leavers Survey, weighted (sample sizes unweighted).

1. Region is defined in terms of the Regional Authorities (and the Argyll and Bute division of Strathclyde).

2. None means no awards in the Scottish Certificate of Education. H means Higher Grade. Direct entry to higher education means entry by autumn of year after left school.

Table A7.10 Highest educational attainment, by broad region, among people aged 23–74 in 2001

%	Attainment[1]		Sample size
Region	H grade or HE qualification	HE qualification	
West	49.1	28.6	4305
Central and Tayside	49.6	30.7	1296
East	55.1	37.0	2224
North and Islands	54.3	32.2	1979

Source: Scottish Household Survey 2001, weighted (sample sizes unweighted in brackets).

1. H grade is Higher Grade; HE is higher education (diploma, first degree, postgraduate degree or professional qualification).

Table A7.11 Socio-economic group, by highest educational attainment, among people aged 16–59, 1981–2000

% in columns within attainment level		Year		
Highest educational attainment	Broad socio-economic group	1981	1991	2000
First degree, higher degree, professional qualification	Professional and managerial	27.7	41.6	44.4
	Intermediate non-manual	41.3	35.0	32.7
	Junior non-manual	5.5	3.4	6.2
	Skilled manual	2.6	1.3	2.3
	Semi-skilled manual	2.6	3.0	2.4
	Unskilled manual	0.6	0.3	0.3
	Unclassified or armed forces	19.6	15.5	11.7
	Sample size	1134	895	1188
HND, HNC, etc.	Professional and managerial	37.3	30.2	27.2
	Intermediate non-manual	16.7	24.4	19.8
	Junior non-manual	16.4	12.1	18.6
	Skilled manual	17.8	14.0	9.7
	Semi-skilled manual	3.3	3.7	8.5
	Unskilled manual	0.6	1.3	0.8
	Unclassified or armed forces	7.9	14.1	15.3
	Sample size	159	311	657
Higher Grade, A level, etc.	Professional and managerial	11.3	14.0	15.7
	Intermediate non-manual	7.6	10.9	9.6
	Junior non-manual	30.0	19.2	21.9
	Skilled manual	6.2	21.3	17.8
	Semi-skilled manual	6.0	8.7	9.7
	Unskilled manual	2.1	1.8	2.6
	Unclassified or armed forces	36.8	24.0	22.7
	Sample size	1116	1879	1469

cont'd over

Table A7.11 cont'd

% in columns within attainment level Highest educational attainment	Broad socio-economic group	Year		
		1981	1991	2000
O Grade, Standard Grade, etc.	Professional and managerial	7.6	9.1	10.2
	Intermediate non-manual	3.7	9.2	6.1
	Junior non-manual	16.2	21.4	15.6
	Skilled manual	32.7	15.5	22.0
	Semi-skilled manual	12.4	13.3	14.3
	Unskilled manual	3.2	5.0	4.5
	Unclassified or armed forces	24.3	26.6	27.2
	Sample size	3568	1434	1926
Scotvec modules, CSE, etc.	Professional and managerial	7.4	11.7	8.2
	Intermediate non-manual	6.6	8.5	6.0
	Junior non-manual	24.4	11.4	10.9
	Skilled manual	10.0	25.3	16.8
	Semi-skilled manual	8.0	10.0	17.7
	Unskilled manual	4.2	4.9	8.6
	Unclassified or armed forces	39.4	28.1	31.9
	Sample size	645	475	798
None of these or no answer	Professional and managerial	5.1	5.9	4.8
	Intermediate non-manual	2.7	4.3	3.6
	Junior non-manual	11.8	8.1	9.6
	Skilled manual	13.4	17.4	8.5
	Semi-skilled manual	16.2	14.4	14.3
	Unskilled manual	10.0	9.8	9.0
	Unclassified or armed forces	40.8	40.0	50.2
	Sample size	5937	3194	1671

Sources: Labour Force Survey 1981, 1991, March–May 2000, weighted (sample sizes unweighted)

Table A7.12 Social mobility by highest educational attainment, among people aged 23–62, 1999

% in columns within segments of Table Mobility	Low or none	O Grade etc.	H Grade etc.	HND etc.	Degree
Mobility at current job					
Downwards	25.7	28.8	28.4	27.1	21.2
Immobile	24.3	13.8	15.2	13.5	17.3
Upwards	50.0	57.4	56.4	59.4	61.5
Sample size	294	332	336	135	288
Mobility at first job					
Downwards	25.7	24.9	19.5	20.4	11.5
Immobile	36.1	27.3	29.0	25.7	41.7
Upwards	38.3	47.8	51.5	54.0	46.8
Sample size	285	312	279	117	229
Mobility between first job and current job					
Downwards	19.8	19.5	13.8	15.8	8.6
Immobile	27.8	21.3	20.6	19.9	31.3
Upwards	52.4	59.2	65.5	64.4	60.1
Sample size	355	400	385	148	318

Source: British Household Panel Survey 1999, weighted (sample sizes unweighted in brackets).

Table A7.13 Geographical mobility, by highest educational attainment, 1999

% in rows Highest educational attainment	Place of birth			Sample size
	Outwith Scotland	In a different region[1] of Scotland	In the same region[1]	
Degree etc.	30.7	40.5	28.8	426
Higher education below degree	13.4	34.9	51.7	209
Highers etc.	12.9	37.2	49.8	603
O Grade etc.	12.6	26.3	61.1	612
Low or none	10.0	23.6	66.4	1043

Source: British Household Panel Survey, waves 1 and 9, weighted (sample sizes unweighted).

1. For definition of these regions, see Table A2.7.

Table A7.14 Percentage of school leavers directly entering higher education, by examination attainment at school, 1980, 1990 and 1993

Numbers of passes in Higher Grade	Year of leaving school		
	1980	1990	1993
One	4.0	7.5	20.4
Sample size	1222	219	286
Two	14.1	14.1	44.0
Sample size	1140	213	270
Three	38.2	29.3	61.3
Sample size	1165	282	239
Four	59.9	47.4	72.2
Sample size	1392	382	261
Five	78.5	73.2	82.2
Sample size	1588	488	361
Six	82.9	84.9	92.1
Sample size	882	436	262

Source: Scottish School Leavers Surveys, weighted (sample sizes unweighted).

Table A7.15 Ages at which parents left school, among school leavers, 1980, 1990 and 1993

% in columns	Year respondent left school		
Ages at which parents left school	1980	1990	1993
Both 17 or older	4.1	7.8	9.6
One 17 or older, not both	7.6	12.8	17.9
One 16, neither 17 or older	13.8	25.9	27.8
One or both 15, neither older	64.2	39.2	29.8
Both no information	10.4	14.3	14.9
Sample size	23158	3586	3469

Source: Scottish School Leavers Survey, weighted (sample sizes unweighted).

Table A7.16 Direct entry to higher education by school leavers, by broad socio-economic group of father and ages at which parents left school, 1980, 1990 and 1993

% entering by autumn of year after left school Father's broad socio-economic group		Year of leaving school		
		1980	1990	1993
Professional and managerial	neither 17	22.4	29.8	45.2
	Sample size	2991	347	294
	one or both 17	45.0	53.4	65.7
	Sample size	1563	445	374
Intermediate non-manual	neither 17	22.5	26.7	40.6
	Sample size	931	157	125
	one or both 17	50.2	48.2	66.2
	Sample size	505	126	152
Junior non-manual	neither 17	15.7	16.3	26.0
	Sample size	1125	127	163
	one or both 17	41.2	27.2	48.8
	Sample size	190	65	85
Skilled manual	neither 17	6.9	11.6	22.6
	Sample size	8192	1044	874
	one or both 17	19.9	25.0	44.5
	Sample size	410	151	234
Semi-skilled manual	neither 17	5.4	7.6	19.2
	Sample size	2586	280	240
	one or both 17	17.8	24.0	35.2
	Sample size	96	27	37
Unskilled manual	neither 17	3.4	5.7	12.9
	Sample size	1175	131	91
	one or both 17	14.1	22.7	38.8
	Sample size	56	15	7

Source: Scottish School Leavers Surveys, weighted (sample sizes unweighted). Omits cases where socio-economic group is armed forces, or inadequate information for socio-economic group.

Table A7.17 Social capital by highest educational attainment, 2000

% with one or more membership or engaging in one or more political action	Type of social capital			Sample size
Highest educational attainment	Membership of community group	Membership of national group	Political action	
Degree	38.7	34.2	80.5	214
Higher education below degree	28.8	22.5	66.8	239
Highers etc.	19.4	17.7	60.8	207
O Grade etc.	19.3	9.3	66.0	315
None	14.1	6.5	44.6	556

Source: Scottish Social Attitudes Survey 2000, weighted (sample sizes unweighted).

People with other qualifications or not supplying information are omitted.

For definitions of membership and action, see text and Paterson (2002a).

SUPPLEMENTARY TABLES FOR CHAPTER 8

Table A8.1 Changes in housing tenure, 1979–99

	Tenure				Public authority sales to sitting tenants in five-year period[2]
	Owner occupied	Public rented	Housing association	Private rented[1]	
Thousands					
1979	699	1073	–	210	1
1984	816	987	45	167	66
1989	1033	877	62	133	123
1994	1258	721	77	155	121
1999	1435	584	130	155	74
% in rows					
1979	35.3	54.1	–	10.6	
1984	40.5	49.0	2.2	8.3	
1989	49.1	41.7	2.9	6.3	
1994	56.9	32.6	3.5	7.0	
1999	62.3	25.3	5.6	6.7	

Source: Scottish Executive (2001d: Table 6.5).

1. Figure for private rented sector in 1979 includes housing association.

2. Total number of sales since previous date shown – for example, 66,000 sales in 1980–84.

Table A8.2 Prevalence of cigarette smoking among children, by age and sex, 1998

Age	Boys		Girls	
	% ever smoked	Sample size	% ever smoked	Sample size
8	13	129	6	136
9	5	139	8	103
10	7	133	5	142
11	12	141	12	138
12	16	144	22	114
13	29	143	29	153
14	38	133	51	125
15	37	135	46	139
All	20	1097	23	1050

Source: Boreham (2000: Table A8.19), using Scottish Health Survey 1998. Weighted (sample sizes unweighted).

Table A8.3 Prevalence of cigarette smoking, by sex, 1980–98

% in columns within sex			Year		
	1980	1986	1990	1994	1998
Male:					
never/occasionally smoked cigarettes	30	36	41	44	44
ex-regular cigarette smoker	24	27	26	25	22
current light[1] cigarette smoker	18	18	18	14	20
current heavy[1] cigarette smoker	27	19	15	16	14
Sample size	1044	774	704	669	3928
Female:					
never/occasionally smoked cigarettes	48	48	50	53	50
ex-regular cigarette smoker	10	17	15	18	18
current light[1] cigarette smoker	25	19	22	18	21
current heavy[1] cigarette smoker	16	16	13	12	11
Sample size	1205	925	886	823	5083

Sources: 1980: Scottish Office (1992a: Table 3.19); 1986–1994: Scottish Office (1997a: Table 3D10); 1998: Scottish Health Survey 1998 (see also Boreham (2000)), weighted (sample sizes unweighted).

1. Light is fewer than 20 per day; heavy is 20 or more.

Table A8.4 Prevalence of cigarette smoking, by sex and age, 1980–98

% current cigarette smoker			Year		
	1980	1986	1990	1994	1998
Male:					
16–24	38	41	28	31	37
25–34	47	37	36	30	39
35–49	44	40	38	33	35
50–59	54	44	31	31	32
60 or older[1]	47	29	30	28	25
Female:					
16–24	40	36	38	29	34
25–34	46	33	36	36	36
35–49	54	43	40	33	33
50–59	51	45	42	27	36
60 or older[1]	24	27	26	22	25

Sources: 1980: Scottish Office (1992a: Table 3.19); 1986–1994: Scottish Office (1997a: Table 3D10); 1998: Scottish Health Survey 1998 (see also Boreham (2000)), weighted.

Unweighted sample sizes in 1998

	16–24	25–34	35–49	50–59	60–74
male	391	763	1174	694	906
female	511	971	1418	878	1305

Sample sizes not available for other years.

1. 60–74 in 1998.

Table A8.5 Prevalence of cigarette smoking, by sex and social class, 1998

% current smoker Social class of chief income earner[1]	Male	Female
I professional and managerial	13	10
Sample size	256	241
II intermediate non-manual	25	25
Sample size	1024	1335
IIInm skilled non-manual	34	28
Sample size	418	1032
IIIm skilled manual	38	35
Sample size	1288	1092
IV semi-skilled manual	51	48
Sample size	605	813
V unskilled manual	45	53
Sample size	191	368

Source: Scottish Health Survey 1998 (see also Boreham (2000)).

1. Registrar General's class.

Table A8.6 Alcohol consumption among people aged 16–64, by age and sex, 1995 and 1998

Mean units per week Age	Male		Female	
	1995	1998	1995	1998
16–24	20.8	23.4	8.4	10.0
Sample size	464	365	538	500
25–34	22.8	20.5	6.3	7.4
Sample size	840	763	1160	968
35–44	19.4	17.7	6.6	7.4
Sample size	811	824	992	1006
45–54	19.7	20.0	5.6	6.2
Sample size	709	690	825	892
55–64	16.5	17.4	4.6	4.4
Sample size	689	682	884	805
All ages	20.1	19.8	6.3	7.1
Sample size	3513	3324	4399	4171

Source: Erens (2000: Table 9.9), using Scottish Health Survey 1998. Weighted (sample sizes unweighted).

Table A8.7 Children's experience of alcohol, by age and sex, 1998

Age	Boys		Girls	
	% had a proper alcoholic drink	Sample size	% had a proper alcoholic drink	Sample size
8	12	129	6	134
9	6	139	6	102
10	11	132	5	142
11	16	141	9	138
12	28	144	23	114
13	40	143	41	153
14	61	133	58	125
15	67	135	68	140
All	30	1096	27	1048

Source: Erens (2000: Table 9.18), using Scottish Health Survey 1998. Weighted (sample sizes unweighted).

Table A8.8 New drug addicts notified to the Home Office, by sex, 1980–95

Year	Male		Female	
	number	mean age	number	mean age
1980	58	–	32	–
1986	424	23.1	192	23.2
1991	509	26.0	218	24.9
1995	1032	24.9	431	24.2

Sources: 1980 and 1986: Scottish Office (1992a: Table 3.18(a)); 1991 and 1995: Scottish Office (1997a: Table 3D8).

Table A8.9 Reported drug misuse among people aged 15–59, 1996

% reporting drug misuse in last 12 months Age:	Male	Female
16–19	26	20
20–24	37	21
25–29	15	11
30–39	12	4
40–59	2	1

Source: Scottish Executive (2001a: Table 6.12), using Scottish Crime Survey 1996.

Table A8.10 Prevalence of any cardiovascular disorder, by social class of chief income earner and sex, 1998

% prevalence[1] Social class of chief income earner[2]	Male	Female
I professional and managerial	18.2	14.0
Sample size	255	242
II intermediate non-manual	23.5	20.8
Sample size	1024	1334
IIInm skilled non-manual	25.9	23.4
Sample size	419	1033
IIIm skilled manual	23.3	25.5
Sample size	1287	1093
IV semi-skilled manual	23.1	26.5
Sample size	607	810
V unskilled manual	30.4	28.8
Sample size	191	368

Source: Falaschetti et al. (2000: Table 2.10), using Scottish Health Survey 1998. Weighted (sample sizes unweighted).

1. Age standardised.

2. Registrar General's class.

Table A8.11 Overall participation in physical activity[1] among people aged 16–74, by social class of chief income earner and sex, 1998

% in columns within sex[2]	Social class of chief income earner[3]						Total
	I	II	IIInm	IIIm	IV	V	
Male							
low	23	31	37	31	40	43	33
medium	42	36	31	25	18	14	28
high	36	33	32	44	42	43	38
Sample size	254	1020	419	1288	605	191	3928
Female							
low	29	32	40	38	39	42	38
medium	43	38	35	35	34	32	35
high	28	30	25	27	27	26	27
Sample size	240	1336	1034	1093	814	368	5092

Source: Pitson (2000: Table 6.8), using Scottish Health Survey 1998. Weighted (sample sizes unweighted).

1. 'High' is 30 minutes or more moderate-plus activity on at least five days per week; 'Medium' is 30 minutes or more on one to four days per week; 'Low' is lower level of activity (in terms of duration, frequency or intensity). See source for definition of 'moderate plus'.

2. Age standardised.

3. Registrar General's class.

Table A8.12 Overall participation in physical activity[1] among people aged 16–74, by age and sex, 1998

% in columns within sex	Age						Total
	16–24	25–34	35–44	45–54	55–64	65–74	
Male							
low	14	20	29	37	56	62	33
medium	32	32	32	29	18	24	29
high	55	48	40	33	26	14	38
Sample size	394	763	825	692	682	572	3928
Female							
low	31	27	28	36	51	67	38
medium	37	41	38	36	30	26	35
high	33	31	34	29	19	8	27
Sample size	523	971	1006	896	808	888	5092

Source: Pitson (2000: Table 6.6), using Scottish Health Survey 1998. Weighted (sample sizes unweighted).

1. 'High' is 30 minutes or more moderate-plus activity on at least five days per week; 'Medium' is 30 minutes or more on one to four days per week; 'Low' is lower level of activity (in terms of duration, frequency or intensity). See source for definition of 'moderate plus'.

Table A8.13 Physical exercise among children aged 11–15, 1990–8

	Exercise in free time 4 or more hours per week	Exercise in or out of school 6 or more hours per week	Sample size
Male			
1990	36.5	not available	1924
1994	35.7	43.5	2373
1998	42.3	49.3	2723
Female			
1990	19.0	not available	2126
1994	18.2	22.9	2504
1998	23.6	29.2	2827

Source: Todd et al. (2000: Tables 26 and 28).

Table A8.14 Ownership of household items, by net annual household income, 2000

% of households in rows Income band (£)[1]	Ownership of household item							Sample size
	Freezer or fridge	Washing machine	Tele-phone	Cars etc.		Computer[2]	Access[3] to internet from home	
				1+	2+			
0–6,000	88.6	88.0	88.3	33.6	4.3	15.3	7.1	1965
6,000–10,000	91.1	91.4	90.7	37.0	4.1	14.4	6.9	3441
10,000–15,000	95.0	96.1	95.5	61.5	9.9	25.7	14.7	3170
15,000–20,000	97.7	99.0	98.4	84.0	23.6	42.2	25.7	2327
20,000+	98.4	99.4	99.5	95.9	52.1	67.7	48.1	4129
All	94.6	95.3	95.0	65.1	21.5	35.8	22.7	15032

Source: Scottish Household Survey 2000, weighted (sample sizes unweighted).

1. Net income after taxation and other deductions from employment, benefits and other sources, brought into the household by the highest income earner, or their spouse, and including any contribution from other household members.

2. Computer in the household's accommodation.

3. Percentage of all households, not only of those with a computer.

Table A8.15 Usual means of travel to work, 1966–99

% in rows	Train	Bus	Car	Bicycle	Foot	Other
1966	4	43	21	2	24	6
1971	3	35	29	2	24	6
1981	3	25	46	1	20	4
1991	3	18	59	1	15	4
1999	3	11	69	2	13	1

Source: Scottish Social Statistics 2001, Table A8.5, using census for 1966–91 and Labour Force Survey for 1999.

Spring 1966–91, Autumn 1999.

Table A8.16 Distance travelled per adult per year, 1985–6 to 1997–9

Miles Age Year	Men				Women				All
	16–29	30–59	60+	All	16–29	30–59	60+	All	
1985–86	7000	8100	3200	6800	5300	4100	2100	3900	5200
1989–91	7800	10500	4300	8300	6700	7100	3300	5900	7000
1992–94	8300	9300	4000	7700	6900	5900	3500	5300	6400
1995–97	9000	10800	5900	9200	5900	7500	4000	6200	7600
1997–99	8700	10400	6500	9000	8400	8200	4400	7000	8000

Source: Scottish Executive (2001a: Table A8.1), using National Travel Survey, and combining years to achieve adequate sample sizes. Rounded to nearest 100 miles.

Table A8.17 Vehicles licensed, road lengths, and casualties, 1980–99

Year	All licensed vehicles (millions)	Road lengths (1000 km)	Number of casualties
1980	1.398	49.4	29286
1985	1.514	50.7	27290
1990	1.788	51.7	27225
1995	1.910	52.8	22194
1999	2.131	53.5	20976

Source: Scottish Executive (2001a: Table A8.16).

There is a discontinuity from 1993, which results in figures from then onwards being about 2.5% lower than they would have been in the old series.

Table A8.18 Internet use, by sex, age, household income and education, 2001

	Whether use internet		Number of hours per week (users only)	
	%	Sample size	Mean hours	Sample size
Sex:				
male	42.1	645	4.3	254
female	34.0	959	3.4	284
Age:				
18–34	59.0	411	4.6	225
35–54	44.0	574	2.9	246
55 or older	13.5	618	4.4	67
Gross annual household income (£)				
0–6,000	15.5	264	7.0	36
6,000–10,000	19.2	242	4.0	37
10,000–15,000	25.4	211	5.0	57
15,000–20,000	31.8	148	3.5	54
20,000–26,000	36.8	130	5.5	51
26,000+	64.1	376	2.8	239
Highest educational attainment				
degree	75.8	228	3.5	168
other higher education	52.7	232	3.0	117
Highers etc.	60.9	183	4.5	97
Standard Grade etc.	37.5	235	4.1	85
lower than Standard Grade	12.5	185	3.2	22
none	10.8	532	5.5	46

Source: Scottish Social Attitudes Survey 2001, weighted (sample sizes unweighted).

Table A8.19 Active membership of churches, 1980–2000

Thousands	Roman Catholic[1]	Presbyterian	Other Christian	Non-Trinitarian	Other religions
Year					
1980	296	988	153	26	25
1985	285	900	151	29	30
1990	284	816	155	35	42
1995	249	726	150	38	50
2000	225	639	150	42	59

Source: Scottish Executive (2001a: Table 10.10).

1. Mass attendance.

Table A8.20 Book reading and television watching, by socio-economic group, 2000

Socio-economic group	Book reading for pleasure (mean hours per week)	Television (mean hours per weekday evening)	Sample size
Professionals and managers	4.2	2.5	276
Intermediate non-manual	4.9	2.7	233
Junior non-manual	4.3	3.1	281
Skilled manual	3.3	3.5	289
Semi-skilled manual	3.7	3.7	298
Unskilled manual	3.7	4.5	115

Source: Scottish Social Attitudes Survey 2000, weighted (sample size unweighted).

Table A8.21 Book reading and television watching, by highest educational attainment, 2000

Highest educational attainment	Book reading for pleasure (mean hours per week)	Television (mean hours per weekday evening)	Sample size
Degree or professional qual.	4.7	2.2	213
HND etc.	4.4	2.8	238
Highers etc.	4.1	2.8	207
O Grade etc.	3.6	3.3	426
None or low	3.9	4.0	553
All	4.0	3.2	1639

Source: Scottish Social Attitudes Survey 2000, weighted (sample size unweighted).

Table A8.22 Public library use among people aged 16–74 who were economically active, by socio-economic group, 2000

% Socio-economic group	Use of public library in past month	Sample size
Professionals and managers	22.6	1276
Intermediate non-manual	34.9	1321
Junior non-manual	28.9	1194
Skilled manual	17.5	1334
Semi-skilled manual	20.3	1027
Unskilled manual	19.5	381
All (including unclassified)	24.7	6567

Source: Scottish Household Survey 2000, weighted (sample size unweighted).

Table A8.23 Public library use, by highest educational attainment, 2000

% Highest educational attainment	Use of public library in past month	Sample size
Degree or professional qual.	37.3	2519
HND etc.	31.5	2688
Highers etc.	27.7	2228
O Grade etc.	23.4	825
None or low	18.4	2222
All	26.8	10482

Source: Scottish Household Survey 2000, weighted (sample size unweighted).

Sources of Data

The detailed sources of the data for the tables in the book are indicated in each of them. There are four broad types of source. One is the population censuses of 1981, 1991 and 2001. The second is other kinds of government publication, including the publications of the General Register Office for Scotland. The third is various social surveys that are conducted regularly, some funded by government and some by research grants from research councils or other sources. All three of these are summarised here. The fourth is other academic writing, some of which draws on these or similar surveys, and some of which is based on ad hoc surveys, details of which are in the cited publications. Within this last type, there are in particular the data compiled by Professor Michael Anderson at Edinburgh University, which are described below in a note kindly supplied to us by him. The purpose of this Appendix is not to provide full accounts of any of the sources, but merely to summarise what they are and to note publications or web sites where more information may be obtained.

POPULATION CENSUS

The tables from the 2001 census of population are available electronically, the first UK census for which this has been possible: see below. Most of the data we have used are found in *Scotland's Census 2001: Reference Volume*, published in 2003 (Registrar General for Scotland 2003b), but some are also taken from the shorter summary report, *Registrar General's 2001 Census Report to the Scottish Parliament* (Registrar General for Scotland 2003a) or from the initial *2001 Population Report* (Registrar General for Scotland 2002c). All three of these are available in full on the web site.

We also use the 1981 and 1991 censuses, all the reports from which were published by the General Register Office. The tables for 1991 come from the *1991 Census: Report for Scotland* (Registrar General for Scotland 1994a), and from *1991 Census Scotland: Economic Activity* (Registrar General for Scotland 1994b). The tables for 1981 come from *1981 Census Scotland: Scottish Summary* (Registrar General for Scotland 1983a), *1981 Census Scotland: Housing and Household Report* (Registrar General for Scotland 1983c) and *1981 Census Scotland: Economic Activity* (Registrar General for Scotland 1983b). In both 1981 and 1991, the tables from the economic activity volumes are based on a 10 per cent random sample of records, but that still gives very large sample sizes.

GOVERNMENT PUBLICATIONS

The main government publications used for 2001 were the annual volumes *Scottish Social Statistics* and *Scottish Economic Statistics*, both published by the Scottish Executive (see http://www.scotland.gov.uk/stats/scotstats.asp). These replaced the annual *Scottish Abstract of Statistics* and the *Scottish Economic Bulletin*, both published by the Scottish Office, the former until 1998 and the latter until 1999. Other general government publications cited are the annual *Scottish Health Statistics*, the reports of the *Scottish Health Survey* of 1995 and 1998, the annual reports for Scotland of the Health and Safety Executive, and the statistical bulletins of the Scottish Education Department and its successors. We have also drawn on the *Annual Report* of the General Register Office for Scotland, which provides demographic information between censuses; in 2001, the old-style report became *Vital Events Reference Tables*, and the new *Annual Report* presented summaries of these. The detailed sources are cited in the text and tables, and are listed in the bibliography at the end of the book.

NOTE ON DEMOGRAPHIC SOURCES FOR SCOTLAND[1]

The principal data sources for Scottish demographic data are almost all derived from the Office of the Registrar General for Scotland. Comparative data for England and Wales are published by the Office of National Statistics (which is also responsible for assembling UK-wide data).

The prime sources for statistics on population numbers and characteristics are the censuses, conducted decennially (except in 1941) since 1801. These are generally reliable enough for most purposes, but there are doubts about the completeness of the 1991 census, which has required significant recalculation of some rates, and this means that some recently published figures (especially with respect to estimates of population change) differ significantly from those previously available. Census data up to 1991 are available in print form, with separate volumes for each county or region as well as various aggregate volumes. The 1991 printed volumes give estimates of roughly consistent populations at regional level back to 1891. The 2001 census results are all available on-line in easily downloadable formats from the Registrar General's excellent website: the index is at http://www.gro-scotland.gov.uk/grosweb/grosweb.nsf/pages/stabb

To take just two examples, the index page for the key 2001 census national tables is at http://www.gro-scotland.gov.uk/grosweb/grosweb.nsf/pages/scotcen6, and this provides downloadable Excel files (CAS001–34 are particularly useful for present purposes). Clicking on Key Statistics for Council Areas and Health Board Areas – http://www.gro-scotland.gov.uk/grosweb/grosweb.nsf/pages/scotcen7 – reveals a mass of excellent data broken down by areas. Local population estimates are also available.

Births, deaths, marriages, divorces and abortions are covered in the Registrar General's *Annual Reports* which have been published annually for years since 1855. Details of what was published varied over time so it is quite difficult to provide consistent data on some points, especially at below national level (though some very detailed local data continued to be published until the late 1970s, after which supplementary microfiche tables were made available). Since 2001 a much briefer report has been produced, but supplemented by a mass of on-line tables, accessed for 2002 through, for example, http://www.gro-scotland.gov.uk/grosweb/grosweb.nsf/pages/02reference-tables. Clicking here under the Summary on Table 1.1 produces an extremely useful first table in Excel format giving all the main indicators back to 1855. Some later tables also include data going back for 10 or 20 years which can then be linked back to the earlier published volumes; some similar data are also published in the *Scottish Abstract of Statistics*.

Data on Scottish net migration flows, which are published for the whole twentieth century in the *Annual Abstract of Statistics* (Table 5.2), are the least robust, because they are only estimated indirectly from estimates of population change and births and deaths, and they thus fluctuate very markedly depending on the accuracy of the most recent census estimates.

SOCIAL SURVEYS

Where surveys are cited in the book without reference to a publication, the information has been taken directly from electronic versions of the survey data, nearly all of which are available from the UK Data Archive at Essex University (www.data-archive.ac.uk). The only exception to that availability are some of the data sets from the Scottish School Leavers Surveys, which were obtained from the Centre for Educational Sociology at Edinburgh University. Except where noted, all the surveys described below were carried out by interview, most of them by the very experienced staff and contractors of the Social Survey Division of the Office for National Statistics (or its predecessors), or of the National Centre for Social Research (or its predecessors). In recent years, that has usually come to mean computer-aided interview, in which the interviewer carries a laptop computer that provides the questions to be read out and into which the interviewer enters the response. This has the advantage that data can then be transferred electronically from the interviewer to the survey managers.

We have used Britain-wide or UK-wide surveys only where the sample size is large enough to allow reliable independent analysis of the Scottish sub-sample.

Labour Force Survey

This is a survey of people (not only adults) living in households in the UK at private addresses or in NHS institutional addresses or in student residences, and it is now carried out by the Social Survey Division of the Office of National Statistics (ONS). It has been running since 1973, and – although there had been earlier occasional surveys – was set up primarily in response to the data requirements of what is now the European Union. The survey ran every two years from 1973 to 1983, in the spring, and from the start covered topics in social policy as well as matters relating directly to the labour market. From 1984 until 1991, it was conducted quarterly throughout the year with a total sample size of around 15,000 households in Great Britain alone, and in March to May was boosted by some 44,000 households in Britain and 5,000 cases in Northern Ireland. For that period, the data are available only for the spring survey. Since spring 1992, it has been run every quarter (March–May etc.), with a sample size of some 60,000 households every quarter, and the quarterly data are now available. We use mainly the spring quarter, to maintain continuity with the earlier surveys, but we occasionally use other quarters for variables that are available only from them. By 'Scottish' members of the sample, we mean people who described their place of usual residence as being Scotland (for example, coded in the recent Labour Force Survey data sets as categories 18 and 19 of the variable GOVTOR).

The sample selection now mostly uses the Postcode Address File to select an unclustered sample, with households selected randomly within addresses. (Before the advent of the quarterly survey, the samples were clustered.) The exception is the area north and west of the Great Glen, in which, because it is sparsely populated, random telephone interviewing is used instead. That introduces a slight bias, because not every household owns a telephone. Nevertheless, from the 2000 Scottish Social Attitudes Survey, which did not use telephone sampling (see below), we can estimate that only 6.6 per cent of individuals in that area live in accommodation where there is no telephone, representing just 0.5 per cent of the whole Scottish population. (For the purposes of this calculation, the area north and west of the Great Glen has been approximated by the parliamentary constituencies of Caithness, Sutherland and Easter Ross, Orkney, Ross, Cromarty and Inverness West, Shetland, and Western Isles.)

The response rates of the Labour Force Surveys have been over 75 per cent. Weights are available to compensate for non-response, and a unique feature of this series of surveys is that the weights are recurrently recalculated retrospectively to make use of better population estimates between population censuses.

Further information about the Labour Force Survey can be found on the ONS web site (www.statistics.gov.uk) and in the survey documentation available from the UK Data Archive. See also Office of Population, Censuses and Surveys (1982, 1992)

Scottish Household Survey

The Scottish Household Survey has been carried out annually since 1999 on behalf of the Scottish Executive. In some respects, it is intended to replicate for Scottish policy makers the role which the General Household Survey has served for British policy makers (see below). The sample size each year is around 15,000 cases. It is a survey of households, and the main interview is done with a randomly selected adult (aged at least 16) within each household. However, certain information is collected from the highest income resident on all other people within the household. The households are selected using the Postcode Address File, and the sampling frame is all households living at private addresses (covering the whole of Scotland); households are selected randomly within addresses. A simple random sample is taken in densely populated areas, and a clustered sample (within census enumeration districts) in less densely populated areas. The response rate has been around 66 per cent, and weights are available to compensate for non-response. Different versions of the weights allow population estimates to be made that describe the population of all households or the population of all adults. Further details are available from the survey's web site, via www.scotland.gov.uk/about/SR/CRU-SocInc/00016002/SHShome.aspx.

British Household Panel Survey

The BHPS is an annual panel survey of adults which, for Britain as a whole, has been running since 1991; it is funded by the ESRC and is carried out by the Research Centre on Micro-Social Change at Essex University. That is, the same people are interviewed each year. The objective at the beginning was to have 5,000 households, and thus about 10,000 adults (aged at least 16), adding in all new adult members of households which these members subsequently formed; the sample was selected from the Postcode Address File, with households selected randomly within addresses. The great strength of a panel study is that it allows change to be tracked at the individual level – for example, how people move in and out of poverty. This sample size was not enough to carry out separate analysis for Scotland, but since 1999 the Scottish sample has been enhanced to about 1,500 households and about 3,000 adults, including the surviving people in Scotland from the original sample. The new sample included full representation of the area north and west of the Great Glen, although the original (1991) sample did not. From the data available to date, we cannot yet use this survey to track individual change in Scotland, but the richness of the interviews makes this an important new source of cross-sectional data for the time being. Weights are available to compensate for non-response, and different weights are available for estimates of the population of households and of the population of all adults. Further information is available from the survey's web site, at www.iser.essex.ac.uk/bhps/index.php.

General Household Survey

The GHS is now carried out by the Social Survey Division of the Office for National Statistics, and collects information about people living in private households in Britain. It started in 1971, and has been carried out annually since then except in 1997–8 and 1999–2000. Its purpose has been to inform a wide range of social policy decisions, and so it is sponsored by a range of government departments in London. The sample size is now around 13,000 households, selected from the Postcode Address File, and it achieves a response rate of over 70 per cent; households are selected randomly within addresses. All adults (aged at least 16) within the household are interviewed. Weighting to compensate for non-response is available only since 2000. Further information is available from the survey's annual reports, published annually under the title *Living in Britain*. The most recent is ONS (2002b), available electronically at the ONS web site (www.statistics.gov.uk).

Scottish Social Attitudes Survey and Scottish Election Survey

The Scottish Social Attitudes Survey has been running annually since 1999, and is carried out by the National Centre for Social Research; it has been funded by the ESRC, the Leverhulme Trust, and some Scottish government departments and agencies. The series is parallel to the long-established British Social Attitudes Survey (Jowell et al. 1999). The sample is selected by means of the Postcode Address File, and is clustered; it is confined to people living at private addresses, and aged at least 18. Households are selected randomly within addresses, and respondents randomly within households. Its sample size is generally around 1,500 individuals. Data have also been used from the Scottish Election Surveys of 1979, 1992 and 1997 (funded by the ESRC or its predecessor, the Social Science Research Council), which used a similar design although based on the electoral register not the Postcode Address File; their sample sizes are only around 1,000 individuals. Weights are available to compensate for non-response. The surveys have mostly been carried out by interview, but in the Social Attitudes Survey a supplementary questionnaire was also returned by post. Further information can be found at the National Centre's web site (www.natcen.ac.uk), or in the publications from the survey, for example Paterson et al. (2001).

Scottish School Leavers Survey

These were founded in 1971 by the Centre for Educational Sociology at Edinburgh University (and in some respects date back to a leavers survey conducted in 1963 by the Scottish Council for Research in Education). Since 1979 they have covered all leavers, although the earlier ones covered only people with some recorded attainment in external examinations. The survey ran every two years from 1979 until 1991. The surveys in the 1970s and early 1980s were funded by the Social Science Research Council and some education authorities; in later years the funding came mainly from the Scottish Office, but also from other government departments. After 1991, the surveys were taken over by Social and Community Planning Research, the predecessor to the National Centre for Social Research. The name of the survey has varied over time, but we refer to it here as the Scottish School Leavers Survey. The sample design has remained broadly constant – as a random sample of people who left school roughly nine months before the date of the survey, details of the sampling frame having been collected from school headteachers. For example, the survey which took place in spring 1991 covered people who left school in summer 1990. Response rates were nearly all over 70 per cent; weights are available to compensate for non-response. The sample sizes have varied from around 20,000 to around 3,500 (dictated by the funding available). Unlike most of the surveys we use, this one has always been carried out fully by post. Further information is available in, for example, Burnhill et al. (1987), Lynn (1995) and Tomes (1988).

Scottish Health Survey

Although most of the use we make of the Scottish Health Surveys of 1995 and 1998 is quoting directly from the published report (as noted under 'government publications' above and in the relevant tables), we have supplemented that by some further analysis of the 1998 survey. (The results of the 2003 survey will not be available in time to be included in this book.) The survey series is funded by the Scottish Executive. The 1995 and 1998 samples were drawn from the Postcode Address File, with households selected randomly within addresses, and the information is gathered by an interviewer and a nurse (because some of it requires medical testing). All people aged two to 74 were eligible for inclusion (a wider range than any of the other surveys we use), but information on children aged two to 12 was collected from a parent, with the child present. The 1998 sample covered around 13,000 individuals, and at least one interview was recorded at 77 per cent of selected households. Weights are available to compensate for non-response. Further information is available at the survey's web site, www.show.scot.nhs.uk/scottishhealthsurvey/index.htm.

Notes

1. This note has been kindly supplied, along with graphs and tables in Chapter 2, by Professor Michael Anderson of Edinburgh University.

APPENDIX 3

Measuring Social Class

The purpose of this Appendix is to explain briefly the measures of social class we have used in this book, and to point to much fuller technical accounts of their histories and derivations. Some history of the classification of occupations in the UK is provided by Marshall et al. (1988: 13–30), Rose et al. (1997), and ONS (2002c).

Socio-economic group (SEG)

For many decades, this was the basis of official measures of class, and it has also been widely used by social researchers. It comes in both full (16-category) and condensed (6–category) versions, both of which are used here, the latter being referred to as 'broad SEG': the categories of these are illustrated in, for example, Table 6.1 and Table A6.2 respectively, and the correspondence between the two is noted in Table App 3.1 below. In both the full and the condensed versions, there is a further category for 'unclassified', which, in the case of broad SEG, also includes people in the armed forces. Furthermore, for the 16–category version in this book, we group self-employed farmers with farm owners, and so we use only 15 substantive categories. Sometimes we further group the categories 7 to 12, 14 and 15 to give a broad 'working class' group.

Socio-economic group is sociologically a more valid measure than the better-known Registrar General's Social Class, which we use here only when data are quoted from other researchers who have used it. Indeed, the 16–category version of SEG is used by Goldthorpe and Mills (2002) as a reasonable surrogate for the more sociologically valid Goldthorpe classes (see below). Both SEG and Registrar General's Social Class are derived from the list of 353 Occupational Unit Groups (OUG) in the Standard Occupational Classification 2000 (a number which has varied somewhat over time: it was 371 in 1990), along with information about employment status and size of organisation. The OUGs are themselves derived from a list of some 26,000 job titles.

Occasionally we quote data from other authors who use the market research categories of 'social grade'. The 2001 Census report shows an approximation to this measure (Table S66), and – for England and Wales – the Market Research Society (2003) has compared the distribution of social grade from the census with the distribution used in the National Readership Survey, and note that a more detailed paper on the comparison by Erhard Meier and Corrine Moy will be published in the *International Journal of Market Research*.

Table App 3.1 Full socio-economic group and broad socio-economic group

Socio-economic group	Category	Broad socio-economic group	Categories of socio-economic group (from second column)
Employers and managers, large establishments	1	Professional and managerial	1, 2, 3, 4, 13
Employers and managers, small establishments	2		
Professionals, self-employed	3		
Professionals, employees	4		
Intermediate non-manual	5	Intermediate non-manual	5
Junior non-manual	6	Junior non-manual	6
Personal service	7		
Foreman and supervisors	8		
Skilled manual	9	Skilled manual	8, 9, 12, 14
Semi-skilled manual	10	Semi-skilled manual	7, 10
Unskilled manual	11	Unskilled manual	11, 15
Other self-employed	12		
Farmers (employers, managers)	13		
Farmers (self-employed)	14		
Agricultural workers	15		
Armed forces	16		

NATIONAL STATISTICS SOCIO-ECONOMIC CLASSIFICATION

This is the scheme that has replaced the SEG classification, and is the only source of information about social class in the 2001 population census, and in government surveys after 2000, such as the Labour Force Survey. It was developed by government statisticians in discussion with sociologists, and is judged by them to be as valid as the class schemes (such as the Goldthorpe scheme below) which have been preferred by sociologists to Registrar General's Social Class (ONS 2002c; Rose et al. 1997). We use only the summary version which has nine categories. The first eight of these are illustrated in, for example, the first eight categories in Table A6.1. The ninth category of the classification is 'never worked or long-term unemployed', people in which category are excluded from that table. The last category in the table – 'full-time student' – would normally be grouped into an 'unclassified' category.

The report of the 2001 population census shows also the result of re-coding the occupation data from the 1991 census to a format which is similar to that which underlies the classification in 2001; this is included in, for example, Table A6.1. Since we also have SEG from 1991 in Table 6.1, a comparison of the two classificatory schemes is possible. As noted in Chapter 6, the trends between 1991 and 2000–1 shown by SEG are similar to the trends shown by the new classification, at least for the broad purposes of this book. ONS (2002c: 25) gives more detail about how an approximate version of SEG may be derived from the full version of the new classification (not the summary version shown in our tables).

GOLDTHORPE CLASSES

This scheme was developed over many years by John Goldthorpe and colleagues at Nuffield College, Oxford, partly in an attempt to deal with some of the conceptual inadequacies of Registrar General's Social Class (Erikson and Goldthorpe 1993: 35–47; Goldthorpe and Hope 1974; Marshall et al. 1988: 21–3). It is used in this book mainly to measure social mobility (the movement of people from the class in which they grew up to the class they occupy as an adult), because versions of the Goldthorpe scheme have become the standard measure internationally for this purpose. We use the seven–category version, but further grouped, as in Table 6.3, into five classes. There is an approximate correspondence between these grouped Goldthorpe classes and the grouped version of SEGs, as may be seen by comparing Table App 3.2 with Table App 3.1. With Goldthorpe classes grouped in this way, many of the discrepancies between Goldthorpe and grouped SEG are removed. The only differences that affect large numbers of people are that SEG 2 ('employees and managers in small establishments', 7.1 per cent of people in 2000, from Table 6.1) is grouped with 'lower-grade professionals and managers' in the grouped Goldthorpe classes but with all the other 'professional and managerial classes' in grouped SEG; and that SEG 7 ('personal service', 6.1 per cent in 2000) is included with 'routine non-manual' in the grouped Goldthorpe classes but with 'semi-skilled manual' in grouped SEG.

Table App 3.2 Approximate correspondence between Goldthorpe classes and socio-economic group

Goldthorpe class	Socio-economic group (category from second column of Table App 3.1)
I Higher-grade professionals and managers in large establishments	1, 3, 4
II Lower-grade professionals and managers in small establishments; supervisors of non-manual workers	2, 5
III Routine non-manual	6, 7
IV Self employed	12, 13, 14
V Lower-grade technicians; supervisors of manual workers	8
VI Skilled manual workers	9
VII Semi-skilled and unskilled workers	10, 11, 15

Comparing Percentages

Three techniques for comparing percentages are common, and all three have been used on occasion in this book: absolute differences, relative chances, and odds ratios. The strengths and weakness of each are outlined in this Appendix. Further discussion can be found in many books and articles on social statistics, for example Heath (2000: 317–8 and 331), Erikson and Goldthorpe (1993: 55–8) and Collett (1991: 25). For illustration we refer throughout to the data below, extracted from the more complex Table A7.6, which describes attainment in school education, 1980–93, according to the social class of the school leaver's father.

Extract from Table A7.6 Highest educational attainment of school leavers, by broad socio-economic group of father, 1980 and 1993

% Father's broad socio-economic group	Criterion[1]	Year of leaving school	
		1980	1993
Professional and managerial	No awards	9.2	0.4
	5 or more O/S passes	66.2	84.1
	3 or more H passes	41.3	56.6
	5 or more H passes	22.2	37.1
	Sample size	4554	634
Semi-skilled manual	No awards	40.8	3.1
	5 or more O/S passes	22.5	45.1
	3 or more H passes	9.4	19.0
	5 or more H passes	3.6	9.6
	Sample size	2681	262

Source: Table A7.6.

1 No award means no awards in the Scottish Certificate of Education. O/S means Ordinary or Standard Grade. H means Higher Grade.

ABSOLUTE DIFFERENCES

Consider, for example, the proportions gaining three or more Higher Grade passes in 1980 and 1993, comparing the professional and managerial class with the semi-skilled manual class. In the first of these classes, the proportion rose from 41.3 per cent to 56.6 per cent, an absolute difference of 15.3 points. In the semi-skilled manual class, the rise was from 9.4 per cent to 19.0 per cent, an absolute difference of 9.6 points. The undoubted advantage of looking at the change in this way is that the absolute figures give us a succinct description of the educational experience of these two classes. The rise was greater in the professional and managerial class and started from a higher base. In short, as a result, this level of attainment became the majority experience in the first class, but remained a small minority experience in the second.

However, the disadvantage is that changes of this sort are largely driven by overall changes in total attainment across all classes taken together, not really by different trajectories within the separate classes. This is most clearly seen for the criterion 'No awards'. Between 1980 and 1993, as the full Table A7.6 shows, the proportions gaining no awards fell sharply in all the socio-economic groups. The proportion was already very low in 1980 for the professional and managerial class, at 9.2 per cent. By contrast, the rate of gaining no awards was still, in 1980, quite high in the semi-skilled manual class, at 40.8 per cent. So any overall reduction in this rate would have been bound to have had a disproportionate effect on the semi-skilled class (and on the other manual classes), simply because there was hardly any room for further improvement in the professional and other non-manual classes. That is indeed what happened. The rate for the professional and managerial class fell from very low to negligible (9.2 per cent to 0.4 per cent), while the rate for the semi-skilled manual class fell from 40.8 per cent to 3.1 per cent. But because, as explained in Chapter 7, this merely reflected a policy of re-defining school attainment in a way that would include nearly everyone, it does not tell us much about different processes in the different classes: it was, by definition, a universal policy.

RELATIVE CHANCES

The second approach tries to take account of these points by calculating the relative change in the percentages in the two classes, acknowledging that different starting points make particular absolute changes mean different things. Thus, returning to the criterion of three or more Higher Grade passes, we find that the 15.3 per cent rise in the professional and managerial class from 41.3 per cent to 56.6 per cent was a relative rise of 37 per cent. In other words, the increase of 15.3 points is 37 per cent of the baseline of 41.3 per cent. Likewise, the relative rise for the semi-skilled class (from 9.4 per cent to 19.0 per cent) was 102 per cent. By this method, then, we would conclude that the rise had been substantially greater for the semi-skilled class than for the other class. We prefer this way of expressing it, on the simple grounds that a rise of 9.6 points from a base of only 9.4 is a more significant change than the larger absolute rise of 15.3 points from the higher base of 41.3. The reason we prefer this relative approach can be seen if we express these as chances for individuals. A typical individual from the semi-skilled class, having increased their chances by over 100 per cent, was more than twice as likely to reach this level of attainment in 1993 than he or she was in 1980, whereas the typical individual in the professional and managerial class increased their chances by only just over one-third.

We have used relative chances frequently throughout the book, but this approach does have one disadvantage: it takes no account of the fact that percentages cannot exceed 100 or be lower than 0. This causes problems when one of the baseline percentages is already very high (or very low) and so cannot change greatly. To illustrate these problems, consider the criterion 'five or more Ordinary or Standard Grade passes'. In the semi-skilled manual class, the proportion rose from 22.5 per cent to 45.1 per cent, an increase of almost exactly 100 per cent. The professional and managerial class could logically not have matched this, because their rate in 1980 was already much higher: 66.2 per cent. Even if everyone in that class had reached this threshold of attainment in 1993, the increase would only have been 33.8 points, and so the relative rise could not have been more than 51 per cent (that is, 33.8 as a proportion of 66.2).

ODDS RATIOS

For that reason, we also compare what are known as odds ratios. These have the advantage of being defined in such a way that there is no longer any ceiling or floor constraint. The odds ratio is defined in several steps:

- First, we start with the probability of something happening, which in practical terms we measure by a percentage. For example, take the case of passing three or more Higher Grades. In 1980, the proportion of the semi-skilled class who reached this level was 9.4 per cent, and so the probability of someone from that class reaching this standard was 0.094.
- The odds are the probability of something happening divided by the probability of its not happening. Still with the same example, the

proportion of the semi-skilled class who did *not* pass three or more Higher Grades was 90.6 per cent (100 per cent - 9.4 per cent). So the probability of their *not* reaching that level was 0.906, and hence the odds of their reaching the level is 0.094 divided by 0.906. The result is 0.104. Note that when something is equally likely to happen and not to happen – so that the probability is 0.5 for each – the odds are 1. A high value of the odds thus means that the thing in question is very likely to happen. A low value means it is unlikely to happen, which is what we have in this example: in 1980, it was unlikely that a student from the semi-skilled class would pass three or more Higher Grades.

- The odds ratio is then used to compare the odds for one group of people with the odds for another group. A typical example would be comparing the same criterion (passing three or more Higher Grades) for two social groups, such as the professional class and the semi-skilled class. We have just seen that the odds on this criterion for the semi-skilled class in 1980 were 0.104. In that same year, the proportion of the professional and managerial class passing three or more Higher Grades was 0.413, and the proportion not doing so was therefore 0.587. So the odds for that class were 0.413 divided by 0.587, which is 0.704. So the odds ratio between the two classes is 0.704 divided by 0.104, which is 6.77.

- In summary (and more abstractly): the odds of some event happening are defined in terms of the chance p that it will happen as $p/(1-p)$. The odds ratio for two social groups is then the odds for that event in the one group, $p_1/(1-p_1)$, divided by the odds for the event in the other group, $p_2/(1-p_2)$.

- An odds ratio at one moment in time does not itself tell us much more than that people from the professional and managerial class were far more likely to reach this level of attainment than people from the semi-skilled class, something which we can readily discern from the table or the other measures we have outlined. The odds ratio comes into its own when we wish, for example, to make comparisons at two points in time. By comparing the odds ratios in this way, we can assess whether inequality has risen or fallen. The odds for the semi-skilled class in 1993 were $0.19/(1-0.19)$, or 0.235, and that for the professional and managerial class were $0.566/(1-0.566)$, or 1.304. So the odds ratio in 1993 was $1.304/0.235$, which is 5.55, somewhat less than the 6.77 in 1980. In other words, it allows us to say that there has been a modest decrease in inequality during that period.

In this example of attaining three or more Higher Grades, we have reached the same conclusion as we reached by the relative chances approach, but without having run the risk of our interpretation being confused by ceiling effects: the odds ratio may take any value from 0 upwards, and two chances are equal only if the odds ratio is 1.

There is the further advantage that the meaning of the odds ratio does not change if the meanings of 'success' and 'failure' are interchanged. That is a potential problem with the relative chances approach. For example, in the case of the criterion three or more Higher Grades, if we compare the percentages not reaching this level instead of the proportions reaching it, we find that the change between 1980 and 1993 for the semi-skilled manual class is a decline of 10.6 per cent (from 90.6 to 81.0), and that the change for the professional and managerial class is a decline of 26.1 per cent (from 58.7 to 43.4). So, expressed this way round, the change seems greater for the professional and managerial class than for the semi-skilled manual class, whereas we saw previously that the change in the chances seemed greater for the semi-skilled manual class. The odds ratios are unaffected by such changes in definition.

The odds ratio approach also does not suffer from the problem identified with the absolute difference approach, namely that changes in particular groups in the population were largely determined by changes across the population as a whole. Finally, the odds ratio has the advantage of being the basis of the advanced statistical modelling techniques of logistic regression and loglinear modelling. Although we do not use these explicitly in this book, many of the research publications which we cite do base their analysis on that: for example, still in the area of educational inequalities, Tinklin and Raffe (1999), and Heath (2000). It seems reasonable sometimes to use techniques in the present book that are consistent with the dominant ones in the literature which explores the issues in greater depth than we do here. Nevertheless, we continue to use the relative chances measure as well, because it is more intuitively appealing and therefore more readily understood than the quite complicated formula for the odds ratio.

References

Abbotts, J., R. Williams, G. Ford, K. Hunt and P. West (1997), 'Morbidity and Irish Catholic descent in Britain: an ethnic and religious minority 150 years on', *Social Science and Medicine*, 45, pp. 3–14.

Alexander, L., C. Currie and J. Todd (2003), *Gender Matters: Physical Activity Patterns of Schoolchildren in Scotland*, Edinburgh: Child and Adolescent Research Unit, Edinburgh University.

Anderson, M. (1992), 'Population and family life', in A. Dickson, and J. H. Treble (eds), *People and Society in Scotland, Volume III, 1914–1990*, Edinburgh: John Donald, pp. 12–47.

Anderson, M. (1996), 'British population history, 1911–1991', in M. Anderson (ed.) *British Population History From the Black Death to the Present Day*, Cambridge: Cambridge University Press, pp. 361–403.

Anderson, M. (2004), 'One Scotland or several: the historical evolution of Scotland's 'population over the past century and its implications for the future', in R. Wright (ed.), *Scotland's Demographic Challenge*, Stirling and Glasgow: Scottish Economic Policy Network, to appear.

Atkinson, A. B. (2000), 'Distribution of income and wealth', in A. H. Halsey and J. Webb (eds), *Twentieth-Century British Social Trends*, London: Macmillan, pp. 348–81.

Bain, M. (2002), 'Patterns and trends in health inequalities', in A. Blamey, P. Hanlon, K. Judge and J. Muirie (eds), *Health Inequalities in the New Scotland*, Glasgow: Health Promotion Policy Unit and Public Health Institute in Scotland, pp. 19–25, www.dph.gla.ac.uk/hppu/publns/HealthInequalitiesReport.pdf.

Barlow, A. (2002), 'Cohabitation and marriage in Scotland: attitudes, myths and the law, in J. Curtice, D. McCrone, A. Park and L. Paterson (eds), *New Scotland, New Society*, Edinburgh: Polygon, pp. 65–91.

Beck, U. (1992), *Risk Society*, London: Sage.

Bell, Daniel (1976), *The Coming of Post-Industrial Society*, Harmondsworth: Penguin.

Bell, David (1999), 'Higher education in Scotland: an economic perspective', research report for the Independent Committee of Inquiry into Student Finance, Edinburgh.

Boreham, R. (2000), 'Smoking', in A. Shaw, A. McMunn and J. Field (eds), *The Scottish Health Survey 1998*, vol. 1, Edinburgh: Scottish Executive, pp. 239–76, www.show.scot.nhs.uk/scottishhealthsurvey/index.htm.

Brotherston, J. (1987), 'The development of public medical care: 1900–1948', in G. McLachlan (ed.), *Improving the Common Weal: Aspects of Scottish Health Services 1900–1984*, Edinburgh: Edinburgh University Press, pp. 35–102.

Bruce, S. and T. Glendinning (2003), 'Religious beliefs and differences', in C. Bromley, J. Curtice, K. Hinds and A. Park (eds), *Devolution – Scottish Answers to Scottish Questions?*, Edinburgh: Edinburgh University Press, pp. 86–115.

Burnhill, P., C. Garner and A. McPherson (1988), 'Social change, school attainment and entry to higher education 1976–1986', in D. Raffe (ed.), *Education and the Youth Labour Market*, Lewes: Falmer, pp. 66–99.

Burnhill, P., A. McPherson, D. Raffe and N. Tomes (1987), 'Constructing a public account of an education system', in G. Walford (ed.), *Doing Sociology of Education*, Lewes: Falmer, pp. 207–29.

Carstairs, V. and R. Morris (1989), 'Deprivation: explaining differences between Scotland and England and Wales', *British Medical Journal*, 299, pp. 886–9.

Census 2001: see note on reference conventions in Preface.

Cinema Advertising Association (1998), *Scottish Screen Data*, London: Cinema Advertising Association.

City of Edinburgh Council (2003), *Edinburgh's Census 2001 City Comparisons*, www.edinburgh.gov.uk/CEC/City__Development/Planning__and__Strategy/Edinburghs__Census__2001/Census__2001__menu.html.

Clark, T., M. Myk and Z. Smith (2001), *Fiscal Reform Affecting Households, 1997–2001*, London: Institute for Fiscal Studies.

Collett, D. (1991), *Modelling Binary Data*, London: Chapman and Hall.

Common Services Agency (2000), *Scottish Health Statistics 2000*, Edinburgh: CSA, www.show.scot.nhs.uk/isd/Scottish__Health__Statistics/shs2001/home.htm.

Common Services Agency (2001), *Scottish Health Statistics 2001*, Edinburgh: CSA, www.show.scot.nhs.uk/isd/Scottish__Health__Statistics/shs2001/index.htm.

Curtice, J. (2002), 'Devolution and democracy: new trust or old cynicism?', in J. Curtice, D. McCrone, A. Park and L. Paterson (eds), *New Scotland, New Society*, Edinburgh: Polygon, pp. 142–65.

Deepchand, K., A. Shaw and J. Field (2000), 'Eating habits', in A. Shaw, A. McMunn and J. Field (eds), *The Scottish Health Survey 1998*, vol. 1, Edinburgh: Scottish Executive, pp. 319–86, www.show.scot.nhs.uk/scottishhealthsurvey/index.htm.

Department of Work and Pensions (2003), *Family Resources Survey 2001–2*, London: DWP, http://www.dwp.gov.uk/asd/frs/.

Devine, M., J. Hall, J. Mapp and K. Musselbrook (1996), *Maintaining Standards: Performance at Higher Grade in Biology, English, Geography and Mathematics*, Edinburgh: Scottish Council for Research in Education.

Dilnot, A. and Emmerson, C. (2000), 'The economic environment', in A. H. Halsey and J. Webb (eds), *Twentieth-Century British Social Trends*, London, Macmillan, pp. 324–47.

Erens, B. (2000), 'Alcohol consumption', in A. Shaw, A. McMunn and J. Field (eds), *The Scottish Health Survey 1998*, vol. 1, Edinburgh: Scottish Executive, pp. 277–318, www.show.scot.nhs.uk/scottishhealthsurvey/index.htm.

Erikson, R. and J. Goldthorpe (1993), *The Constant Flux: A Study of Class Mobility in Industrial Societies*, Oxford: Clarendon Press.

Ermisch, J. (2000), *Personal Relationships and Marriage Expectations: Evidence From the 1998 British Household Panel Study*, Working Paper 2000–27, Colchester: Institute for Social and Economic Research.

Falaschetti, E., A. McMunn, P. Primatesta and M. Brookes (2000), 'Cardiovascular disease prevalence and risk factors', in A. Shaw, A. McMunn and J. Field (eds), *The Scottish Health Survey 1998*, vol. 1, Edinburgh: Scottish Executive, pp. 11–66, www.show.scot.nhs.uk/scottishhealthsurvey/index.htm.

Gallacher, J. (2002), 'Parallel lines? Higher education in Scotland's colleges and higher education institutions', *Scottish Affairs*, no. 40, pp. 123–40.

Gallie, D. (2000), 'The labour force', in A. H. Halsey and J. Webb (eds), *Twentieth-Century British Social Trends*, London: Macmillan, pp. 281–323.

Gardner, J. and A. Oswald (2001), 'Internet use: the digital divide', in A. Park, J. Curtice, K. Thomson, L. Jarvis and C. Bromley (eds), *British Social Attitudes: The Eighteenth Report*, London: Sage, pp. 159–73.

Gershuny, J. and K. Fisher (2000), 'Leisure', in A. H. Halsey and J. Webb (eds), *Twentieth Century British Social Trends*, London: Macmillan, pp. 620–49.

Giddens, A. (1984), *The Constitution of Society*, Cambridge: Polity.

Giddens, A. (1998), *The Third Way*, Cambridge: Polity.

Goldstein, H. and A. Heath (eds) (2000), *Educational Standards*, Oxford: Oxford University Press.

Goldthorpe, J. and K. Hope (1974), *The Social Grading of Occupations*, Oxford: Clarendon.

Goldthorpe, J. and C. Mills (2002), 'Trends in intergenerational class mobility in Britain in the late twentieth century', paper prepared for the meeting of the ISA Research Committee, Berkeley, 14–16 August.

Gutmann, A. (1987), *Democratic Education*, Princeton: Princeton University Press.

Halsey, A. H. (2000), 'Introduction: twentieth-century Britain', in A. H. Halsey and J. Webb (eds), *Twentieth-Century British Social Trends*, London: Macmillan, pp. 1–23.

Halsey, A. H. and J. Webb (eds) (2000), *Twentieth-Century British Social Trends*, London: Macmillan.

Hanlon, P., D. Walsh, D. Buchanan, A. Redpath, M. Bain, D. Brewster, J. Chalmers, R. Muir, M. Smalls, J. Willis and R. Wood (2001), *Chasing the Scottish Effect*, Glasgow: Public Health Institute in Scotland, www.phis.org.uk/pdf.pl?file=pdf/chasing scottish effect.pdf.

Haskey, J. (1999), 'Cohabitational and marital histories of adults in Great Britain', *Population Trends*, 96, pp. 13–23.

Health and Safety Executive (2002), *Statistics Briefing: Safety, Enforcement and Occupational Ill Health 2001–2, Scotland*, Bootle: HSE.

Heath, A. (2000), 'The political arithmetic tradition in the sociology of education', *Oxford Review of Education*, 26, pp. 313–31.

Heath, A. and C. Payne (2000), 'Social mobility', in A. H. Halsey and J. Webb (eds), *Twentieth-Century British Social Trends*, London: Macmillan, pp. 254–78.

Hills, J. (2001), 'Poverty and social security: what rights? whose responsibilities?', in A. Park, J. Curtice, K. Thomson, L. Jarvis and C. Bromley (eds), *British Social Attitudes: The Eighteenth Report*, London: Sage, pp. 1–28.

Hinds, K. and L. Jamieson (2002), 'Rejecting traditional family building? Attitudes to cohabitation and teenage pregnancy in Scotland', in J. Curtice, D. McCrone, A. Park and L. Paterson (eds), *New Scotland, New Society*, Edinburgh: Polygon, pp. 33–64.

Hirst, P. and G. Thompson (1999), *Globalisation in Question: The International Economy and the Possibilities of Governance*, Cambridge: Polity.

Hobsbawm, E. (1994), *Age of Extremes: The Short Twentieth Century 1914–1991*, London: Michael Joseph.

Hobsbawm, E. (2002), *Interesting Times: A Twentieth Century Life*, Harmondsworth: Penguin.

Iacovou, M. (2001), *Leaving Home in the European Union*, Colchester: Working Papers of the Institute for Social and Economic Research, University of Essex, iserwww.essex.ac.uk/pubs/workpaps/index.php.

Iacovou, M. and R. Berthoud (2001), *Young People's Lives: A Map of Europe*, Colchester: Working Papers of the Institute for Social and Economic Research, University of Essex, iserwww.essex.ac.uk/pubs/workpaps/index.php.

Iannelli, C. and L. Paterson (2003), 'Education and social mobility in Scotland', paper presented at the Nuffield College Sociology seminars, 22 January.

Inland Revenue web site, www.inlandrevenue.gov.uk/stats/personal_wealth/menu.htm.

Johnston, M. and R. Jowell (2001), 'How robust is British civil society?' in A. Park, J. Curtice, K. Thomson, L. Jarvis and C. Bromley (eds), *British Social Attitudes: The Eighteenth Report*, London: Sage, pp. 175–97.

Jowell, R., J. Curtice, A. Park and K. Thomson (eds) (1999), *British Social Attitudes: The Sixteenth Report*, Aldershot: Ashgate.

Laiho, J. and S. Purdon (2000), 'Accidents', in A. Shaw, A. McMunn and J. Field (eds), *The Scottish Health Survey 1998*, vol. 1, Edinburgh: Scottish Executive, pp. 131–66, www.show.scot.nhs.uk/scottishhealthsurvey/index.htm.

Lee, J. (1963), *This Great Journey*, London: MacGibbon and Kee.

Leon, D., S. Morton, S. Cannegeiter and M. McKee (2003), *Understanding the Health of Scotland's Population in an International Context: A Review of Current Approaches, Knowledge and Recommendations for New Research Direction*, report by London School of Hygiene and Tropical Medicine for Public Health in Scotland, February, www.phis.org.uk/pdf.pl?file=pdf/part1.pdf.

Lynn, P. (1995), *The 1993 Leavers*, Edinburgh: Scottish Office.

Market Research Society (2003), *2001 Census Outputs by the MRS Social Grade*

Approximation, London: MRS, www.mrs.org.uk/networking/cgg/cggsocialgrade. htm.

Marshall, G., D. Rose, H. Newby and C. Vogler (1988), *Social Class in Modern Britain*, London: Unwin Hyman.

Marshall, G., A. Swift and S. Roberts (1997), *Against the Odds? Social Class and Social Justice in Industrial Societies*, Oxford: Clarendon Press.

McCrone, D. (1992), *Understanding Scotland*, London: Routledge, 1st edn.

McCrone, D. (2001), *Understanding Scotland*, London: Routledge, 2nd edn.

McLaren G. L. and M. R. S. Bain (1998), *Deprivation and Health in Scotland: Insights from NHS Data*, Edinburgh: Common Services Agency.

Modood, T. (1997), 'Employment', in T. Modood and R. Berthoud (eds), *Ethnic Minorities in Britain*, London: Policy Studies Institute, pp. 83–149.

Mueller, W. and R. Pollak (2001), 'Social mobility in West Germany: the long arms of history discovered?', paper prepared for the meeting of the ISA Research Committee, Berkeley, 14–16 August.

Office of National Statistics (2001), *Regional Trends*, vol. 37, London: ONS.

Office of National Statistics (2002a), *Social Trends*, vol. 32, London: ONS.

Office of National Statistics (2002b), *Living in Britain 2001*, London: HMSO.

Office of National Statistics (2002c), *The National Statistics Socio-economic Classification: User Manual*, London: ONS, www.statistics.gov.uk.

Office of Population, Census and Surveys (1982), *Labour Force Survey 1981*, London: HMSO.

Office of Population, Census and Surveys (1992), *Labour Force Survey 1990 and 1991*, London: HMSO.

Paterson, L. (1997a), 'Student achievement and educational change in Scotland, 1980–1995', *Scottish Educational Review*, 29, pp. 10–19.

Paterson, L. (1997b), 'Trends in higher education participation in Scotland', *Higher Education Quarterly*, 51, pp. 29–48.

Paterson, L. (1998), *A Diverse Assembly: The Debate on a Scottish Parliament*, Edinburgh: Edinburgh University Press.

Paterson, L. (2000), Discussion of paper by M. Cresswell on public examinations, in H. Goldstein and A. Heath (eds), *Educational Standards*, Oxford: Oxford University Press, pp. 109–15.

Paterson, L. (2001), 'Education and inequality in Britain', paper given at the annual meeting of the British Association, Glasgow, 4 September, www.institute-of-governance.org.

Paterson, L. (2002a), 'Social capital and constitutional reform', in J. Curtice, D. McCrone, A. Park and L. Paterson (eds), *New Scotland, New Society*, Edinburgh: Polygon, pp. 5–32.

Paterson, L. (2002b), 'Civic democracy', in G. Hassan and C. Warhurst (eds), *Anatomy of the New Scotland*, Edinburgh: Mainstream, pp. 56–64.

Paterson, L. (2002c), 'Scottish social democracy and Blairism: difference, diversity and community', in G. Hassan and C. Warhurst (eds), *Tomorrow's Scotland*, London: Lawrence and Wishart, pp. 116–29.

Paterson, L. (2002d), 'Governing from the centre: ideology and public policy', in J. Curtice, D. McCrone, A. Park, and L. Paterson (eds), *New Scotland, New Society?*, Edinburgh: Edinburgh University Press, pp. 196–218.

Paterson, L. (2003), *Scottish Education in the Twentieth Century*, Edinburgh: Edinburgh University Press.

Paterson, L. and D. Raffe, (1995), ' "Staying-on" in full-time education in Scotland, 1985–1991', *Oxford Review of Education*, 21, pp. 3–23.

Paterson, L., A. Brown, J. Curtice, K. Hinds, D. McCrone, A. Park, K. Sproston and P. Surridge (2001), *New Scotland, New Politics?*, Edinburgh: Edinburgh University Press.

Pitson, L. (2000), 'Adult physical activity', in A. Shaw, A. McMunn and J. Field (eds), *The Scottish Health Survey 1998*, vol. 1, Edinburgh: Scottish Executive, pp. 167–202, www.show.scot.nhs.uk/scottishhealthsurvey/index.htm.

Putnam, R. D. (2000), *Bowling Alone*, New York: Simon and Schuster.

Raab, G. (1998), *Participation in Higher Education in Scotland 1996–97*, Edinburgh: Scottish Higher Education Funding Council.

Raab, G. and H. Storkey (2001), *Widening Access to Higher Education in Scotland: Evidence for Change from 1996–97 to 1998–99*, Edinburgh: Scottish Higher Education Funding Council.

Raftery, A. E. and M. Hout (1993), 'Maximally maintained inequality: expansion, reform and opportunity in Irish education, 1921–75', *Sociology of Education*, 66, 41–62.

Registrar General for Scotland (1961), *Report on the Sixteenth Census of Scotland*, Edinburgh: HMSO.

Registrar General for Scotland (1981), *Annual Report 1981*, Edinburgh: HMSO.

Registrar General for Scotland (1983a), *Census 1981: Scottish Summary*, Edinburgh: HMSO.

Registrar General for Scotland (1983b), *Census 1981: Economic Activity*, Edinburgh: HMSO.

Registrar General for Scotland (1983c), *Census 1981: Housing and Household Report*, Edinburgh: HMSO.

Registrar General for Scotland (1994a), *Census 1991 Scotland: Report for Scotland*, Edinburgh: HMSO.

Registrar General for Scotland (1994b), *Census 1991 Scotland: Economic Activity*, Edinburgh: HMSO.

Registrar General for Scotland (2002a), *Vital Events Reference Tables*, Edinburgh: General Register Office, www.gro-scotland.gov.uk/grosweb/grosweb.nsf/pages/reftabs.

Registrar General for Scotland (2002b), *Scotland's Population 2001*, Edinburgh: General Register Office.

Registrar General for Scotland (2002c), *2001 Population Report*, Edinburgh: General Register Office.

Registrar General for Scotland (2003a), *Scotland's Census 2001: The Registrar General's 2001 Census Report to the Scottish Parliament*, Edinburgh: General Register Office, www.gro-scotland.gov.uk/grosweb/grosweb.nsf/pages/censushm.

Registrar General for Scotland (2003b), *Scotland's Census 2001: Reference Volume*, Edinburgh: General Register Office, www.gro-scotland.gov.uk/grosweb/grosweb.nsf/pages/censushm.

Rodger, R. (1989), 'Introduction', in R. Rodger (ed.) *Scottish Housing in the Twentieth Century*, Leicester University Press, pp. 1–24.

Rose, D., K. O'Reilly and J. Martin (1997), 'The ESRC review of government social classifications', *Population Trends*, 89, pp. 49–59.

Royal Commission on the Distribution of Income and Wealth (1977), *Third Report on the Standing Reference*, London: HMSO.

Runciman, W. G. (1964), *Relative Deprivation and Social Justice*, London: Routledge.

Runciman, W. G. (ed.) (1978), *Weber: Selections in Translation*, Cambridge: Cambridge University Press.

Savage, M. (2000), *Class Analysis and Social Transformation*, Buckingham: Open University Press.

Schuller, T. and C. Bamford (1998), *Initial and Continuing Education in Scotland: Divergence, Convergence and Learning Relationships*, Edinburgh: Centre for Continuing Education, Edinburgh University.

Schuller, T., D. Raffe, B. Morgan-Klein and I. Clark (1999), *Part-Time Higher Education*, London: Jessica Kingsley.

Scottish Executive (2001a), *Scottish Social Statistics 2001*, Edinburgh: Scottish Executive.

Scottish Executive (2001b), *Scotland's People: Results from the 1999–2000 Scottish Household Survey, Volume 3, Annual Report*, Edinburgh: Scottish Executive.

Scottish Executive (2001c), 'Transport across Scotland: some Scottish Household Survey results for parts of Scotland', *Statistical Bulletin*, Trn/2001/4, Edinburgh: Scottish Executive.

Scottish Executive (2001d), *Scottish Economic Statistics 2001*, Edinburgh: Scottish Executive.

Scottish Executive (2001e), *Scottish School Leavers and their Qualifications: 1998–99*, Statistical Bulletin, 22 May, Edinburgh: Scottish Executive.

Scottish Executive (2001f), *Scottish School Leavers and their Qualifications: 1998–99*, Statistical Bulletin, 22 May, Edinburgh: Scottish Executive.

Scottish Executive (2002a), *Standard Tables on Higher Education and Further Education in Scotland: 2000–01*, Statistical Bulletin, September, Edinburgh: Scottish Executive.

Scottish Executive (2002b), *Students in Higher Education in Scotland: 2000–01*, Statistical Bulletin, Edinburgh: Scottish Executive.

Scottish Executive (2002c), *Scotland's People: Results from the 2001 Scottish Household Survey, Volume 5, Annual Report*, Edinburgh: Scottish Executive.

Scottish Executive (2002d), *Students in Higher Education in Scotland: 2000–01*, Statistical Bulletin, 13 June, Edinburgh: Scottish Executive.

Scottish Executive (2002e), *Standard Tables on Higher Education and Further Education in Scotland: 2000–01*, Statistical Bulletin, September, Edinburgh: Scottish Executive.

Scottish Executive (2002f), *Scottish House Conditions Survey 2002*, Edinburgh: Communities Scotland.

Scottish Executive (2003a), *Health in Scotland 2002*, Edinburgh: Scottish Executive.

Scottish Executive (2003b), *First Destination of Graduates and Diplomates in Scotland: 2000–01*, Statistical Bulletin, 30 January, Edinburgh: Scottish Executive.

Scottish Executive (2003c), *Scotland's People: Results from the 2001/2002 Scottish Household Survey, Volume 7, Annual Report*, Edinburgh: Scottish Executive.

Scottish Executive (2003d), *Participation Rates in Education by 16 to 21 Year Olds in Scotland: 2000–01*, Statistical Bulletin, 13 May, Edinburgh: Scottish Executive.

Scottish Further Education Funding Council (2003), *Student and Staff Performance Indicators for Further Education Colleges in Scotland 2001–02*, Edinburgh: SFEFC.

Scottish Higher Education Funding Council (2001), *Performance Indicators in Higher Education*, Edinburgh: SHEFC.

Scottish Office (1988), *Scottish Abstract of Statistics 1987*, Edinburgh: HMSO.

Scottish Office (1992a), *Scottish Abstract of Statistics 1991*, Edinburgh: HMSO.

Scottish Office (1992b), *Scottish Higher Education Statistics*, Statistical Bulletin Edn/J2/1992/18, Edinburgh: Scottish Office.

Scottish Office (1992c), *School Leavers' Qualifications 1989–90*, Statistical Bulletin Edn/E2/1992/5, Edinburgh: Scottish Office.

Scottish Office (1993), *Scottish Abstract of Statistics 1993*, Edinburgh: HMSO.

Scottish Office (1995a), *Scottish Higher Education Statistics 1993–94*, Statistical Bulletin Edn/J2/1995/13, Edinburgh: Scottish Office.

Scottish Office (1995b), *Scottish School Leavers and their Qualifications 1983–84 to 1993–94*, Statistical Bulletin Edn/E2/1995/14, Edinburgh: Scottish Office.

Scottish Office (1996a), *Scottish Higher Education Statistics 1994–95*, Statistical Bulletin Edn/J2/1996/12, Edinburgh: Scottish Office.

Scottish Office (1996b), *Scottish School Leavers and their Qualifications: 1984–85 to 1994–95*, Statistical Bulletin Edn/E2/1996/9, Edinburgh: Scottish Office.

Scottish Office (1997a), *Scottish Abstract of Statistics 1996*, Edinburgh: HMSO.

Scottish Office (1997b), *Participation in Education by 16 to 21 Year Olds in Scotland: 1985–86 to 1995–96*, Statistical Bulletin Edn/C3/1997/10, Edinburgh: Scottish Office.

Scottish Office (1997c), *Scottish Higher Education Statistics 1995–96*, Statistical Bulletin Edn/J2/1997/12, Edinburgh: Scottish Office.

Scottish Office (1998), *Scottish Abstract of Statistics 1998*, Edinburgh: Scottish Office.

Scottish Office (1999), *School Attainment and Qualifications of School Leavers in Scotland: 1997–98*, Statistical Bulletin Edn/E2/1999/4, Edinburgh: Scottish Office.

Scottish Qualifications Authority (2003), *Standards at Higher over Time*, Glasgow: SQA.

Scottish Screen (1998), *Scottish Screen Data*, Glasgow: Scottish Screen, www.scottishscreen.com/downloads/SSD1.pdf.

Shaw, C. and J. Haskey (1999), 'New estimates and proportions of the population cohabiting in England and Wales', *Population Trends*, 95, pp. 1–17.

Smith, E. and S. Gorard (2002), 'What does PISA tell us about equity in education systems?', Occasional Paper Series Paper 54, Cardiff: School of Social Science, Cardiff University, www.cardiff.ac.uk/socsi/equity.

Smout, T. C. (1992), 'Patterns of culture', in A. Dickson and J. H. Treble (eds) *People and Society in Scotland, Volume III, 1914–1990*, Edinburgh: John Donald, pp. 261–81.

Social Disadvantage Research Centre (2003), *Scottish Indices of Deprivation*, Oxford: Oxford University, www.scotland.gov.uk/library5/social/siod-00.asp.

Swaffield, J. (2000), 'Women's pay', *CentrePiece: The Magazine of the Centre for Economic Performance*, 5 (1), pp. 20–3.

Tinklin, T. and D. Raffe (1999), *Entrants to Higher Education*, Edinburgh: Centre for Educational Sociology.

Todd, J., C. Currie, R. Smith and G. Small (2000), *Health Behaviours of Scottish Schoolchildren*, Edinburgh: Child and Adolescent Research Unit, Edinburgh University.

Tomes, N. (1988), 'Scottish surveys since 1977', in D. Raffe (ed.), *Education and the Youth Labour Market*, Lewes: Falmer, pp. 266–73.

Trow, M. (1973), *Problems in the Transition from Elite to Mass Higher Education*, Washington: Carnegie Commission on Higher Education.

Turner, A. (2001), *Just Capital: The Liberal Economy*, London: Macmillan.

Vallet, L.-A. (2001), 'Change in intergenerational class mobility in France from the 1970s to the 1990s and its explanation', paper prepared for the meeting of the ISA Research Committee, Berkeley, 14–16 August.

Watson, M. (2003), *Being English in Scotland*, Edinburgh: Edinburgh University Press.

Wightman, A. (1996), *Who Owns Scotland?*, Edinburgh: Canongate.

Wightman, A., and P. Higgins (2000), 'Sporting estates and the recreational economy in the Highlands and Islands of Scotland', *Scottish Affairs*, 31, pp. 18–36.

Index